Palgrave Studies in Life Writing

Series Editors
Clare Brant
Department of English
King's College London
London, UK

Max Saunders
Department of English
King's College London
London, UK

This series features books that address key concepts and subjects, with an emphasis on new and emergent approaches. It offers specialist but accessible studies of contemporary and historical topics, with a focus on connecting life writing to themes with cross-disciplinary appeal. The series aims to be the place to go to for current and fresh research for scholars and students looking for clear and original discussion of specific subjects and forms; it is also a home for experimental approaches that take creative risks with potent materials.

The term 'Life Writing' is takenbroadly so as to reflect the academic, public and global reach of life writing, and to continue its democratic tradition. The series seeks contributions that address contexts beyond traditional territories – for instance, in the Middle East, Africa and Asia. It also aims to publish volumes addressing topics of general interest (such as food, drink, sport, gardening) with which life writing scholarship can engage in lively and original ways, as well as to further the political engagement of life writing especially in relation to human rights, migration, trauma and repression, sadly also persistently topical themes. The series looks for work that challenges and extends how life writing is understood and practised, especially in a world of rapidly changing digital media; that deepens and diversifies knowledge and perspectives on the subject, and which contributes to the intellectual excitement and the world relevance of life writing.

More information about this series at
http://www.palgrave.com/gp/series/15200

Alexandra S. Moore • Elizabeth Swanson
Editors

Witnessing Torture

Perspectives of Torture Survivors and Human Rights Workers

Editors
Alexandra S. Moore
Binghamton University
Binghamton, NY, USA

Elizabeth Swanson
Babson College
Babson Park, MA, USA

Palgrave Studies in Life Writing
ISBN 978-3-319-74964-8   ISBN 978-3-319-74965-5 (eBook)
https://doi.org/10.1007/978-3-319-74965-5

Library of Congress Control Number: 2018942222

© The Editor(s) (if applicable) and The Author(s) 2018
This work is subject to copyright. All rights are solely and exclusively licensed by the Publisher, whether the whole or part of the material is concerned, specifically the rights of translation, reprinting, reuse of illustrations, recitation, broadcasting, reproduction on microfilms or in any other physical way, and transmission or information storage and retrieval, electronic adaptation, computer software, or by similar or dissimilar methodology now known or hereafter developed.
The use of general descriptive names, registered names, trademarks, service marks, etc. in this publication does not imply, even in the absence of a specific statement, that such names are exempt from the relevant protective laws and regulations and therefore free for general use.
The publisher, the authors and the editors are safe to assume that the advice and information in this book are believed to be true and accurate at the date of publication. Neither the publisher nor the authors or the editors give a warranty, express or implied, with respect to the material contained herein or for any errors or omissions that may have been made. The publisher remains neutral with regard to jurisdictional claims in published maps and institutional affiliations.

Cover illustration: Untitled (Crying Eye), 2016, by Muhammad Ansi

Printed on acid-free paper

This Palgrave Macmillan imprint is published by the registered company Springer International Publishing AG part of Springer Nature.
The registered company address is: Gewerbestrasse 11, 6330 Cham, Switzerland

In memory of Patricio Rice and Orlando Tizon, indefatigable fighters for justice, and in honor of Sister Dianna Ortiz, beacon for the abolition of torture.

This volume is dedicated to the global community of torture survivors and to those who work with them toward restoration, redress, and an end to the practice of torture, everywhere.
For Chloë, Samantha, and Marcelle

Alone at Night

Orlando P. Tizon

Alone at night in my cell
I look for the stars through
the dark hair of night.
I hear the waves of the sea
Beating, beating martial music,
Calling
And the wind brings the salt
Spray of the sea, the tang
Of the islands,
Fishes, rocks, corals, mangrove,
Salty moon
Nets, boats, bamboo poles
The sweet sharp, salty wind
Brings back fishermen's songs
Voices
Friends calling in the night
Patient but awake.

Davao Detention Center
Davao, Philippines
June 5, 1984

Prologue

Elizabeth Swanson

Rhetorics of Torture in the Public Sphere

I became involved with human rights activism at the age of fourteen, but it would be twenty-five years before I met a person who had survived torture. Many human rights activists and academics never meet someone who has survived a grave violation such as disappearance, torture, rape, or genocide, and certainly the vast majority of survivors never meet those who speak on their behalf in the arena of international human rights advocacy. Indeed, at its highest institutional levels, and in spite of the intrepid on-the-ground work of advocates and humanitarian agents, much human rights work is divorced from the intimate struggles, pain, and trauma experienced by individual humans, focused instead upon reporting on and negotiating with governments, armed resistance groups, non-governmental organizations (NGOs), corporations, diplomats, and others about the treatment of groups of people: dissidents living under repressive regimes; ethnic minorities mistreated by state apparatuses; detainees confined without trial in the "war on terror"; women and girls violated and oppressed the world over.

In spite of the fact that I had been an activist with Amnesty International's Urgent Action Network for more than twenty years, and although my professional life was focused upon teaching and writing about human rights from a cultural perspective, it was not until I was invited to participate in a panel at a One Day Forum on Torture at Catholic University in Washington, DC in June 2003 that I met a group of people who had survived torture.[1] The events of this day illuminated significant issues regarding the relationship between survivors of human rights violations and the community of human rights activists/academics/clinicians who have not experienced such violations; such issues can best be identified through the Cartesian split between mind and body that marks the construction of these two groups in the public sphere, and that also informs the rhetorical modes in which they are known to speak most frequently. In spite of all we have learned about the limits of the philosophical division between mind and body (also responsible for separating emotion from intellect, and public from private space) from postmodernists, feminists, and multiculturalists, among others, it remains surprisingly conventional in the human rights arena in ways that correspond predictably to national, racial, and gendered identity positions.

My own introduction to the issue of torture came in 1981, when I read a small ad at the back of *Writer's Digest*, a journal for poets and writers. The ad, from the writer's organization PEN International, asked for letters on behalf of a dissident writer, currently imprisoned and suffering torture for his work. An aspiring writer and naïve US teenager, I was properly shocked and promptly ordered further materials on the subject from PEN. The descriptions I read of writers persecuted for expressing their ideas in a variety of literary and journalistic forms were accompanied by a reference to Amnesty International, which I also contacted. Receiving my first Urgent Action Network member kit, I began the letter writing that I have continued ever since.

Years later, as an assistant professor of English at a small college of management and entrepreneurship in the Boston area, I found a supportive home for my joint interests in literature and human rights, and was engaged in teaching courses in both areas, when a colleague forwarded to me a call for a panelist with expertise in the cultural representation of torture. The panel, "Torture: From Clandestine Prison to Popular Culture," was part of a One Day Forum on Torture sponsored by the Torture

---

[1] The terminology of "survivor" and "non-survivor" is complicated by the fact that within the community of torture survivors, "non-survivor" may refer to one who died as a result of his or her torture, rather than one who has not been tortured. For the purposes of defining its membership, the Torture Abolition and Survivor Support Coalition International (TASSC) includes anyone who has been tortured, or who is the family member or partner of one who has been tortured, as a "survivor." In this essay, I will use the term "non-survivor" to refer to human rights workers who have not experienced torture, and "victim" to describe those who did not survive their torture.

Abolition and Survivor Support Coalition International (TASSC), an international human rights NGO founded and run by survivors of torture. I was eager to share my work with the diverse community of survivors and human rights workers (journalists, legislators, physicians, psychologists, attorneys, advocates, academics) participating in the conference. The make-up of my panel is worthy of mention: chaired by an historian who was the life-partner of a torture survivor, the panel also included a young academic who, like me, had never shared her work on human rights and literature with an audience that included torture survivors. Prior to our session, this woman articulated her nervousness about the presentation, and her sense that it was presumptuous to speak as an academic about torture to those who have survived it. This is one common mark of the tenuous relationship between survivors and non-survivors who are concerned with human rights: the sense that one who has not experienced torture has no right to speak about it—at least not in front of or directly to those who have. The sentiment comes from a healthy desire to honor the painful experiences of others that may seem unimaginable to one who has not had similar experiences, and to defer to the knowledge that comes with that experience. It also bears traces of the kind of guilt that marks positions of relative privilege and/or authenticity in any context, but particularly in terms of race, class, and, in this case, painful experience.

In my presentation, I discussed a genre of film that I identified as the *counter-historical drama*, a mode of popular film that gained prominence in the 1980s, dedicated to telling stories of mass human rights violations in global "hotspots" using a combination of documentary and classical Hollywood film conventions.[2] The hallmark of the genre is its focus upon a white, western, usually male protagonist who journeys through a global political danger zone such as El Salvador (Oliver Stone's *Salvador*, 1981); Chile (Costa Gravas' *Missing*, 1982); Indonesia (Peter Weir's *The Year of Living Dangerously*, 1982); South Africa (Richard Attenborough's *Cry Freedom*, 1987); Burma (John Boorman's *Beyond Rangoon*, 1995); Tibet (Jean-Jacques Annaud's *Seven Years in Tibet*, 1997); China (Jon Avnet's *Red Corner*, 1997); and so on. The plot is split in classical Hollywood style between the foreground story of the individual protagonist and the backdrop plot of the oppressed national collective. While the films overtly claim to protest the rights violations that occur in the sites of the films'

---

[2] This work was published as the first chapter of my book *Beyond Terror: Gender, Narrative, Human Rights* (Rutgers, NJ: Rutgers University Press, 2007).

settings, either by countering an official version of events or by restoring a lost or suppressed account, audience identification is paradoxically directed to the fate of the protagonist, who not only manages to maintain bodily safety even while the "natives" around him are brutalized and killed, but whose storyline typically achieves closure while the narrative of rights violations and those who suffer them is left open, unresolved. I showed clips from *Salvador* and *Cry Freedom* to illustrate these points, and made the claim that while such successful films could potentially inform mass audiences of the causes and effects of specific human rights violations, and even stimulate historical consciousness and political activism, they relinquish that potential to the demands of the box office and the notion that audiences in the west require a white protagonist with "star power" as a lens through which to identify with the events in the film.

The first response to my talk came from a survivor from Central America, who articulated that he appreciated the reading of *Salvador*, as it had been one of his favorite films, and, inasmuch as he felt gratified that a film that addressed US intervention in El Salvador in the early 1980s had even been made, he had not at the time considered the kinds of critiques that I offered in my analysis. The substance of his remark, however, was to draw a parallel between my reading of the films and the One Day Forum itself: survivors, mostly people of color, many from the so-called third world, speaking mostly in testimonial mode, stuck in the endless repetition of testifying to the atrocity they had experienced without achieving closure. Academics and activists on a dais, mostly of European descent and from the United States or Europe, speaking in analytical modes, and achieving a measure of closure in being able to "walk away with a book."

Not surprisingly, his comment generated heated discussion. Several points are worth noting; foremost among them, that his assessment was factually correct in its address of the demographic of the room, the structure of the conference, and the division in modes of speech between survivors and non-survivor human rights workers. Less clear, however, was the accuracy or usefulness of the kinds of investments or distances he attributed to survivors and academics, respectively. The first person to respond to his comment was an historian who expressed outrage at the assumptions contained in his assessment. This woman testified to having lost her marriage as a result of the work she undertook to document the recent history of US intervention in—coincidentally—El Salvador. She challenged the assumption that academics do not invest emotion in their work, even if the product of that work is most often delivered in analytical form. At the same time, the woman who shared my panel whispered in my ear, "I knew I shouldn't have come." When the panel ended, the survivor who had made the comment approached me to say that he hadn't meant so much to critique the academics (and lawyers, journalists, clinicians, legislators, activists) in the room as to invite *survivors* to move beyond the testimonial mode to advance *analyses* about human rights goals and problems from a variety of perspectives. He wondered why the panels at the Forum had not comprised a mix of survivors and non-survivors.

This comment and the dialogues it generated illuminate a great deal that can help us to make better sense of the relationship between human rights workers and those who have survived human rights violations, as well as of the rhetorical modes in which their work is most often delivered to a wider public. They reveal significant aspects of the investments and identifications made by people with different relations to human rights work, and they offer ideas about how to move forward more productively and ethically with the shared goal of eradicating torture and other grave abuses of human rights.

Survivors of human rights violations are well accustomed to being the objects of others' discourse: the discourse of the governments or non-governmental agents who rendered them vulnerable to torture or other violence; the discourse of politicians and diplomats who may talk about and make policies related to events that comprise their experiences; the discourse of human rights activists who presumably work on their behalf; the discourse of lawyers and judges who may be assigned to or, alternatively, dismiss their cases; the discourse of physicians, psychiatrists, psychologists, and social workers whom they may encounter in the traumatic aftermath of their violation; the discourse of academics who research, theorize, and write about the violation of rights in general, and perhaps even the particular rights violations that produced their pain. Some of those discourses have been sensitive to their experiences and knowledge, and have approached them in ethical, inclusive terms; others have not.

What would it mean for torture survivors to know something about the emotional, ethical, and professional investments of those who work on their behalf, who speak about them? How might it help a torture survivor, who in order to gain a measure of justice and/or personal healing has been compelled to expose the most intimate, personal, painful details of her life, to be met with accounts from those who speak and write about her that also offer some measure of personal vulnerability and exposure? Acknowledging that the distribution of pain and violence remains unbearably uneven in the global sphere, what would it mean for those who are enabled by the privilege of professional status to retain a protective shield in the discursive realm (which likely accrues from a range of other privileges) to shed that armor and to share some part of their personal, intimate, vulnerable investments? And what would it mean for activists and professionals who work with torture survivors to understand them not solely as patients, clients, or objects of study, but as agents of their own lives? How might human rights workers who are non-survivors learn from survivors' expertise, not solely in the realms of pain, trauma, and suffering, but often in the same disciplines—history, health, law, policy-making, education—in which they encounter one another?

This volume—the proceeds of which are donated to TASSC—collects a group of essays from a variety of disciplines that address these questions. In blurring the rhetorical divide that often separates survivors and non-survivors, while maintaining a careful sense of their relative positionings, the authors offer an expanded idiom of witnessing torture that we explore more fully in the introduction that follows. First, however, a word on the shape of the book. The process of soliciting essays for this volume began at that One Day Forum on Torture in 2003, and has continued since. We worked closely with TASSC to identify survivors and human rights workers who would be interested in participating with the express rhetorical and discursive goals of the volume in mind. Bringing together a group of writers so diverse in nationality, life and work experience, language, and other identity characteristics presents a set of challenges that can be said to mirror the challenging contexts of torture itself: people in various circumstances with relation to their national and/or immigration status, their professional or disciplinary backgrounds, and—not least—their ability to speak or to write publicly about such issues. TASSC figures prominently in the book's genesis and in its contents, and we recognize the organization as one among *many* such efforts to support survivors in determining the paths of their own futures and in the ongoing campaign to abolish torture. The work assembled here does not make any claim to be geographically or politically representative of torture as a global phenomenon, but rather results from the evolving circumstances and exigencies of networks of survivors and advocates. Some who would have liked to write for this volume could not because of ongoing legal or political issues; however, the voices represented here, as with much life writing, gesture toward the larger collectives and communities of which they are part.

Editors' Introduction

Alexandra S. Moore and Elizabeth Swanson

On the Social and Institutional Contexts of Witnessing: Expanding the Frame of Life Writing about Torture

Henri Alleg, the journalist arrested, interrogated, and tortured by French paratroopers during the Battle of Algiers, begins his memoir of the experience with self-effacement: "In this enormous prison, where each cell houses a quantity of human suffering, it is almost indecent to talk about oneself."[1] The statement reflects key aspects of survivor testimony and points to the need for an expansive and nuanced reading of witnessing torture. Alleg's sense of what is "almost indecent" captures the paradoxical necessity and inevitable inadequacy of sharing his story. On the one hand, first-person witnessing brings the abhorrent workings of the torture chamber to light, providing evidence to refute the claims perpetrators regularly make to their victims that "no one will hear, believe, or remember you." On the other hand, as many scholars and witnesses have demonstrated, even when first-person accounts reveal what was ostensibly hidden, they are also always partial—freighted with the challenge of making pain and traumatic experience legible, of representing a singular experience that (because there are identifiable patterns to torture) may also be generalizable, of remembering through the prism of trauma, and of the speaker's possible re-traumatization in the telling. Life writing about torture, then,

---

[1] Henri Alleg, *The Question*, trans. John Calder (Lincoln: University of Nebraska Press, 2006 [1958]), 33.

is at once marked by and resistant to the dissolution of the subject that torture tries to accomplish. What follows the decision to "talk about oneself" is thus not a simple recounting of experience, but a complex meditation on how one reconstitutes oneself as a speaking subject, and how one's psychological and physical experience might be represented and understood within a matrix of social relations, linguistic conventions, and, not least, egregious harms.

To stop there, however, would be to restrict the reading of Alleg's account, to relegate the torture survivor solely to the realm of suffering, and to delimit that realm from full emplacement within the larger social and political contexts in which torture and its aftermath take place. It also would reinforce the rhetorical divide between survivors—who, as the Prologue to this volume discusses, are often called upon to attest to phenomenological "truths" of torture—and those with professional expertise—lawyers, policy-makers, health-care workers, teachers, and human rights activists and observers—who are authorized to analyze torture in specific historical, legal, cultural, and institutional contexts. We can see this divide between the personal and affective testimonial discourse of witnessing on the one hand, and analytical discourses of professional expertise on the other, and also reflected in the standard form of the human rights report, in which individual stories are set apart typographically from more neutral documentary and analytical language in order that individualized stories of atrocity might animate the data. Although there are obvious reasons that human rights literature, reporting, and public discourse have remained divided between the testimonial literature of survivors and analytical academic/activist work, this division presents the following problems and limitations that this volume aims to address:

- First, the divide in genre, however inadvertently, constructs torture victims and survivors, and their life writing, as objects of political and analytical discourse, exacerbating the silencing and loss of agency that are a hallmark of survivor experience. Such a divide might unwittingly contribute to social blindness about what Darius Rejali has called stealth torture—that is, torture that does not leave any mark, such as techniques of sensory deprivation, stress and duress, or mock executions, as opposed to premodern forms of torture that scarred

and maimed—particularly when it involves democratic regimes.[2] It also elides those persons who occupy multiple subject positions, as survivor, as activist/academic/clinician working on human rights, and as citizen.
- Second, the lack of analytical commentary from survivors in the literature about torture reinforces assumptions about the necessity, attainability, and value of scholarly neutrality and objectivity, ostensibly achieved by maintaining a certain distance from one's subject, that have been challenged by postmodern philosophies and methodologies across disciplines, and that remain to be critically examined in the arena of human rights.
- Third, the absence of analytical commentary from those who have themselves experienced such grave violations of rights means that a major intellectual and activist resource for the prohibition of torture remains unmined. In parallel, ignoring the affective, psychological, and phenomenological dimensions of the work of (non-survivor) human rights workers curtails a fuller understanding of the sociality of torture and healing, and of solidarities and divergences in the struggle against torture. When life narratives of torture comprise solely survivors' testimonies of pain, our understanding of the broad interpersonal and socio-political dimensions of torture is greatly diminished.
- Fourth, as we confront the use of torture as a tool used by democratic and authoritarian, state and non-state actors, it is crucial to ground our understanding of torture in political and social contexts in order to examine the ideologies that sustain it. If the only recognized witnesses to torture are its victims and perpetrators, our understanding of its ideological and institutional foundations, and thus our capacity to dismantle those foundations, is severely limited.

Striving for such an expansive contextual apparatus for witnessing torture, survivor, performance artist, and activist Hector Aristizábal emphasizes

---

[2] See, for instance, Rejali's larger argument about the coupling of stealth torture and democracy, as well as his more specific argument that "Stealth torture denies precisely this home in the body, tangling victims and their communities in doubts, uncertainties, and illusions" (*see* Darius Rejali, *Torture and Democracy* [Princeton, NJ: Princeton University Press, 2007], 32).

the importance of multiple forms of life narratives. Because one of the techniques of torture is to convey its ostensible secrecy and unknowability, for torture's victim, Aristizábal writes, "[i]n that moment of utter surrender, when everyone else had abandoned me, when my own body and mind had betrayed me, only he [the perpetrator] was there."[3] Dismantling the lasting power of the dark chamber for Aristizábal necessitates de-personalizing it, not to evacuate himself from but to re-situate himself within the scene: "I need to think of that man as *the* torturer, not *my* torturer, and to understand that he belonged to the army, to the system of repression, and not to me."[4] Aristizábal effects that transformation by re-narrativizing and performing his own experiences, and we follow his lead here by expanding the scope of life writing about torture to include voices that reflect personally and analytically on those systems of repression, as well as on pathways of healing and redress.

* * *

This volume responds to the limitations of the conventional divide between life writing and analysis described above through fourteen essays insisting that complex modes of witnessing torture can only take place through attention to torture's combined phenomenological and political effects; to the relationship between torture and its larger social and institutional contexts; to torture's prolonged impact on the individual and society; and to the relationship between survivors and other social actors working within institutions of torture, repression, recovery, redress, cultural representation, and education. Our authors demonstrate that torture can be neither adequately represented nor countered by the archetypal scene described by Stephanie Athey that features "an isolated subject, a torturer, and an array of graphic techniques."[5] In this model, there are only two witnesses—victim and perpetrator, each of whom represents a kind of limit case for humanity: the human capacity to bear pain and the human capacity to inflict pain directly upon another person. When torture is imagined to take place solely through this dyad, witnessing is similarly

---

[3] Hector Aristizábal and Diane Lefer, "Out of the Inner Wilderness: Torture and Healing," in *We Shall Bear Witness: Life Narratives and Human Rights*, ed. Meg Jensen and Margaretta Jolly (Madison: University of Wisconsin Press, 2014), 65.
[4] Ibid. Original emphases.
[5] Stephanie Athey, "The Torture Device: Debate and Archetype," in *Torture: Power, Democracy, and the Human Body*, ed. Shampa Biswas and Zahi Zallouia (Seattle: University of Washington Press, 2011), 139.

limited to the perpetrator's justifications for torture and the survivor's attempt to document experience and to withstand the sense Jean Améry has described that "with the very first blow that descends on him he loses something we will perhaps temporarily call 'trust in the world.'"[6] Scholars focused on this emblematic model of torture, Athey argues, "lift the practice out of its historical, social, and institutional complexity."[7] The fact that much testimonial literature is rich with analysis of the larger contexts in which the survivor's torture occurred is often discounted, as is the fact that frequently the survivor has in fact been targeted *because* he or she is an intellectual, activist, or professional.[8] The degree to which human rights literature is split between survivor testimonials and academics', activists', or clinicians' analyses represents the harmful reduction of survivors' identity to the category of "survivor," erasing that which they do and are before, after, and beyond their experience of torture.

To expand the register of witnessing torture in the chapters that follow, survivors (from Argentina, Ireland, the Philippines, Sudan, and the United States) analyze their experiences in historical, religious, legal, and institutional contexts, and non-survivor human rights workers (psychologists, lawyers, artists, activists, and teachers who have worked with survivors from across the globe) offer self-reflective examinations of the institutional, political, and emotional dimensions of their work. These rhetorical and generic shifts make possible forms of witnessing torture within its multifaceted contexts that are otherwise foreclosed. In doing so, the authors included in this volume underscore the uses of and responses to torture as profoundly socio-political, implicating the broad polities in whose name torture occurs. More specifically, the chapters that follow understand torture not as a series of isolated anomalies from within the

---

[6] Jean Améry, *At the Mind's Limits: Contemplations by a Survivor on Auschwitz and Its Realities*, trans. Sidney Rosenfeld and Stella P. Rosenfeld (Bloomington: University of Indiana Press, 1980), 28.

[7] Athey, "The Torture Device," 141.

[8] An example is the "testimonial" of Jacobo Timerman, journalist and editor of the well-respected Argentine newspaper *La Opinion*, whose persistence in publishing writs of habeas corpus during the "Dirty War" resulted in his disappearance and torture by the Argentine military. His *Prisoner without a Name, Cell without a Number* (1981) is considered a classic of testimonial literature; however, passages related to his torture and ill-treatment are outnumbered by chapters analyzing the rise of fascism in Argentina and its parallel to the Nazi era in Germany. In many senses, the book is more a political analysis than a testimonial, or is at least an even mix of the two; however, it is known—and arguably taught—as testimonial. Améry's account cited earlier similarly includes extensive social and political commentary.

flow of civilization, but rather as an age-old political tool tied to institutions that may seem autonomous or even at odds, but that are themselves often linked to one another through personnel, politics, and ideology. Just as the authors recognize the long history of torture's use by political regimes, so, too, do they draw attention to what Carolyn Forché has described as the longue durée of atrocity—its aftermath.[9]

As opposed to what comes *after* torture, as though its ending may be clearly demarcated, *aftermath* implies the lasting effects of torture on its participants and on the societies in which they exist, effects which are non-teleological and cannot be known in advance. The authors also write self-reflectively from their various geopolitical, disciplinary, and institutional positions, noting that the norms governing these positions give shape to the very definitions of what torture and enforced disappearance might mean, as well as to the kinds of recovery and forms of redress that might be possible. Writing from within and about various institutions (such as a network of survivors, the academy, or a professional association) also makes possible collective witnessing of the uses and effects of torture and the role of different institutions in supporting torture, struggling against torture, or promoting healing and redress for survivors. Collective witnessing in this volume does not take the form of a single author combining multiple experiences under the sign of her own "I," as in Rigoberta Menchú's life writing, but rather of life writing that is firmly rooted in larger institutions and systems of harm, representation, and redress. Significantly, as several essays point out, such redress must begin simply with acknowledgment of the occurrence of torture, given that, as Elaine Scarry taught long ago, the denial of torture by its perpetrators and the larger societies in which they operate is one of the central components of torture itself.[10]

Finally, the essays here underscore the importance of both imagination and affect in ethically witnessing torture and its scalar effects: on the individual, on the communities to which the tortured and the perpetrators belong(ed), and on the large social contexts in which aftermaths of torture take shape. Our contributors do not argue for imagination and affect

---

[9] Carolyn Forché, "Reading the Living Archives: The Witness of Literary Art," in *Theoretical Perspectives on Human Rights and Literature*, ed. Elizabeth Swanson Goldberg and Alexandra Schultheis Moore (New York: Routledge, 2012), 137.

[10] Elaine Scarry, *The Body in Pain: The Making and Unmaking of the World* (Cambridge, MA: Harvard University Press, 1985), 9.

simply to secure empathic identification with torture's victims, but rather to recognize that torture always occurs within a social matrix and, thus, always implicates a polity—and that both its perpetration and its eradication are grounded in personal and collective imaginaries.

* * *

In Alleg's initial reluctance to tell his story, we hear reverberations of the title of his book, *The Question*. Resisting disclosure both refuses violent interrogation and seems to anticipate inquiry by someone other than an interrogator into the value of one man's story, in this case a story of survival of a month-long torture regime. To build upon the connection (more pronounced in the original French) between torture and interrogation that Alleg's title invokes, if "the question" is designed to elicit an ostensible truth that the subject withholds but the tortured body (once subjectivity has been wounded or destroyed) releases, then the narrative of its aftermath would also seem to reveal something authentic and otherwise buried about the human condition: the ability to survive, the process of living-with, the manifestation of an everyday life again after the massive disruption of torture.

First, then, *The Question* has a juridical function: it testifies to the fact of torture. Alleg's credibility as a French journalist and editor, his anticolonial politics notwithstanding, amplifies the book's message that the French forces used torture as a tactic during Algeria's liberation war. Indeed, as Alleg states later in the book, "My particular case is exceptional in that it has attracted public attention. It is not in any way unique."[11] In other words, its exceptionality is rooted in the use of torture against a European rather than an Algerian target of French forces, revealing the potent identity politics that have always informed the perpetration, visibility, and redress of torture. The book stands with texts such as Jacobo Timerman's *Prisoner without a Name, Cell without a Number*, Jean Améry's *At the Mind's Limit*, and Alicia Partnoy's *Little School*, among others, that also resonate philosophically to characterize torture, in Diana Taylor's words, as that which "attacks personhood, suspends the rules, and unmakes the world of the victim,"[12] and as that which

---

[11] Alleg, *The Question*, 34.
[12] Diana Taylor, "Double Blind: The Torture Case," *Critical Inquiry* 33, no. 4 (Summer 2007): 710.

crosses the limit, threatening to corrode Enlightenment distinctions between the human and inhuman and eviscerating international agreements differentiating between the legitimate and illegitimate use of force [...] overrid[ing] the rule of law and [...] nullif[ying] all legal mechanisms designed precisely to safeguard against cruelty and violence.[13]

Each of these texts, then, provides testimony to the fact of torture, its mechanics, while also exploring the multiple registers of its individual, social, and institutional effects.

In her important argument about how witnessing can offer a model for understanding subjectivity and ethical relations, Kelly Oliver focuses on these two forms of witnessing—evidentiary and philosophical—in relation to truth:

> There is a tension inherent in the notion of witnessing in the sense of eyewitness to historical facts or accuracy on the one hand, and witnessing in the sense of bearing witness to a truth about humanity and suffering that transcends those facts. It is important to note that witnessing has both the juridical connotations of seeing with one's own eyes and the religious or now political connotations of testifying to that which cannot be seen, or *bearing witness*. It is this double meaning that makes witnessing such a powerful alternative to recognition in reconceiving subjectivity and thereby ethical relations. The tension between eyewitness testimony and bearing witness, between historical facts and what we might call psychoanalytic or phenomenological truth, between subject position and subjectivity is the dynamic operator that moves us beyond the melancholic choice between either dead historical facts or traumatic repetition of violence.[14]

In Oliver's account, it is the relationship between *witnessing* (in the evidentiary or juridical sense) and *bearing witness* (in the ethical, sociopsychological sense) that provides the foundation for understanding subjectivity in terms of one's potential for social meaning, as well as for ethical relations among subjects. Rather than conceptualizing subjectivity as taking place through the act of recognition—such that one becomes a subject when one is recognized by the Other—Oliver develops a model that distributes subjectivity across relations of witnessing and the "response-ability" that witnessing demands. According to this formulation,

---

[13] Taylor, "Double Blind," 711.
[14] Kelly Oliver, "Witnessing and Testimony," *Parallax* 10, no. 1 (2004): 81.

witness as "response-ability" is foundational to the construction and maintenance of subjectivity itself, inasmuch as it enables the following three categories of interaction: (1) the subject's right and ability to address others; (2) the subject's right and ability to respond to others; and (3) others' responsibility to respond to her "in a way that opens up rather than closes off the possibility of recognition by others."[15]

This notion of response-ability helpfully addresses Alleg's anxiety about speaking of his own experience of torture, given how it is situated within the malevolent psychodynamics of the secret prison. In more general terms, this expanded notion of bearing witness can help to negotiate the proprietary registers of pain, suffering, and authenticity when it comes to both survivors' and non-survivor advocates' positioning in relation to the larger field of "torture." Work in this arena is plagued with anxiety (visible or not) about the legitimacy of one's own pain in relation to that of others; the legitimacy of emotional, as opposed to physical, suffering; and the legitimacy of "secondary" trauma in the act of witnessing another's pain. Overall, such anxieties are enflamed by the delimiting idea of authenticity in which hierarchies of pain, suffering, and experience are made and remade, opening or foreclosing upon opportunities to articulate or to share in the social field of torture.

Oliver's concept of response-ability provides language and a map for negotiating these various anxieties in order to allow multiple relations to the phenomenon, experience, and subject of torture to emerge, relations that move beyond psychoanalytic or political recognition. It is an ethical rejoinder (a combination of responsibility toward and response to the speaker and what she discloses) that acknowledges the speaker, narrative, and context, and implicates the reader/listener/spectator in the situation at hand. Response-ability, in other words, can potentially unlock the hierarchy implicit in recognition, which figures as a choice one may or may not make about the Other, with the Other's subjectivity dependent in some way upon the outcome of that choice. It can also intervene in the self-censoring, such as that to which Alleg alludes, that can result from consciousness of such a hierarchy. Because witnessing and responding are multiple, layered, dynamic, and contextualized processes, according to Oliver, subjectivity itself is a process of social making among diverse actors, rather than a singular occurrence that takes place between self and Other.

---

[15] Kelly Oliver, *Witnessing: Beyond Recognition* (Minneapolis: University of Minnesota Press, 2001), 15.

This conception of subjectivity dramatically alters the reading and reception of a text like *The Question,* recasting readers as stakeholders in the consciousness of torture, and redistributing vulnerability from Alleg alone to those who share response-ability for his testimonial.

Whereas witnessing of atrocity serves as a model for understanding subjectivity for Oliver—who emphasizes that her purpose is not "extolling the virtues of testimony per se"[16]—we build on her account of witnessing to focus its implications for understanding torture. More specifically, we emphasize the processes (interpersonal, institutional, ideological) within which witnessing and response-ability take place—such as through the messy personal–professional tasks of translation, psychological therapy, artistic creation, teaching, and legal activism—as well as broadening the range of participants in those processes who are usually considered witnesses. Each of these endeavors requires interpersonal and collective effort (among survivors and in partnership with non-survivor human rights workers) as well as a personal and professional will to witness torture's aftermath in order to countermand it. Stated slightly differently, the chapters demonstrate how historical, clinical, juridical, translational, artistic, and academic responses to torture bear traces of torture's assaults on both the individual and society, and not just on those who have been tortured. The essays here encourage us to read these traces as other forms of witnessing torture's effects by destabilizing the rhetorical separation between survivors and human rights workers in their disciplines.

How do we understand Alleg's narrative in relation to this argument? As already noted, Alleg's account might read solely as the reluctant disclosure of the individual's almost unbearable suffering, leaving Jean-Paul Sartre's Preface to place Alleg's story in its political and philosophical contexts. Sartre refers to *The Question* as the "proof" France has needed to confront the moral challenge that the use of torture in the name of patriotism and anticolonialism presents:

> Up to now it was only those returning from military service, particularly priests, who have been able to bear witness [...] With the publication of *La Question*, everything is changed.[17]

Sartre considers the devastating effects of torture on its perpetrators and what it reveals about human nature, as well as how torture fits within the French military arsenal—and that of other democratic governments.

[16] Oliver, "Witnessing and Testimony," 80.
[17] Jean-Paul Sartre, Preface to Henri Alleg, *The Question*, xxx, xxxi.

"Disavowed—sometimes very quietly—but systematically practiced behind a façade of democratic legality," he writes, "torture has now acquired the status of a semi-clandestine institution."[18] For Sartre, *The Question* reveals the "indissoluble partnership"[19] between the colonizer and the executioner and, thus, the moral vacuum within France's claims to Algeria. Yet it is precisely by citing details of rank, training, procedure, and so forth from Alleg's narrative that Sartre makes his argument. Thus, the Preface directs us to Alleg's text itself as providing witness *and* context: for his suffering (including beatings, electric shocks, and waterboarding) and for the workings of the military force that utilized torture to try to stop the Algerian liberation movement.

Whereas readers traditionally turn to Sartre's Preface to consider the political *question* (that is, "what is the role of torture in contemporary politics?"), leaving Alleg to testify to his personal experience of suffering, we submit that Alleg's narrative in and of itself offers a substantive and rigorous discussion of the political and institutional contexts of that experience. Indeed, Alleg emphasized this larger reading of the title in a 2007 interview with *Democracy Now!*'s Amy Goodman. As the headline of the interview, "French Journalist Henri Alleg Describes His Torture Being Waterboarded by French Forces During the Algerian War," makes clear, the 86-year-old Alleg is being called upon to describe his suffering in order to support the arguments against the legality of waterboarding as a so-called "enhanced interrogation" technique in the war on terror. The lead-in to the story is President George W. Bush's nomination of Judge Michael Mukasey to become Attorney General of the United States in light of Mukasey's "refusal to condemn waterboarding as a form of torture." Although Goodman prompts Alleg, whom she calls a "real-life survivor of torture," to describe how waterboarding feels and what he experienced, Alleg quickly rejects the question—is waterboarding torture?—as neither appropriate nor necessary:

> So I am really astonished that this is a big question in the States about this, because the real question is not waterboarding or not waterboarding, it is the use of torture in such a war, and this use of torture, torture in general.[20]

[18] Ibid., xxxvi.
[19] Ibid., xliii.
[20] "French Journalist Henri Alleg Describes His Torture Being Waterboarded by French Forces During the Algerian War," Interview with Henri Alleg by Amy Goodman, *Democracy Now!* (5 November 2007), https://www.democracynow.org/2007/11/5/french_journalist_henri_alleg_describes_his, accessed 27 February 2017.

Indeed, the argument might cogently be made that the continued exclusion of survivors of torture from nearly all mainstream national and international scholarly and policy debates on human rights constitutes a major detriment to these fields. The passage of the Military Commissions Act (2006), which removed the right of habeas corpus and the presumption of innocence for so-called enemy and unlawful combatants, and which altered the definition of torture codified in the United Nations Convention against Torture (to which the United States is signatory), is a case in point.[21] Aside from US Senator John McCain, no survivor of torture was consulted in the drafting and ratification of that bill, which, as legal scholars have overwhelmingly asserted, not only gutted a foundational legal principle (habeas corpus) and further degraded the United States' standing in the international arena by abrogating standards in the Third Geneva Convention on the treatment of prisoners of war, but also virtually ensured that more persons—regardless of the status of "guilt" or "innocence," notoriously difficult to discern and assign in the slippery arenas of terrorism and counter-terrorism—would be subjected to the unconscionable harm of torture by expanding the definition of allowable methods of coercive interrogation.

Perhaps the vast body of "expertise" so unwillingly acquired by torture survivors might have had an important place in this debate, had one or more of them been consulted.[22] And perhaps it would be considered efficacious to consult one or more survivor as an "expert" in such cases if the

---

[21] *See* Military Commissions Act of 2006, S3930.

[22] TASSC International issued the following statement with regard to the Military Commissions Act:

> The Torture Abolition and Survivors Support Coalition International (TASSC), each member of which is a survivor of torture, denounces the Military Commissions Act of 2006 and calls for its repeal. This legislation constitutes an attack on the constitutional right to habeas corpus the Geneva Conventions, the War Crimes Act, the U.N. Convention Against Torture and protection from punishment derived from coerced testimony. In addition, it grants immunity to those who have ordered and practiced torture. It is a disgrace to the basic values proclaimed by the people of the United States.

> The members of TASSC know torture from the inside out. We also know from our own lived experience what it means to have a friend or family member disappeared or held by a government that permits no avenue of return.
> We know as well what it is to live where government officials are granted impunity, rather than held accountable for the crimes they have committed.

literature by survivors were not so neatly cordoned into the generic category "testimonial": an untheorized, affective account of physical and psychic pain. And perhaps it would be more difficult to write and support such legislation if non-survivor experts on torture had also been invited to share their work with survivors, articulating how it has shaped their understanding of both individual worth and national identity.

Of course, any collection of life writing about torture will be necessarily, productively partial and incomplete. We make no claims on behalf of a coverage model of the subject; rather, we hope this collection will expand the public conversation about torture by broadening its forms and participants, especially in emphasizing that witnessing torture need not solely transform the speaker "from the position of victim to that of plaintiff" to be meaningful and effective.[23] In addition, we hope the essays assembled here demonstrate the rich potential of conceptualizing life writing in interrelated analytical, affective, and often collective registers.

One additional aspect of the perspectives—and lack of perspectives—in this volume deserves attention. Although techniques of torture are often traceable across specific geopolitical alliances that indicate how regimes learn to torture in particular ways, those patterns are tailored to their immediate contexts and subjects. A crucial aspect of that tailoring concerns the sexualization of torture and the gendering of its targets, particularly when rape, sexual assault, and sexual humiliation are employed to feminize persons of all genders. For instance, Diana Taylor has analyzed the sexualized violence of the Argentinian Dirty War in ways that we can compare to other contexts by examining the gendered ideologies that fuel torture: "the gendered violence taking place in the discourse of the symbolic *Patria* was being played out on the 'real' bodies of the victims in order to shape a new symbolic entity: the national being."[24] Despite the prevalence of sexualized torture techniques and the substantial literature devoted to gender and torture, and perhaps because of the difficulty of crossing rhetorical divides regarding such intimate violence, our volume does not include an essay on this topic.

We who are survivors of torture call upon all those who believe in justice and human decency to work on behalf of human decency and against the undemocratic, anti-human rights provisions of the Military Commissions Act of 2006 enacted by the U.S. Congress.
Statement issued September 2006.

[23] Anne Cubilié, *Women Witnessing Terror* (New York: Fordham University Press, 2005), 109.

[24] Diana Taylor, *Disappearing Acts* (Durham, NC: Duke University Press, 1997), 151.

However, we understand the gendering of torture and the ideologies that inform its perpetration as warrants undergirding all of the life writing contained in this volume.

Finally, the expanded register of witnessing and life writing that we propose here does not simply divulge a truth about the individual's experience, nor give voice to the human capacity to inflict and endure pain, so much as it deepens our understanding of how torture works in its larger social matrix and, following the lead of survivors, what might be done to prevent or to respond to it.

Acknowledgments

First, this book would not exist were it not for the life, work, and example of Sister Dianna Ortiz, OSU, founder and long-time director of the Torture Abolition and Survivors Support Coalition International (TASSC), the United States' only NGO founded and run by survivors of torture. Sister Dianna's testimonial to her torture at the hands of North American and Guatemalan agents in a Guatemalan torture chamber can be read in her searing memoir, *The Blindfold's Eyes: My Journey from Torture to Truth* (Orbis Books, 2002). TAASC continues to be on the forefront of the struggle against torture and in support of survivors internationally.

The idea for this volume came into being in 2003, as the US-led "war on terror" was ramping up, and it became clear that Coalition forces were engaging in torture. Sister Dianna, the late Orlando Tizon, who served for many years as Associate Director of TASSC, and Judy B. Okawa, a psychologist who has devoted her career to supporting survivors, and who ran the Program for Survivors of Torture and Severe Trauma in Washington, DC, have guided the work from the beginning, and we gratefully acknowledge their contributions.

Our cover image, Untitled (Crying Eye), 2016, was painted by former Guantánamo prisoner Muhammad Ansi, after the Periodic Review Board initially denied his application for release. Originally from Yemen, Ansi spent nearly fifteen years without charge in Guantánamo before he was sent to Oman in 2017. Although Guantánamo artists are careful to depict images that will not jeopardize their chances of repatriation, Ansi later revealed that he imagined his mother's eye, crying when his first hearing was unsuccessful. We are grateful to Erin

Thompson, curator of Ode to the Sea: Art from Guantánamo, for her dedication to exhibiting Guantánamo artwork and for her assistance in the use of this image.

Finally, we thank the Babson College Faculty Research Fund for generous support, Cassandra Ford for her assistance in assembling the manuscript, the anonymous readers of our manuscript for their extremely helpful comments, and Ben Doyle and Camille Davies at Palgrave for their commitment to the volume.

Contents

Alone at Night   vii
Orlando P. Tizon

Prologue   ix
Elizabeth Swanson

Editors' Introduction   xv
Alexandra S. Moore and Elizabeth Swanson

Acknowledgments   xxix

Part I   **Torture in Context and Translation**   1

1   **Torture: The Catastrophe of a Bond**   7
Carlos Alberto Arestivo

2   **Torture in an Historical Context: Notes from Sudan**   21
Mohamed Elgadi

3   **The Unspeakable Agony of Inflicted Pain: Torture, Betrayal, Redress**   37
Robert Francis Garcia

| 4 | Translating Trauma, Witnessing Survival
Laurie Ball Cooper | 47 |

Part II Witnessing Torture and Recovery: Survivors, Health Professionals, Institutions — 57

| 5 | The Role of Health Professionals in Torture Treatment
Linda A. Piwowarczyk | 61 |
| 6 | Assessing the Treatment of Torture: Balancing Quantifiable with Intangible Metrics
Orlando P. Tizon | 71 |
| 7 | The Little Red Cabinet of Tears: The Impact upon Treatment Providers of Bearing Witness to Torture
Judy B. Okawa | 89 |
| 8 | Beyond Institutional Betrayal: When the Professional Is Personal
Ellen Gerrity | 111 |

Part III Disappearance and Torture, Redress and Representation — 137

| 9 | Everardo and the CIA's Long-Term Torture Practices
Jennifer Harbury | 143 |
| 10 | Survivors and the Origin of the Convention for the Protection of All Persons from Enforced Disappearance
Patricio Rice | 157 |

11	The Tenacity of Memory: Art in the Aftermath of Atrocity Claudia Bernardi	169
12	Teaching about Torture, or, Reading between the Lines in the Humanities Madelaine Hron	183
13	Legal Appeal: Habeas Lawyers Narrate Guantánamo Life Terri Tomsky	211
14	**Did We Survive Torture?** Mansoor Adayfi	231

Epilogue: From Solitude to Solidarity 237
Dianna Ortiz, O.S.U.

Index 241

Notes on Contributors

Mansoor Adayfi originally from Yemen, was held without charge for fourteen years at the US Naval Base in Guantánamo Bay. In 2016, he was released to Serbia. He is the author of the recent *New York Times* Opinion piece, "In Our Prison on the Sea," and he is currently completing a book about his time in Guantánamo.

Carlos Alberto Arestivo is a Paraguayan psychiatrist. In 1978 during the Stroessner regime, he was imprisoned, held incommunicado and in isolation, and tortured physically and psychologically on suspicion of supporting those opposed to the government. Arestivo was released in response to pressure from international organizations, including Amnesty International. He currently works with a non-profit organization in Paraguay that promotes human rights and provides mental health services. After the election of a new government, he was appointed as a human rights commissioner for the country.

Laurie Ball Cooper is a Senior Immigration and Pro Bono Coordinating attorney at Ayuda, a non-profit legal and social services provider in the Washington, D.C. area. She has previously served as an associate in the international human rights practice group at Cohen, Milstein, Sellers & Toll and as a Senior Staff Attorney at the Legal Aid Society of the District of Columbia. While at the Legal Aid Society, she represented low-income tenants in eviction matters and administrative hearings as well as in affirmative litigation before the DC Superior Court and at the DC Court of Appeals. Ms. Ball Copper previously served as a Skadden Arps Fellow and Immigration Staff Attorney at the Tahirih Justice Center. She was a Law

Clerk to the Honorable M. Margaret McKeown, US Court of Appeals for the Ninth Cicruit, from 2010-2011, and served as a volunteer interpeter with TASSC from 2000-2005.

Claudia Bernardi is Professor of Community Arts, Diversity Studies, Critical Studies, and the Graduate Program of Visual and Critical Studies at the California College of the Arts. An internationally known artist, Bernardi works in the fields of art, human rights, and social justice. In her work over the past two decades, she has combined installation, sculpture, painting, and printmaking. Additionally, she has focused her art praxis in developing and facilitating community and collaborative art projects with communities that have suffered state terror, violence, forced exile, and who are victims of human rights violations. Born in Buenos Aires, Argentina, Bernardi lived through the Argentine military junta that ruled the country from 1976 to 1983. She left Argentina in 1979. In 1984, a forensic anthropology team was established in Argentina to supply evidence of violations of human rights carried out against civilian populations. Bernardi participated as mapmaker, and collaborated with the Argentine Forensic Anthropology Team in exhumations of mass graves in El Salvador, Guatemala, Argentina, and Ethiopia. Bernardi is the founder and director of the School of Art and Open Studio of Perquin, El Salvador, serving children, youth, adults, and the elderly. The approach is rooted in the partnership created between art, artists, and local institutions and NGOs. This model of education and community building through art, known now as the Perquin Model, has been successfully implanted in Colombia, Guatemala, Mexico, Canada, Germany, Switzerland, Northern Ireland, and Argentina. For the last three years, Bernardi has been working with unaccompanied, undocumented, Central American migrant minors currently detained in high-security facilities in the United States.

Mohamed Elgadi is a Sudanese human rights activist who received asylum in the United States after being detained in one of the government-operated torture centers known in Sudan as the Ghost Houses. After he escaped Sudan, Elgadi co-founded the Group Against Torture in Sudan (GATS) and the Darfur Alert Coalition (DAC) in Philadelphia. Long-time Coordinator of the Amherst, MA local chapter of Amnesty International, Elgadi works in social services in Northampton, MA, and teaches in the School of Professional and Continuing Studies (SPCS) at Springfield College.

Robert Francis Garcia considers himself a "pedagogue." When he was head of Popular Education for People's Empowerment (or PEPE, an NGO in the Philippines), he wrote the book *Of Maps and Leapfrogs: Popular Education and Other Disruptions* (PEPE, 1999), which holds that pedagogy is the strongest weapon against demagoguery. He also founded a human rights group called PATH, worked with the United Nations, and taught Community Development at the University of the Philippines, where he currently lives. He is also the author of *To Suffer Thy Comrades: How the Revolution Decimated Its Own* (Anvil Press, 2001), a chronicle of his torture experience under the Communist Party of the Philippines–New People's Army (CPP-NPA), for which he received a Philippines National Book Award.

Ellen Gerrity has been involved in traumatic stress research and practice for more than thirty-five years, working as a researcher, senior National Institute of Mental Health (NIMH) research administrator, clinician, and policy advisor. At NIMH, she headed the trauma research program for several years before being assigned for five years to the US Senate to serve as Senior Mental Health Policy Advisor for US Senator Paul Wellstone, working on mental health and addiction treatment parity legislation and many other health and social justice issues. Gerrity is currently an Associate Professor in the Department of Psychiatry and Behavioral Sciences at Duke University Medical Center, and the Associate Director and Senior Policy Advisor of the Duke University–UCLA National Center for Child Traumatic Stress, the coordinating center for the National Child Traumatic Stress Network. She received the NIH Director's Award for her work in support of traumatic stress research, and the 2008 Public Advocacy Award from the International Society for Traumatic Stress Studies, and is the Senior Editor of *Mental Health Consequences of Torture* (Kluwer Academic/Plenum, 2001).

Jennifer Harbury began her career in a small legal aid bureau on the Texas–Mexican border, which led to her involvement in the Mayan resistance to the Guatemalan oligarchy's brutal repression of its indigenous people. Her husband, Efrain Bamaca Velasquez (known as Commandante Everardo), was captured in 1992, tortured for two and a half years, then murdered without trial. Harbury conducted hunger strikes in Guatemala and in front of the White House in Washington, DC to try to force officials in both countries to tell her the truth about what had happened to her husband. Her efforts uncovered information about Central Intelligence Agency (CIA) involvement in torture throughout Latin America. She is the author of *Bridge to Courage: Life Stories of Guatemalan Companeros & Companeras* (Common Courage

Press, 1995); *Searching for Everardo: A Story of Love, War, and the CIA in Guatemala* (Warner Books, 1997); and *Truth, Torture, and the American Way* (Beacon Press, 2005), which documents the long-time use of torture by the CIA. In 1995, Harbury received a Letelier-Moffitt Human Rights Award, and in 1997 the Cavallo Award for Moral Courage, which she shared with Richard Nuccio, the US State Department official who leaked the information about the CIA's cover-up of and complicity in the torture and murder of her husband Everardo.

Madelaine Hron is Associate Professor in the Department of English and Film Studies at Wilfrid Laurier University in Canada. She is the author of *Translating Pain: Immigrant Suffering in Literature and Culture* (University of Toronto Press, 2009), as well as of various articles related to human rights issues, African literature, trauma, and violence, in such varied journals as *Research in African Literature*, *Peace Review*, *Journal of Literature and Trauma Studies*, *Forum in Modern Language Studies*, *Disability Studies Quarterly*, *French Literature Studies*, and *Slavonic and East European Review*. She is also a long-time supporter of the Canadian Center of Victims of Torture in Toronto, Canada.

Alexandra S. Moore is Professor of English and Director of the Human Rights Institute at Binghamton University. Her publications include *Vulnerability and Security in Human Rights Literature and Visual Culture* (Routledge, 2015) and *Regenerative Fictions: Postcolonialism, Psychoanalysis, and the Nation as Family* (Palgrave Macmillan, 2004). She has also co-edited several volumes and a special journal issue: *The Routledge Companion to Literature and Human Rights* (with Sophia A. McClennen, Routledge, 2015); *Teaching Human Rights in Literary and Cultural Studies* (with Elizabeth Swanson Goldberg, MLA, 2015); *Globally Networked Teaching in the Humanities* (with Sunka Simon, Routledge, 2015); *Theoretical Perspectives on Human Rights and Literature* (with Goldberg, Routledge, 2011), and Human Rights and Cultural Forms, a special issue of *College Literature* (with Goldberg and Greg Mullins, 2013). Her current research is on black sites from the war on terror and the stories they tell.

Judy B. Okawa is a licensed clinical psychologist who established and directed the Program for Survivors of Torture and Severe Trauma in the Washington, DC area in 1998. She testified a number of times before congressional subcommittees on the impact of torture on the individual, and served as an expert witness in court for numerous asylum cases. Okawa has provided trauma training at the international and national level to professionals in many fields on how to cope with vicarious trauma and how to assist survivors in recovering from torture. She served on the Executive Council of the National Consortium of Torture Treatment Programs and on the board of the Pacific Survivor Center in Honolulu. She consulted for several years for the Torture Abolition and Survivors Support Coalition International (TASSC). Her work with asylum seekers was recognized with a Human Rights award from the United Nations Association in Washington, DC.

Linda A. Piwowarczyk is a co-founder and Director of the Boston Center for Refugee Health and Human Rights. She specializes in the mental health evaluation and treatment of refugees and torture survivors. This has been her life work for over twenty years. Since 2002, Piwowarczyk has served on the Executive Committee of the National Consortium of Torture Treatment Programs (NCTTP) and is currently its President. In May 2017, she accepted the Human Rights Award on behalf of the NCTTP from the American Psychiatric Association. She is a recipient of the Sarah Haley Memorial Award for Clinical Excellence from the International Society for Traumatic Stress Studies, and the Local Legends Award from the National Library of Medicine that honors female physicians. A Distinguished Fellow of the American Psychiatric Association, she has presented on the topic of torture locally, nationally, and internationally, and has published articles on the subject in various medical journals.

Patricio Rice✝ is originally from Ireland, and served as a Catholic priest among the poor in Buenos Aires, where he was abducted and tortured by the military regime in 1976. With pressure from the Irish government, his religious order, and the Inter-American Commission on Human Rights, he was released and deported. He returned to Argentina, however, to continue his pastoral mission among the poor, and he remained an active voice against human rights violations and an advocate for the disappeared in Latin America. As co-founder and Executive Secretary of FEDEFAM, the Executive Latin American Federation of Families of the Disappeared, between 1981 and 1987, Rice was instrumental in crafting the UN International Convention for the Protection of All Persons from Enforced Disappearance.

Elizabeth Swanson is Professor of English at Babson College and has published widely on the subject of literature and human rights. Author of *Beyond Terror: Gender, Narrative, Human Rights* (Rutgers University Press, 2007), she is co-editor, with Alexandra Schultheis Moore, of

---

✝ Deceased

Theoretical Perspectives on Literature and Human Rights (Routledge 2011) and *Teaching Human Rights in Literary and Cultural Studies* (MLA Press, 2015), and with James Brewer Stewart of *Human Bondage and Abolition: New Histories of Slaveries Past and Present* (Cambridge University Press, 2018). She has been a human rights activist since the age of fourteen, when she wrote her first letter for Amnesty International, and has for the past ten years worked with survivors of sex trafficking and gender-based violence in Southeast Asia to create dignified, sustainable life and livelihood solutions.

Orlando P. Tizon* was arrested on September 21, 1982 in Davao City, on the island of Mindanao, southern Philippines, during the regime of President Marcos. At that time, he was working as a community organizer and educator among the rural poor in the Philippines. During the first three weeks of his imprisonment, the military who arrested him kept him blindfolded and incommunicado in a military camp outside Davao City. He suffered beatings, endless interrogations, mock execution, and solitary confinement for more than three months. In April 1986, after the people power revolution, the Aquino government granted him amnesty and released him from prison. Soon after, he emigrated to the United States, attended graduate school, and earned a doctorate in Sociology. Tizon served as a staff member of the Torture Abolition and Survivors Support Coalition International (TASSC) in Washington, DC, and as Coordinator of the Helping Hands program for torture survivors.

Terri Tomsky is an Assistant Professor in the Department of English and Film Studies at the University of Alberta in Canada. Her research examines memory politics in postcolonial and postsocialist literatures. She is the co-editor (with Eddy Kent) of *Negative Cosmopolitanism: Culture and Politics of World Citizenship after Globalization* (McGill-Queen's University Press, 2017). She has published articles in *parallax*, *Journal of Commonwealth Literature*, *Life Writing*, *Biography*, and *Australian Journal of Human Rights*, as well as contributed chapters to several book collections, including *The Transcultural Turn: Interrogating Memory Between and Beyond Borders* (De Gruyter, 2014), *Cosmopolitan Animals* (Palgrave Macmillan, 2015), and *Security and Hospitality in Literature and Culture: Modern and Contemporary Perspectives* (Routledge, 2016).

* Deceased

PART I

Torture in Context and Translation

In her recent essay, "The Torture Device: Debate and Archetype," Stephanie Athey argues that a better understanding of how torture functions—an understanding crucial to dismantling the ideologies that sustain torture—depends upon critical attention to torture's social and political contexts. Athey analyzes news reports and legal scholarship that address torture, and finds that both typically feature an archetypal portrayal of torture as a confrontation between torturer and tortured that takes place in what J. M. Coetzee has called "the dark chamber."[1] Delimiting the representation of torture to this basic structure and space entails a simultaneous refusal to embed it in ideology, political and social institutions, psychosocial dynamics that extend beyond perpetrator and victim, and particular places. Part of the tantalizing spectacle of torture offered by the conventional torture narrative depends upon the perverse drama one imagines between two persons who function at once individually and representationally of power and powerlessness. The cultural imaginary produced through this scenario, in turn, generates the desire to peek into that dark chamber, a desire identified by Coetzee as dangerous on its own terms, but also inasmuch as it offers only the same representational loop for the writer or artist who seeks ethical means of expressing it. Even when torture is real or historical as opposed to fictionalized, adherence to the archetype still enhances its metaphorical resonance. Whether suffering is spectacularized or presented with restraint, the torture narrative hinges

---

[1] J. M. Coetzee, "Into the Dark Chamber: The Novelist and South Africa," *New York Times*, January 12, 1986: 13.

upon how effectively the victim as witness conveys the ostensible truth of her individual suffering—with effectiveness defined according to the degree of adherence to the conventional narrative. Thus, Athey argues, the archetype of torture "narrows our understanding of the systemic and communal nature of torture" and "closes off from scrutiny all political, social, and economic networks that support the activity."[2] We add to Athey's argument that this archetypal dyad also forecloses understanding of the networks and institutions upon which redress and solidarity depend and, thus, other positions from which witnessing can take place.

This section features four chapters that insist upon complex modes of life writing to convey understandings of torture that are deeply rooted in personal experience and professional training. The authors inhabit multiple perspectives that reflect how personal and professional positionality shape one's entry into the torture narrative. Those multifaceted perspectives also underscore the need to forge anti-torture alliances that extend beyond the confines of immediate situations of either torture or redress. In short, these essays address the ways in which torture and its aftereffects are never cut off from the larger social matrix, and are instead always embedded psychosocially, ideologically, historically, and materially in the societies in which they occur.

Our first chapter, by Paraguayan survivor and psychiatrist Carlos Alberto Arestivo, analyzes what torture is and how it works from a psychosocial perspective that is at once personal and clinical. His approach emphasizes the ways in which the personality of an individual, whether perpetrator or victim, is constituted through social and societal relationships and, therefore, deeply marked by techniques of personal destruction. Moreover, he understands the centrality of those relationships through his own experience under torture by the Stroessner regime and in treating others who suffered with him, as well as through his professional expertise in the psychological stages of torture. Although he rarely speaks in the first person, using it only in relation to his work with a fellow survivor, Arestivo's essay is marked by an intimate knowledge of how the psyche attempts to survive torture through interpersonal bonds, even when the only available bond is with the perpetrator.

---

[2] Stephanie Athey, "The Torture Device: Debate and Archetype," in *Torture: Power, Democracy, and the Human Body*, ed. Shampa Biswas and Zahi Zalloua (Seattle and Walla Walla: Whitman College and University of Washington Press, 2011), 131, 145.

Chapters 2 and 3, also by torture survivors, examine religious and political ideologies used to sustain torture in Sudan and the Philippines, respectively. In Mohamed Elgadi's "Torture in an Historical Context: Notes from Sudan," the author describes his brutal treatment by Omar al-Bashir's regime in the context of the long history of torture in Sudan and, especially, under the guise of religious sanction. Elgadi's contribution emphasizes torture as a political strategy that may take similar forms by perpetrators in different parts of the world, but is nevertheless employed in specific situations and toward discrete political ends. His personal story and its wider context remind us that torture is never simply a struggle of one person's mental and physical fortitude against excruciating pain and suffering wielded by another. Rather, it always depends upon personnel, equipment, discursive patterns, evaluations, and performances that root torture in particular ideologies, histories, and institutions. Rather than attest solely to the mental and physical assaults he experienced, Elgadi writes as an educator and activist who resists torture's isolationist effects by re-contextualizing the dark chamber in ideology, history and politics.

Whereas torture narratives typically detail the abuses of the state against its designated opponents, our third chapter, "The Unspeakable Agony of Inflicted Pain: Torture, Betrayal, Redress" by Robert Francis Garcia, addresses the use of torture by an insurgent movement against its own members. This political shift, whereby comrade becomes perpetrator, doubles the experience of betrayal that the pairing of torture and interrogation invariably produces. Elaine Scarry identifies interrogation as a key component of torture, and although we, like Athey, disagree that this pairing must always and necessarily exist in order for an act to constitute torture, interrogation was central to the torture that Garcia recounts here. When coupled with interrogation, torture "systematically prevents the prisoner from being the agent of anything and simultaneously pretends that he is the agent of some things," Scarry notes.[3] In the case of interrogation that leads to involuntary confession, "he is to understand his confession as it will be understood by others, as an act of self-betrayal."[4] Thus, when the Communist Party of Southern Tagalog accused Garcia and other members of disloyalty to the movement and employed torture to force the naming of ostensible collaborators, the tortured not only experi-

---

[3] Elaine Scarry, *The Body in Pain: The Making and Unmaking of the World* (New York: Oxford University Press, 1985), 47.
[4] Ibid.

enced the self-betrayal that Scarry identifies as integral to torture's work, but its magnification through the justifiable betrayal they felt by the Party and the comrades for whom they had risked so much. If, as Scarry argues, torture *unmakes* the prisoner's world by actively deconstructing its social web of meaning, then the betrayal by one's organization exacerbates this condition and makes survivors' attempts to re-weave those webs of meaning and support all the more difficult. They lost the political, social, and material camaraderie that had defined their lives for years, and, because they were members of a guerrilla insurgency, they cannot turn easily to the state for redress. Although recounting that double betrayal does not suture the political ties that were broken, Garcia's account clearly demonstrates his experience as a form of political abuse, as opposed to the individualized exchange embodied in the archetypal torture narrative.

Many survivors emphasize that organizations such as the Torture Abolition and Survivors Support Coalition International (TASSC) are crucial to building new meaning-making webs of self-identification and security, as well as to providing the ground for wider torture abolition campaigns. Such organizations offer a forum in which survivors from different local contexts share, support, and determine the paths of their own healing and politics. This solidarity depends upon the careful translations of survivors' individual experiences to one another and to outside audiences. In our fourth chapter, "Translating Trauma, Witnessing Survival," Laurie Ball Cooper provides a careful and detailed examination of the emotional and ethical challenges of the work of oral translation in these contexts. Although translators in general are tasked with "projecting a voice without assuming it," as Ball Cooper writes, in the case of torture testimonials the task is laden with the weight of suffering that must be witnessed and translated, but not coopted or spectacularized. In this precise meditation upon her own responses to these challenges, Ball Cooper highlights the interpersonal dynamics that shape translation's process and products, as well as found relationships that extend beyond the immediate testimonial situation in question. The translator's job necessarily rejects the conventional wisdom that torture is unimaginable and inexpressible. Thus, her essay provides a nuanced view of how witnessing emerges and takes shape from specific rhetorical situations and their actors.

We note that translation—not simply in the strict sense of interlinguistic communication, but also in the broader terms of intercontextual and interpersonal exchange—is integral to rethinking witnessing as a dynamic process that produces new subjects and knowledge. In *Trauma Culture:*

The Politics of Terror and Loss in Media and Literature, E. Ann Kaplan defines translation in cross-cultural contexts as a "network of interexchange, not simply a set of binary relations."[5] Here we extend that notion to focus on the dynamic relationship between speaker, translator, and listener that oral translation makes possible. Ball Cooper's essay not only provides an example of this process, emphasizing less the testimony itself than the relationships it garners, but also points to "translation" as a mode of reading. Ball Cooper's careful consideration of her own positionality in relation to that of the survivors for whom she translates models the questions that readers, too, must address when entering into a torture narrative in any language.

Together these chapters identify facets of an expanded register of witnessing necessary for an ethico-political future that we discuss more fully in our introduction to this volume. Kaplan outlines one of the fundamental tenets of witnessing that extends beyond recognition or acknowledgment, and that helps to explain the work performed by the essays in this section: "'Witnessing' involves not just empathy and motivation to help, but understanding the structure of injustice—that an injustice has taken place—rather than focusing on a specific case."[6] Foundational works by Scarry and Darius Rejali (2007) identify the common forms torture takes, its historical evolution, and, in Rejali's monumental study, its regular use by democratic governments. The essays in this section exemplify the process of placing a singular experience within a larger, systemic, and institutional context, asking readers to attend to understanding how torture operates in a given political situation and against its designated targets.

---

[5] E. Ann Kaplan, *Trauma Culture: The Politics of Terror and Loss in Media and Literature* (New Brunswick, NJ: Rutgers University Press, 2005), 104.
[6] Ibid., 23.

CHAPTER 1

Torture: The Catastrophe of a Bond

Carlos Alberto Arestivo

Translated by Laurie Ball Cooper

Drawing on his personal experiences of torture in Paraguay as well as his training as a psychiatrist, Dr. Carlos Alberto Arestivo launches this volume with an overview of what torture is, how it works toward the dissolution of the subject, and its broad social implications. His dual perspective as a survivor and clinician, and his ability to navigate between those positions, reflect the ways in which his understanding of his own experience is profoundly shaped by his medical training. In addition, he situates his experience in the context of the Stroessner dictatorship and connects his analysis of that repressive regime to the larger apparatuses of torture worldwide. Arestivo's attention to both the psychological dimensions of torture and its political contexts affords an examination of two crucial dimensions of torture's rootedness in the larger social matrix: torture's interpersonal dynamics and its embeddedness (as a political strategy, a set of techniques, and lasting scars) in societal institutions and ideologies.

An earlier version of this essay, "Appunti sul lato oscuro nella relazione torturatore/torturato," was presented at "Simposio interdisciplinare su cultura e situazione psicosociale in America Latina," University of Hamburg, September 19–22, 1991

C. A. Arestivo (✉)
Asunción, Paraguay

Arestivo's description of how torturers learn their craft, as well as how their techniques dissemble the victim's social self, underscores the psychosocial effects of torture on individuals—perpetrators and those they torture—and their societies. That the focus of torture is on dissemblage of the victim's social world and the destruction of his or her personality reveals that in its terrible, intimate encounters, torture makes personal the desire of one worldview to vanquish another. Perhaps most devastatingly, Arestivo's essay concludes that when all other social bonds have been destroyed through torture, the last one remaining to the tortured is the one that has involuntarily been made with the torturer.

* * *

The concepts set forth in this work are based upon bibliographic references to the situations of torture in Argentina, Chile, Uruguay, and Greece; direct testimonies of torture survivors; an improvised consultation in the actual prison of "The Ambush," Paraguay, where I was imprisoned for three months in 1978; and my own direct experiences in the torture sessions of the Department of Investigations of the Capital Police.

Torture is a cruel and inhuman act, produced by one or more perpetrators who find themselves in a situation of absolute power of life or death over another person, who finds him- or herself submitted, without any defense or any chance to impede the torture, flee, or defend him- or herself. That person can only endure or suffer, according to his or her psychological and physical resistance.

Many torture survivors manifest psychological repercussions that may be predictable according to variables such as his or her history, identity, or social and political ideals, or that may be extraordinarily random because of his or her organic capacity and particular life circumstances. Torture seeks to produce torment, all types of pain and suffering, vexations and humiliations, and, on the most basic level, fear. Torture attacks all the vulnerable aspects of a human being in this systematic and severe way in order to break the sufferer's defenses.

In effect, torture of political prisoners or prisoners of conscience has as its goals extracting a confession and, above all, destroying the prisoner's personality. At the same time, torture aims to have a psychosocial effect through the commotion that it produces when a member of a determined social group is captured and tortured. The climax of fear and terror expands like waves, maintaining the population in a state of permanent tension and collective fear, generating distrust as well as isolating families and social groups.

The Subculture of Fear: The Irresponsible Subject

The Paraguayan people suffered many decades of repressive government under the Stroessner regime, which was characterized by the *instauración*, or what might be called strategies of generalized terror and cruelty against the regime's political opponents. When we read the words of François Roustang in "Vínculo di libertà" ["Bond of Liberty"] describing the absolute narcissist from the perspective of the psychology of the masses, it appears that he is describing the profile of General Stroessner, expressing (among other things) that this character

> did everything that he wanted and possessed all the powers, all the women that he wanted, and all the subjects. In addition to this, his discretionary power of life and death was like the confirmation of his omnipotence.[1]

Roustang goes on to reference Elias Canetti's work in "Mass and Power":

> This narcissist, threatened with death by those for whose lives he has at his disposal, becomes a species of the super-living: it is possible to maintain power but you must 'subsist' with the incessant fear of being assassinated. […] Now then, the only manner in which to prevent this said fear is killing all the subjects as each and every one of them is his potential murderers. The narcissist who loves only himself cannot avoid detesting all others, fearing them, distrusting them, wishing them the worst of the worst—in other words, he has transformed into a paranoid person.[2]

The logic of creating a climate of fear, through persecutions, detentions, torture, exile, and even death itself is to seek the destruction of the entire social network that has given rise to trust and solidarity between people. Stroessner created this situation as a strategy to maintain his power, creating in addition an operation in which it was necessary to present a façade of democracy and the legality of his government. To do this, he first permanently suspended constitutional guarantees, created a division in the principal opposition party, and, with the necessary bribes, created a "democratic" parliament with one of those new splinter parties. Later, and with the promise of democratizing the country, he seduced the

---

[1] François Roustang, *Vínculo de libertad* (Asuncion, Paraguay: Centro de Documentacion y Estudios, 1989), 1.
[2] Roustang, *Vínculo de libertad*, 1.

other opposition parties to elaborate a new constitution, which permitted the dictator to perpetuate his power and lead in an authoritative fashion due to the very presence of *liberticidas* laws[3] in the constitution that legalized the abuse of human rights.

This abuse of human dignity was perpetuated through a system in which a few—those who displayed power and were guaranteed total impunity—abused, persecuted, captured, banished, or assassinated others. In addition, this impunity allowed them to make use of the state's resources to enrich themselves. The social response in this situation was characterized by a collective fear that restrained or paralyzed the expression of ideas, thoughts, or critiques that could have been in dissent from the acts of the government. As a consequence, defense mechanisms were created to adapt to this situation of generalized anguish—of course, for now we are expressing what occurred at the level of the masses, without considering in this work the different protests against the government which various groups attempted in different periods and which ended in terrible massacres.

Many people, little by little, accepted the situation with expressions of general distrust. They distrusted their family, friends, and neighbors due to their fear of *delación* [denunciation or betrayal]. Most parents prohibited their children from speaking out, much less becoming involved in politics or any type of social movement. Human rights were considered a subversive discourse; it was safer not to think or speak about politics. This subculture of fear created polarizing phenomena in communities. There were those who gave the orders and their families and those close to them, who were made up of those who sponsored and acted out authoritarianism with arrogance—these were the politicians and generals who blindly submitted themselves to tyranny. These people were those who made themselves rich consuming and conquering the other. These people were those

---

[3] Editors' note: The Oganization of American States' Inter-American Commission on Human Rights defines *liberticidas* as the anti-freedom statutes 294 and 209: the so-called Defense of Democracy and the Defense of Public Peace and Personal Freedom laws, respectively, which outlawed communist and other leftist political parties and severely punished individual members. As the Commission's report on Paraguay states, with these laws, "Freedom of thought and expression is stringently limited, as are the right of assembly, political rights—and even the right to work, which is enshrined in the Constitution itself. The lack of precision in defining punishable conduct grants broad discretionary powers to the judicial authority responsible for applying the law." The laws were repealed in 1989 under General Rodriguez. *See* the Annual Report of the Inter-American Commission on Human Rights 1989–90: Paraguay, OEA/Ser.L/V/II.77 rev.1, doc. 7, 17 May 1990. Available at http://www.cidh.org/annualrep/89.90eng/chap4f.htm

who were exempt from the rigors of the law, with substantial bribes, scorning those who did not integrate into their group. At the other extreme, there were the dissenters, explicitly those for whom the repressions already noted waited. Finally, there were the indifferent ones, who in reality were those who adapted to this situation.

All of this determined the loss of moral values in our country; created social fear; impeded the establishment of alliances or social bonds that were part of people's psychological security; and generated distrust, isolation, and self-censure, factors which separate the individual from all that is social. In this way, the individual was forced to renounce his own thoughts, which at the same time makes development of political discourse difficult, allowing the *espúreos* [spurious or false] directors[4] to decide for him. This process leaves man poor and residual, an irresponsible subject who cannot survive the consequences of his principles, discourse, and word responsibly. The social body becomes ill. This model of authoritarianism, arrogance, disrespect for the person, bribery, and corruption, together with a culture of corruption, is supported by impunity and observed in people's everyday conduct in distinct areas of life, such as family, work, school, and so on, even though the tyranny ended a couple of decades ago. The almost imperceptible changes in the conduct of our people are also the effect of the culture of fear.

THE DECISION TO BE A TORTURER

Torture is situated in this context as a useful instrument with which to sustain a repressive government, and, as such, forms part of a plan, a strategy, of governing in which torture ceases to be a contingent phenomenon. Torture implies a scientifically prepared process; it requires trained, suitable, and efficient human resources. For this reason, the role of the torturers requires training. The torturer is a person selected or self-nominated for this role, which implies an aggressive capacity. Despite this, the torturer is a common, mediocre person who, as many authors have indicated, has not achieved or had great goals in life, and who, through this "work," seeks to be an object of the leader's libidinal deposit. In addition to this, the torturer obtains in this way a privileged life. In this way, the torturer triumphs, through his egotistical efforts, over the "social subject."

---

[4] Translator's note: Possibly a specifically Paraguayan reference to the *junta directiva*.

At the same time, the torturer can be the father of a family considered to be "good" by the community. (This occurred in Paraguay, where one of the famous torturers recognized for his cruelty was, until his detention, the charge of the president of the Commission of Priests of a religious college.) The torturer is not mentally ill (not a sadist or a psychopath), even though there are detectable features of his personality. He is a subject who has consciously decided to assume the function of torture and has been trained and prepared for this work. In some countries (e.g., the United States and Greece), there are schools for torturers, and experts in the technology of pain are sent in to teach techniques of torture.

The training of torturers involves a series of situations, which are interesting to imagine. Some American authors investigated torture in Greece and described the necessary conditions and situations for one to become a torturer: one needs to find oneself in a situation of total obedience (such as in the military or police force) and submit oneself to severe punishments if one does not precisely follow the orders of one's superiors. Future torturers endure suffering and humiliation in their preparations in order to internalize their lessons. Another aspect of their training consists of making sure that the torturer does not feel guilty or sensitive when faced with this horrific act. To achieve this, the torturer is persuaded and convinced that he is protecting the community from a miserable being that wishes to destroy the system; the enemy is seen as an *un*human being, a monster or an animal that does not deserve compassion. He is the subject of death, like a deified being—a consumer who is satisfied in plunder and robbery. The torturer is an expert in producing pain, knowing the most vulnerable and sensitive zones of the body, how far he can go, and the limits—although sometimes he errs. A final element that favors the role of the torturer is the great impunity that he enjoys, which permits him to feel both invulnerable and omnipotent, knowing that he is feared and that he himself is the producer of that fear.

TORTURE: ETIOLOGY OF CLINICAL MANIFESTATIONS THAT FOLLOW

Generally, the "treatment" lasts weeks or months, or even years, when there is a systematic and continuous threat, and through this very fear people tend to reject, isolate, or marginalize the victim or survivor. The survivor then suffers constant stress, which produces psychological and physical exhaustion. Over time that exhaustion generates psychological defense mechanisms which in principle appear to be isolated symptoms, but which usually cease to be symptoms and become part of the individual's conduct even after the cause of these symptoms disappears.

Pain softens a person, hypersensitizes her, leaving her apprehensive and radically afraid. It damages her. The humiliations, mistreatment, and vexations work against her self-esteem, often causing the person to hate and despise herself. The lack of communication, apart from the fear, provokes anxiety and distress, and causes so much desperation that it sometimes succeeds in destroying the personality. The victim, according to her own history, comes out from this anguish connecting with experiences that evoke valid, internalized human relationships which confirm her "social body." This process of connection constitutes a saving hallucination, a clinical phenomenon that has been introduced conceptually by F. Roustang. The hallucinogenic or delirious phenomenon should not be read as a traumatic psychosis, it should be placed as a psychopathological manifestation *sui generis*. Traumatic psychoses are in most cases produced by a natural phenomenon, and generally the trauma appears suddenly and does not last a long time. The person is not impeded from fleeing or defending herself; there is not a lack of communication, nor is there clear intent, humiliation, and vexation. What is more, there is a tendency for solidarity among people when traumatic psychoses are at issue. Torture is something more than this. It is a deplorable act produced by man, wherein the survivor is submitted to a structured process of destruction and where all factors which hold the survivor to her existence in the world are systematically attacked. The survivor's physical structure is attacked to produce pain, mutilate her, or humiliate her. The torturers attack the prisoner's psychological and social structures through the use of incommunicado detention, fear and guilt, and through the destruction of the survivor's self-esteem.

Another way of emerging from the situation of torture occurs in those individuals who in their histories have not succeeded in internalizing significant relationships that constitute the social body, but instead have prioritized internalizing their ideological discourse. These subjects therefore lack this human experience. They do not manage to connect with human characters and succeed only in destroying their own ideals, entering into the game of the torturer, who has in this case achieved his objectives.

The individual does, however, possess a great strength, a capacity to fight against adversity, and an admirable ability to adapt. She adapts to the most difficult situations, endures the most atrocious pain, and seeks desperately to relate to whomever she can, including the torturer himself, because even though the torturer is cruel, he constitutes in this moment a significant person associated with the survivor's primary experience. In this way, the survivor seeks a bit of calm. However, the constant change of reclusive places and torturers begins to drain the survivor's adaptive capacity and favor stress, which always increases in the face of that which is new. This alert state that the situation generates and its accompanying constant fear impede sleep or make it difficult for the prisoner to fall asleep. Even if she manages to do so due to sheer exhaustion, the guards enter to impede her sleep violently. Lack of sleep consumes physical and psychological energies. Lack of sleep makes the prisoner crazy.

The survivor of torture has been slowly and systematically branded on all of her vulnerable points. It is possible that she does not have an historical reference for this situation which would allow her to relate or associate, except to the situation of helplessness and defenselessness with relation to her childhood of primary experience set forth already.

Many psychopathological manifestations that appear in this situation warrant deeper study, because they escape psychopathological concepts and the psychiatric mainstream. Although the symptoms exhibited appear similar to other manifestations, the global understanding of these manifestations is confused, and it is due to this confusion that survivors do not always respond to classic psychotherapy treatments.

Tortured: Anguish and Attempts at a Solution

People who are deprived of their liberty in a demonstrative, violent, and showy way, for their political motives or because they helped dissidents, enter systematically into the process of torture already described. When they recover their liberty, sometimes they sink into a state of panic; paradoxically, they feel safer inside of the "inferno." They have learned, more or less, to get by in a dangerous situation. Once outside, in a situation of relative tranquility, where the danger is apparently relative, their phantoms appear and their lives become the inferno, because in the prison the danger was real, and now that there is no danger, victims lack the skills to confront these phantoms.

A political prisoner (and engineer by profession) incarcerated for more than eighteen years, with whom I shared the time that I was a prisoner, learned to be a tailor during his confinement. He had suffered atrocious torture for years, according to his story given while we shared a cell, and then they had left him in peace. His status was good from a psychiatric standpoint. Two months after I gained my liberty, he also gained his. After a little bit of time, he called me to give him professional help. I found him in a state of panic: shaking, with a fixed stare, refusing to undress out of his wife's clothing, babbling, extremely docile, and suffering from days of insomnia. He had undoubtedly suffered a deep regression, to the point that we had to intern him in his own home with therapeutic assistants and psychopharmacological treatments, until we were able to stabilize him and send him abroad as a refugee.

When a survivor recovers his liberty, there is fear and distrust in the social environment. His friends reject and avoid the survivor, creating in him a deep isolation; we call this situation the "leper's syndrome." His body is tired, without direct pain now; however, the pain is inscribed on his body. He sees his entire life project promptly erased and remains without projects because his present is confused—it is so charged with his past that it does not allow him to think. His self-esteem is broken.

Two weeks after the coup d'état in Paraguay (February 2–3, 1989), formerly tortured people came together to form a human rights entity called the Assembly for the Right to Life. In this first meeting of almost forty people, something that I have noted as "therapeutic" occurred, although it was not planned. The meeting was very emotional. Many of my patients were there, who had not wanted to speak about their painful experiences in the torture chambers in group therapy or individual sessions. Despite this, almost all of them began telling their stories spontaneously, almost as if they were returning to experiment by creating a special climate that favored this cathartic situation. This is what I considered the therapeutic moment, not just for the cathartic situation itself, but instead for the solidarity and restraint of distress that were produced through this re-feeling and re-living, contained for so long without a safe space or ears qualified to hear.

The tortured person needs to gather up that which has been spoiled, re-arm this personality, and meet someone who accepts, appreciates, and values him, including that which was done to him. The tortured person needs something more than psychopharmaceuticals; he needs a new meeting with himself and others.

This work, a little disorganized and *desprolijo* [messy], provides the context and the reference point for that which I wish to set forth: I am going to pause the film at the scene of a dramatic meeting between a torturer and a survivor, a dramatic encounter between complete power, in the form of the torturer, and total powerlessness, embodied in the survivor. The person who is going to be tortured is totally immobilized, she cannot flee or defend herself. She can only yell if they do not muzzle her. She can only think quickly, searching for an exit from this stressful situation, but these simultaneous thoughts crowd together in a flood, confusing the person who is to be tortured. Panic enters and it is impossible to imagine. Stress is at its maximum.

A surgeon facing a patient about to be submitted to surgical intervention also has absolute power of life or death over someone who is totally defenseless. The surgeon cares for the patient so that the patient does not suffer, for this the surgeon uses anesthesia. The patient trusts the surgeon and is (one hopes) delivered peacefully in the end. The surgeon takes care to produce minimal surgical trauma and ensures that the patient suffers minimal stress. Through this relationship there emerges a certain affection, a recognition of gratitude.

As opposed to this relation of gratitude and trust, when the torturer confronts the prisoner, he takes care that the prisoner is always lucid, and sometimes drugs the prisoner with amphetamines to increase his vigilance and to free more energy. The torturer makes sure that his work is precise, meticulous, and done in such a way as to produce maximum pain while leaving minimal traces. The torturer takes pains to ensure that the prisoner reaches his maximum level of stress. This moment is the consummation of the prisoner's fear, and of all the ritual preparation for this act.

Psychological Phases and Processes in a Situation of Torture

When the prisoner comes before an extreme circumstance, such as immersion in putrid water with the urine, excrement, and vomit of those who preceded the him in this same experience, the prisoner lives out a peculiar situation. Torture by immersion in a *pileta* or small pool is one of the most atrocious torments, at the limits where death itself is confronted and sometimes even sought as a salvation or an escape, but is rarely found. With the victim's hands and feet immobilized, his mouth is plunged into a pool in those ancient baths. A specialist, the torturer, straddles the stomach of the prisoner and takes the prisoner's hair to submerge him. The prisoner can last only a few minutes, fighting and struggling; the body tries everything to untie itself. Another collaborator immobilizes the prisoner's legs, which hang over the opposite edge of the pool. The prisoner continues struggling, swallowing putrid water.

The prisoner's lucidity is elevated by the huge release of adrenalin. When the torturer notices some kind of signal, perhaps cyanosis, thanks to his refined and exquisite training, the torturer brings the prisoner to the surface. The prisoner is permitted some gulps of air, and then later the torturer carries out acts that are almost stereotypes of *reanimación*, like using his fists to hit the prisoner in the stomach to produce vomit of swallowed water. The prisoner uses his strength to reclaim a little air in an extraordinary effort, then vomits, urinates, and defecates. Taking advantage of this state of confusion, the torturer proceeds with an interrogation to obtain information or to pressure the prisoner to sign a declaration compromising himself or others, given that the prisoner cannot use his own psychological autonomy at this point. This situation is repeated many times, producing a progressive deterioration manifested in extreme physical weakness, psychological exhaustion, and displays of psychological injury.

This is how the climax of the torture session arrives in what presents itself as a manifestation of mental, moral, and religious emptiness. This marks, at the same time, the extreme disintegration of the personality. There comes a moment when the prisoner, who is still lucid even though he is completely exhausted, realizes that he cannot continue to fight. The prisoner tightens his abdominal muscles and, already without strength, searches for death, trying to drown, breathing below the water, and when this does not succeed, becoming desperate, enters the first phase, which we will call *illusion*. The prisoner cries out internally for God, whether he believes or does not believe alike; he feels like a child abandoned by all; the prisoner cries out for his mother. However, neither God nor the prisoner's mother appears to save him from this atrocious suffering. The prisoner opens his eyes and only has in front of him the one man who can save him, this torturer who is killing him. There is no alternative, the prisoner must trust the torturer and so he trusts… In this second phase, which we will call *trust*, the tortured person, who needs and desires this social fabric already discussed, establishes a perverse alliance with his torturer, destroying little by little his political ideals built over the course of his history. The prisoner has been defeated. Torture breaks the subject, as Roustang wrote, and the prisoner's own body converts into a horrifying object for himself and the perfect world that has wrought it. The prisoner has disappeared slowly and, paradoxically, prepares himself despite his own will to accept this trust in whatever salvation may come. Trust in this moment seems, due to the drama and the intensity, to stay marked as an imprint associated with the primary experience of torture, in a profound regression.

Those tortured people who have, as we said before, internalized a significant social fabric in addition to their political principles manage to enter a third phase, which we can call *refuge*. This phase is manifested in disconnection from this situation of extreme anguish: suddenly, the prisoner feels nothing and no longer suffers. The prisoner's body completely relaxes, he no longer fights for his life, nor does he swallow water. Although the prisoner is lucidly disassociating himself, his body continues to be submerged, but the prisoner is somewhere else. The subject is submerged in a warm world full of fantastic experiences. He finds refuge in those human relationships that inhabit his internal world, true defensive hallucinations. He continues to be lucid: he feels that they take him out of the water, that they hit him in the stomach, that he vomits, and that they ask him questions. However, the prisoner feels all of this at a distance, as if it were not directed at him. Here they finish the session and abandon the prisoner.

There is always a police medic on hand for any kind of emergency—a doctor, also a torturer—in case they fail. This is because they do not want to kill the person, but rather just to destroy the personality. Here, the session ends. This third phase proclaims the failure of the torturer, proclaims the limit that the violent system fails to recognize, and reveals the failure of omnipotence, of which the entire authoritarian system is constituted. The strong social body, significantly that of social subjects, constitutes the singular element of the limit upon authoritarian ideologies that can be redeemed from the clinic. And yet, at the end of the session, the prisoner remains alone in a corner, trembling. Suddenly, he lets out (or rather, emits) a yell like a child being born, an incomprehensible and impulsive cry—in this way, he re/enters the harsh reality. The torturers reappear, bringing a blanket, a cup of coffee, with a "kind-hearted" smile. He who was a torturer now is taking care of the prisoner, and the prisoner becomes confused.

Up until this point, I wanted to describe the phases of the process of torture. In conclusion, I would like to focus attention on the second phase of *trust*. This phase consists of a restless phenomenon that is not always understood or accepted, and that is systematically denied by tortured people. From outside, anyone realizes that when survivors relay their experiences, a certain hate, rancor, and fury are displayed toward the torturer. At the same time, under the cover of this catastrophe, there appears a hidden protection for the torturer, an attempt to justify the unjustifiable. Could it be that this strange bond, so intensely dramatic, brings forth another bond so primitive that it manages to confuse the bond itself?

CHAPTER 2

Torture in an Historical Context: Notes from Sudan

Mohamed Elgadi

Dr. Mohamed Elgadi, a Sudanese refugee, torture survivor, and US citizen, is a human rights activist and college educator. In this essay, he examines how political authorities draw on religion as a justification for torture. Although his case study is Islamic governments, his argument is not limited to a single religion. He begins by tracing torture in Sudan back to pre-Islamist eras and up to its contemporary uses, in order to argue that torture in Sudan has "no single originary moment." His brief overview underscores the ways in which, although torture has not historically been limited to Islamist rule, Islamist regimes have also not hesitated to invoke religious law to justify torture. Elgadi then focuses on the use of torture by Islamist authorities in Sudan since the military coup of 1989.

This historical background provides the context for Elgadi's description of "My Ghost House Life," when, in 1992, he was held and tortured in one of Omar al-Bashir's detention centers in Khartoum. Set up to perversely mimic a khalwa, or religious school, the detention center was designed to enforce particular Islamic doctrines and to quash political and human rights opposition to the government. Elgadi identifies aspects of torture that are familiar to scholars of how, as Elaine Scarry has detailed, torture transforms the victim's pain into a symbol of the torturer's power. These techniques include

M. Elgadi (✉)
Amherst, MA, USA

© The Author(s) 2018
A. S. Moore, E. Swanson (eds.), *Witnessing Torture*, Palgrave Studies in Life Writing, https://doi.org/10.1007/978-3-319-74965-5_2

the use of euphemism, the creation of torture rituals, and, especially in religious contexts, the indoctrination of perpetrators to see themselves as divinely protected, as well as the self-abnegating effect of torture on prisoners who are equally forcefully indoctrinated so as to understand their suffering as a result of divine punishment, particularly for the sin of their supposed deviance from religious purity.

Elgadi concludes with a more hopeful argument that, notwithstanding the religious invocations to excuse or promote torture, the political use of torture might galvanize its opposition in two ways. First, recognizing the incompatibility of torture and a just society can spur public opposition against abusive, pseudo-religious regimes; and, second, it can generate a productive critique of religious penal codes that violate fundamental human rights.

* * *

Evidence of torture has been present from the earliest histories of ancient civilizations; indeed, it can be traced back more than four millennia. The documents and drawings found in ancient Egyptian temples have told us about the terrible fate of prisoners of war during the time of King Ramses II. In one of the most horrific scenes documented on a wall sculpture almost 4000 years ago, the image of prisoners being beaten is very close to one of the torture methods known as "The Party" in modern Islamists' lexicon of torture in Sudan.[1] Followers of the Prophet Muhammad in the early seventh century were mainly slaves from Mecca, and the torture endured by Ammar bin Yasir was one of the living examples from that era taught to children in Muslim schools as a good example of standing up for one's beliefs.[2] The polytheists of Mecca, led by Abu Lahab, the uncle of Prophet Muhammad, inflicted severe torture on Ammar and other members of his family who embraced the new religion of Islam. The torture of slaves was very common and part of the daily practices seen in most public markets in ancient Arabia. In spite of the strong opposition to torture by the Islamic state during

---

[1] Anuraag Sanghi, "3 Battles That Changed World History – and India," *2ndlook*, last modified February 28, 2009, accessed May 7, 2014, http://2ndlook.wordpress.com/2009/02/28/3-battles-that-changed-world-history-and-india/.

[2] "Ammar bin Yasir," accessed January 18, 2014, http://www.al-islam.org/ammar-bin-yasir-kamal-al-sayyid/ammar-bin-yasir.

the reign of the Prophet Muhammad in Medina, just a few decades after his death the use of torture was embraced by those in power as a tool of oppression. Sadly, torture continues to be marshaled by many Arab and Muslim societies today to serve political ends.

In Sudan, the Islamic invaders in the seventh century enslaved members of the black African population, and stories of torture emerge from the old history of the Sudanese sultanates and kingdoms. The controversial Paqt Treaty of 652 imposed on the Nubians of north Sudan required them to hand over to the Muslim invaders 400 slaves every year. In this way, Sudan had become a hunting ground for slaves, a practice that continued even after the treaty was abolished in 1315. From the mid-seventh century until the mid-nineteenth century, the Umayyad, Abbasid, and Ottoman empires introduced new dimensions in the institutionalized torture of African slaves. For example, slaves were whipped to force them to walk across the harsh African Sahara to the north African slave markets. It was very common for a caravan of 1000 slaves "hunted" in the Bahr Ghazal region and the southern parts of Sudan to reach its final destination in Ghadames, Tripoli, or Cairo with only 100–200 survivors. Torture also appears in the popular folk tale of "Umm Kardos Mountain," set during the Daju Kingdom (twelfth century) in the eastern Darfur region. The Daju sultan was known for his cruelty, the tale goes. His sadism rose to a new level when one day he ordered the people to dig up the mountain to move it, in order to join it with another series of mountains in the far west. (This is not to say that there was not resistance to such cruelty; in the story, the wise woman Um Kardos managed to get rid of the Sultan and his torturous practices by a clever deceit when she fed his presumptuous and egocentric attitude and offered him a ride on a wild beast that ended up killing him.) Well-documented cases of torture are found, too, at the onset of Turkish rule of Sudan in 1821, when it was practiced in the name of religion against those who failed to pay taxes to the Ottoman Empire. Turkish authorities also introduced the horrific slow killing instrument known as Khazouk, or execution by impalement, as the historian M. S. Algaddal notes.

Unfortunately, torture was not abolished in the aftermath of the Mahdist revolution in 1885, perhaps because it was institutionalized during the time of its predecessor, Khallifa Abdullahi, who might be considered the father of systematic torture in the modern history of Sudan. During his thirteen-year rule he tortured his dissidents using strange and cruel methods not found in any history of torture. He ordered his prisoners to be put inside a small room with no food or water, and then ordered the door and windows to be sealed and boarded up using *toub* (bricks). This method, known as *tattwib* (from *toub*), was used to slowly kill a number of his military leaders when he suspected their disloyalty.[3] The massacre of the "Bataheen" tribe[4] stands as another shameful landmark in the history of Sudan. What kind of a leader was it who stood for long hours observing the slow killing of sixty-seven rebels by skinning their feet and dragging them to be hanged or cross-amputated (the infamous *khillaf* amputation)?

After Sudan gained independence from Anglo-Egyptian rule in 1956, and before the October Revolution of 1964, very little was known and documented about the use of systematic torture. A Sudanese Communist leader attributes the development of the current torture establishment in Sudan to the period of General Aboud (1958–64), who employed mass arrest and exile, in addition to a scorched-earth land policy, against rebels in the south.[5] We can also note the systematic building of the current torture establishment during the early days of the dictator Numeri (1969–85), who established an independent and specialized government department to oversee torture. The department took its own power directly from the Revolution Commands Council (RCC), whose members had training at the School of the Americas through a special working relationship established with the Central Intelligence Agency (CIA) in the early 1980s.

These brief examples and history remind us that torture in Sudan has no single originary moment. It is not a relatively new phenomenon linked to the dictators who ruled over the last six decades; however, it does have a long entanglement with Islamic political authority. This was evident when the Mahdiya state in the late nineteenth century adopted some of the Islamic Shari'a laws of Hudud, or "crimes against God," that establish and promote torture. A century later, the Muslim Brotherhood political party reintroduced Shari'a laws by convincing the dictator Numeri (1969–85) that they would be the best tool for subduing the growing opposition.

---

[3] Mohammed Saeed Algaddal, *almhdiah walhbshah; drasah fi alsyasah aldakhliah walkharjiah ldoulah almhdiah 1881–1898* (Lebanon: Dar Eljil Publishing, 1992).

[4] Algaddal, *almhdiah walhbshah*, 1992.

[5] Personal communication with Ustaz/Tigani Eltayeb-Aden, Yemen, 1994.

Torture in Sudan after 1989

After the military coup of the National Islamic Front (NIF) in 1989, a new era of torture began under a dogmatic religious program to build up the Islamic state in Sudan, and to suppress and subdue all other opinions—Islamic and secular—that stood in its way. The regime appointed Nafie Ali Nafie, a university professor and one of the infamous aggressive cadres of the NIF. It was rumored in Sudan that Nafie had had a highly technical training in torture in Iran.[6] Under his supervision, the para-legal prison system known as "ghost houses" was officially established in July 1989, exactly one day after the military coup. As reported by *Al-Wafd* in 1993, the following statement was made by a former security officer who worked inside the current torture machine, until he ended up himself as a torture victim because of doubt and suspicion of his loyalty:

> Ghost houses are secret places belonging to the General Security apparatus which were designated for the political detainees [...] what is happening inside these places is simply unbelievable [...] beyond the human imagination.[7]

At one point in 1993, the Group Against Torture in Sudan (GATS)[8] reported and confirmed the locations of over twenty "ghost houses" in the capital city Khartoum alone. The central location was a "ghost house" in the east of Khartoum, near the former Citibank building, off al-Makk Nimir Street. In the past, the house had been a government residence designated to one family; however, it was made to hold 171 activists during the time I was detained there in 1992.

The importance of this historical background stems from linking and connecting the different historical faces of torture—again, both religious and secular—to the current one being perpetrated by the dictatorial regime of Omar al-Bashir. In its attempts to show its religious ideological superiority over other schools, the Muslim Brotherhood (MB) in Sudan proved beyond doubt that it is, in fact, no different from any other torture regime, religious

---

[6] This training had taken place during the 1985–89 democratic period, when the NIF was preparing for its 1989 military coup. This is public information in circulation among most of the human rights and political movements in Sudan. The NIF has not yet admitted it.

[7] *Al-Wafd* newspaper, December 27, 1993, page 9, Cairo, Egypt (Arabic publication).

[8] See *Group Against Torture in Sudan*, accessed March 27, 2013, www.GhostHouses.blogspot.com

or secular. The use of systematic torture against peaceful dissidents, no matter what the religious justification, renders this religious regime in keeping with other brutal, outlaw regimes. Indeed, when it comes to torture there is no difference, as we will see in the next section of this essay, between the religious Inquisition sponsored by the Catholic Church of the Middle Ages and the Sudanese Islamist torturers of the twenty-first century. In spite of the clashing ideologies of the Inquisition and Islamism, both are united in crushing their challengers, who are called the same, if only in different languages: heretic or *kafir* (infidel).

My Ghost House Life

For a tourist or one who was not familiar with what was going on in Sudan after the 1989 military coup that installed Omar al-Bashir as President, the scene at the Citibank Ghost House would look like any of those in a *khalwa*, or Qur'anic school—although of course there was no *khalwa* needed when the British rulers planned and built that neighborhood for their own administrative staff in the early 1900s. The house continued to accommodate senior staff of the Sudanese government after Independence, until it was taken over by one of the Civil Service departments before ending up as the absurd "*khalwa*-like" scene in which I was interned.

This scene at the Citibank Ghost House is one dimension of the "Civilizational Project," as the MB called its radical Islamic vision for Sudan. "Students" squatted on the floor, holding the Qur'an and reading from different chapters, some in small groups, reciting in the same way an *imam* or *sheikh* would be doing when leading prayer. Despite this apparent similarity, a couple of things were different in that late-afternoon scene. The average age of the "students" was over forty years, ranging from twenty to seventy (in Qur'anic school it is five to twelve); there was no *sheikh* (teacher) sitting on the floor to supervise and lead the "class"; and the place itself was different from any teaching *khalwa*. It was a three-room building opening into a large living room (a salon, as it is known in Sudan) that included two bathrooms, and all windows were boarded from the outside, such that light bulbs were turned on all day (and night, too). Another major element that would rule out the *khalwa* was the presence of bathrooms in an Islamic place of worship or place for reading the Qur'an. Unlike the mosques in the United States, and in some other Muslim countries, Sudanese mosques (and teaching *khalwa*, too) are designed to have the bathrooms as far as possible from the main court of prayer. In that Sudanese scene, over eighty persons were jammed on the floors and so close by the two toilets that one needed to step over tired bodies to enter the small, dirty room to relieve oneself. No, this was not a *khalwa*. This was the infamous government-operated torture center known by people in Sudan as the Citibank Ghost House (because of its proximity to the former Citibank building).[9] The scene was chaotic in a way that I did not fully digest until I saw it reflected on the face of a citizen who was detained after he decided to rest under the shade of a tree by the gate of the Ghost House. Thinking it was just a regular family house, he was astonished by the harsh order of one of the guards that he stay away, which he declined. He was immediately arrested and severely beaten, before being literally thrown inside my large cell. There, he later opened his eyes on this Kafkaesque scene that was very much like one described in the recent feature film *Rosewater* (2014), based upon the memoir of a journalist who was detained and tortured in Evin prison in Iran.[10] After a few days of shock, the citizen began to speak and tell his story, saying that he thought he must be in a dream or nightmare.

Such mimicry of the *khalwa* in the torture chamber was not an innovation by the modern Sudanese government; in fact, torture has been used throughout history to help one religious school prevail over another. One example is from the relatively recent history of Spain. The Spanish Inquisition in the late fifteenth century, which targeted mainly Jews and Muslims, used torture chambers supervised by priests. Most of the current schools of torture adopted and adapted methods that were used at that time. One example here is the infamous waterboarding, which was actually based on the

> *toca*, also called *interrogatorio mejorado del agua*, and which consisted of introducing a cloth into the mouth of the victim, and forcing them to ingest water spilled from a jar so that they had the impression of drowning.[11]

---

[9] Prior to the visit of the United Nations' special Human Rights Rapporteur to Sudan in 1995, the eighteen torture cells were removed and all detainees were moved somewhere else. The place still belongs to the Security Apparatus, located at the corner of El Nugumi, Ali Dinar, and 17th streets, east of Makk Nimir street. Torture survivors plan to designate it as a memorial museum when the country is finally free of the al-Bashir dictatorship.

[10] Maziar Bahari, *Then They Came for Me: A Family's Story of Love, Captivity, and Survival* (New York: Random House, 2011).

[11] George Ryley Scott, *The History of Torture through the Ages* (New York: Columbia University Press, 2003), 172.

Significantly, these priests who were conducting torture insisted that confession be taken from the victim after the end of the torture session. They wanted to convince their religious conscience that the "subject" had confessed freely and not under/during the actual act of torture. Apparently this "free-will confession" was a prerequisite of the sentencing to be issued by the bishop's representative.[12] This illogical behavior on the part of religious officials was no different from the kind I personally experienced and witnessed at the Citibank Ghost House. The only difference was that the modern Islamist torturer at the Citibank Ghost House was not looking for a confession, like his counterpart, the Inquisition-era Spaniard; rather, he was targeting the imaginary Satan that he perceived in my resistance to accepting his version of Islam.

The cruel minds of the Islamist leaders who seized power in 1989 introduced the ghost house system to crush the human rights movement and to punish opposition activists. President Omar al-Bashir, the head of the regime, insisted on denying the existence of these secret torture centers, even when his Minister of Justice and Attorney General, Abdelaziz Shiddu, admitted that they did exist. And while the Minister recognized the Ghost Houses, he still claimed that they were designed for the "comfort of detainees."[13]

The torture "party" (the softening-up phase characterizing the Islamist torture school in Sudan) is one example of how these detention centers are made "comfortable" for detainees. This absurd name was given by the Sudanese torturers to mimic young people's extravagantly loud musical parties. As one former detainee put it, "The only music at these parties is cries of pain, swear words, lashing sounds and electrical shocks."[14] The "party" is usually conducted by a group of guards who outnumber the prisoners, under supervision of a high-ranking torturer. Acting in the capacity of an outside evaluator, this torturer instructs the junior torturers on when, how, and on whom they should focus to reach the person he had identified as the weakest member of the group, the one who can be broken. In my own case, the Head of the Security Apparatus instructed his party team while they were "working" on me and my human rights colleagues when we were arrested in 1992:

[12] *Ibid.*
[13] See the Amnesty International documentary *Scarred Nation*, which was originally produced by Journeyman Pictures under a different name, *The Harsher Face of Islam*, www.journeyman.tv/?lid=9694 accessed February 27, 2013.
[14] See "The Party: A Sudanese Torture Story," accessed March 27, 2013, www.youtube.com/watch?v=M8eDuH1SCQ0. Comment made on YouTube website in response to that documentary.

> In every group for which you have succeeded in arresting its members, there is a weak ring or circle [and] you have to single him out [...] carefully study the group you brought in tonight while you are working on them, and *insha'Allah* [God willing] you will get useful information.

That is not much different from another statement I later learned about, one that was given by another torturer, who lectured:

> Before starting the torture session, you must have been finished studying the victim thoroughly to point out strength and weak sides in his/her personality, and accordingly to determine what most effective method of torture to carry on.[15]

The only difference here was in ethnicity and religion. The first one was a black Sudanese Muslim torturer, and the second was a white South African Christian torturer.

REFLECTION AND EVALUATION

It is very interesting to try to understand the world of a torturer and how he arrived at that point in his life (they are almost always males). Take, for example, naming torture a "party." Is this designation something borrowed from a perverted understanding of spirituality? I am thinking here of images from the Middle Ages in Persia, depicting Jahannam with Satan standing at the gates to the afterlife with a big smile, dancing and laughing at the "sinners" while they are getting grilled. Maybe this is why they call torture in Sudan the "party," because Islamists are so obsessed with the concept of an afterlife. In his remarkable book on torture and torturers, John Conroy reviewed many psychological studies that shed light on the making of a torturer. One example was the training of Greek military police during the horror years of the military coup, 1967–74. The suffering and hard times they went through during training made them deal with people under investigation as "enemies of the state" and "worms"; these constructions, in turn, made it possible, and indeed "morally correct," to beat them up. The torturers even used the term "tea party" to describe torture training or a torture job (another funny thing that

---

[15] International Rehabilitation Council for Torture Victims, *Torture Journal* 4, no. 3 (1994).

reminds me of my Tea Group, as we were called in the Ghost House, referring to the condition we were in when got arrested; this contrasts with another, the "Araki Group," who were drinking the hard local liquor *arak* when arrested).[16]

The character of the Islamist torturer is not unique, as some may think. It is no different from most of those selected to do such a dirty job within any political or religious group. They get recruited to a core, elite group within the Party based on their outstanding obedience and loyalty. This core group is based on the history of the Muslim Brotherhood in Egypt, specifically the formation of the "Private Apparatus"—a kind of "special forces" unit—in 1939. They are not necessarily distinguished in military training, but are selected for their political and ideological orientation: many of the Islamist torturers took the job and were promoted based on their hatred for "liberals" in general and the political Left in particular. Just like their colleagues in other countries, they too give nicknames to their torture methods and to the places they practice their dirty business. They called the Citibank location in Khartoum "al-Waha" (oasis!). For some of the torture methods they invented, they selected names such as "Tayyara Gammat" (airplane take-off) or "Sit Alaraki" (female *arak* seller), among others.

Sometimes you hear stories about torturers who respect or admire their strong victims who stand up and do not give in during the horrific pain. I did not witness this. They saw us as just a *Tabour* (fifth column) helping their infidel enemies: crushing prisoners with no mercy does not permit any sympathy with their bravery. I think part of the torturers' obvious anger over the resistance of their victims is that it resembles in their sick minds the heroic resistance of the first Muslims in Mecca in 609 CE, in particular Ammar ibn Yasir,[17] one of the first followers of the Prophet Muhammad who suffered a great deal at the hands of Mecca elites. The more the prisoner shows resistance and defiance, the more the Islamist torturer of the twenty-first century gets angry and hurts him, just as happened to Ammar in the seventh century.

To clarify: I met two types of torturer at Citibank: first, the "professional" torturer, whose training was initially as part of the legal system of the police department before the 1989 military coup. Those in this category,

---

[16] John Conroy, *Unspeakable Acts, Ordinary People: The Dynamics of Torture* (New York: Alfred Knopf, 2000), 95–96.

[17] Akramulla Syed, "Hazrat Ammar ibn Yasir (Radiyallahu Anhu), Sahaba Stories, Yathrib (Madina al-Munawara)," last modified November 17, 2016, accessed May 7, 2014, http://www.ezsoftech.com/stories/companion6.asp

generally speaking, were less feared unless they believed you had some information they wanted. The second category, the meaner one, was the "ideologized" torturer who had joined the security team for his blind partisan obedience. You know this type immediately when you meet them: "Their mark is on their faces," per the Qur'an (Ch. 48:29); however, not exactly as the Holy Book meant by describing righteous people in this verse. You can see in their faces that dangerous look of a sadist who actually enjoys inflicting pain and suffering because he strongly believes he is doing his work in the name of Allah. The moans and screams of the victims represent their victory over Satan; therefore, the more the prisoners resist, the more the torturers get angry over their own devilish enemy. This is why it is very important in a ghost house to be able to identify who is your torturer: a professional, or an Islamist ideologue.

Torture Menu

Once when I was discussing in a public forum in the United States the horror of the ghost houses, I noticed among the audience a representative of the Sudanese regime who was sheepishly smiling when I used the term "Torture Menu." He insisted that he had no connection with the torture establishment, in spite of the fact that he had admitted he was a member of *al-Gihaz* (Apparatus), as the National Intelligence and Security Services (NISS) is known in Sudan. I imagined him sharing the English term "menu" with his subordinates and maybe asking them to use it instead of the Arabic word *lista*, which was used by the torturer Abuzeid. Torturers in general and Islamists in particular are very concerned with creating their own rituals when they inflict torture. Take the use of this weird method to conduct their dirty business as if it were part of the food order in a restaurant, or as in a prescription for medication. After the initial evaluation conducted while the "party" was going on, a Torture Menu would be created according to the strengths/weaknesses that were noticed by supervisors during the chaotic, savage orgy (i.e. the "party"). Like in any evaluation report, the Torture Menu included the Evaluation Recommendations to be carried out daily by a team of sadistic experts, especially after curfew so that the screams of pain could not be heard in that business-district block. The interrogation takes place at night at the main offices of the NISS, and that is when most of the bodily damage happens; however, that is not to say that such damage was not also inflicted during the day at the ghost house. I witnessed and/or tasted over thirty torture methods used during the four-month period I was detained in that place: beating (the "party"); systematic beating that causes head injury; strangling; burning (feet roasting); flogging; El Telefono (continuous slapping); oxygen deprivation (especially to asthmatic detainees); genital mutilation (testicle crushing); starvation; medicinal torture by injecting hallucinatory drugs; repetitive loud noise during solitary confinement; electroshock; anal penetration using solid objects; and more. This list of physical tortures was supplemented by many cruel methods of psychological torture that led to the mental collapse of some cellmates, who attempted suicide as a way to ease the pain.

Even as the torturers were evaluating their victims, however, another evaluation was going on at the same time. The prisoners, after spending enough time in the ghost house, quickly responded to this hidden method of evaluation and managed to convince their oppressors that their torture techniques worked. Using survival instincts, some detainees of Citibank Ghost House actually discovered a relationship between the Torture Menu and the Qur'an! This relationship was as follows: the more you read the Holy Book and participate in religious *Halaqa* (religious circles), the less torture you would receive in the long run. Or even better, as I personally tested, do the non-mandatory religious rituals of fasting on Monday and Thursday[18] to give the impression that you have caved in and are completely brainwashed. No physical or mental resistance. Fully surrendered! This is academically known as "Evaluation of the Evaluation" and sometimes called Meta-Evaluation.[19] It is usually reached and conducted when the detainee finds that the main reason for being tortured was to break his resistance. So, what the hell? Why live in that horrendous pain and suffering while they are literally breaking your body? Let the torturer believe that you have become as much of a sheep as he is, that you would follow his version of Islam and become another blindly obedient crusader. The torturers assumed that the Qur'an could be used as a brainwashing tool—and it can, in addition to other atrocious tools that are used to break the body. Still, simultaneously, the detainees responded by doing their own counter-evaluation. The only difference in this from the academic Meta-Evaluation is that it is done secretly from one side by the

---

[18] Muslims believe that the Prophet Muhammad used to fast on these two days as a way of meditation.

[19] Michael Quinn Patton, *Qualitative Research & Evaluation Methods*, 3rd ed. (Newbury Park, CA: Sage Publications, 2002).

detainees. The Torture Menu and the Holy Qur'an were used simultaneously as a way to assess how much the detainee was responding to the indoctrination treatment. The more you are seen to be involved in Qur'an study groups, the less you are offered items on the Torture Menu, revealing how defiant and smart victims can survive in the face of their perpetrators. I have personally witnessed and performed this subversive resistance technique and it did work while I was a "guest" in that place for four months. I believe it saved my body extra damage!

There was, however, one rather consequential side effect of this performance of religious commitment: some detainees, becoming fully spiritually immersed in reading the Qur'an, praying more, and fasting twice a week, started to feel guilt, that they must have done something wrong in their life and this is why Allah was making them suffer (read: get tortured). Instead of continuing the subtle resistance while faking surrender, they fall back into the trap of internalized oppression. No wonder that a quote of Karl Marx has lived across the centuries, and will continue to live: "Religion is the sigh of the oppressed creature, the heart of a heartless world, just as it is the spirit of a spiritless situation. It is the opium of the people."[20] Crucially, my point is not solely about the misuse of religion in Sudan. No matter what the religion, it can be used to excuse or to promote torture, as well as to resist it.

In his book on the Islamist movement in Sudan, Fathi Al-Daw (2012) studied the history of the Muslim Brotherhood since it seized power in 1989.[21] Al-Daw explains in detail how the Brotherhood introduced the "culture of ideological torture" into a pluralistic society like Sudan. The arrogant feeling of superiority that members can get through comprehensive special religious courses of indoctrination when they join the MB organization makes them look down upon others, including mainstream Muslims. In addition to complete isolation, a special harsh training is offered to prepare these future torturers, which may be no different from that of secular police units, as in the case of the military regime in Greece.[22] However, the secrecy of the training, which is usually carried out in remote, isolated areas, along with its special harshness, makes the

---

[20] Karl Marx, "A Contribution to the Critique of Hegel's Philosophy of Right," *Deutsch-Französische Jahrbücher*, 7 & 10 February 1844 (Paris). Translator unknown.

[21] Fathi Al-Daw, *The Trench: Secrets of State of Corruption and Oppression in Sudan*, 2nd ed. (Cairo, Egypt: Rose Island Library, 2012). Arabic publication.

[22] John Conroy, *Unspeakable Acts, Ordinary People: The Dynamics of Torture* (New York: Alfred Knopf, 2000), 88–96.

member in the final stage of initiation feel that he is loyal to a higher, divine authority, that no one can stand in his way.[23] This belief, that the act of torture is authorized by a divine authority, may help to explain the lack of regret for their actions expressed by members of this special unit. As Ibrahim Elsanousi, a Muslim Brotherhood leader in Sudan, asserted:

> If the torture we committed was right, then Allah will reward us for what we did. If it's wrong, Allah will forgive us because we did it for the benefit of Islam and Sudan. This is a normal/natural thing.[24]

No feeling of remorse, shame, or asking for repentance from Allah, since they are so certain that they are the agents of God. The quote is similar to the sentiments expressed by another religious torturer, this time from Argentina: "What I did I did for my Fatherland, my faith, and my religion. Of course I would do it again."[25]

The failure of the Muslim Brotherhood project in Sudan, politically and religiously, was not only in the ghost houses' savage evaluation system. This failure moved outside the buildings of the torture machine and prevailed in every aspect of life. People outside the ghost houses, too, who were living under harsh oppression for twenty-five years, started to conduct their own evaluation. The resistance to the regime came from within, and it is no longer only a few *tabour* or communists. Much of the country joined the resistance via their meta-evaluation in resisting this brutal, corrupt regime that shamelessly chops off the hand of a homeless person (*shamasi*) who steals to feed himself and that pardons members of the regime who embezzle millions of dollars. If anything good may come out of this brutal ghost house torture system, it would be that many voices now are questioning the savage Shari'a *Hudud* laws, which truly created the foundation of the current torture establishment. In an unprecedented step, torture survivors issued a press release calling for the elimination of the Shari'a penal code, and considering "any advocacy

---

[23] Mahmoud Sadek, "The Muslim Brothers Militia" (Facebook), last modified December 1, 2012, accessed February 9, 2014, www.facebook.com/permalink.php?story_fbid=377610638999941&id=153851778042496.

[24] "Islamists' Justification of Torture and Rape," *Group Against Torture in Sudan*, last modified February 9, 2014, accessed February 9, 2014, www.ghosthouses.blogspot.com/2014/02/islamists-justification-of-torture-rape.html.

[25] Marguerite Feitlowitz, *A Lexicon of Terror: Argentina and Legacies of Torture* (New York: Oxford University Press, 1998), 212.

of the Islamic *Hudud* legislation as full support of the current torture atrocities."[26] It is not enough to condemn the crime of torture. Sudanese and international human rights organizations need to be as clear as the torture survivors and identify, evaluate, and then resist the deep historical and ideological roots that are feeding this crime.

---

[26] "GATS Calls for the Elimination of Sharia Penal Codes," *Group Against Torture in Sudan*, last modified December 29, 2010, accessed October 22, 2014, http://ghosthouses.blogspot.com/2010/12/gats-calls-for-elimination-of-sharia.html.

CHAPTER 3

The Unspeakable Agony of Inflicted Pain: Torture, Betrayal, Redress

Robert Francis Garcia

Writer, teacher, and human rights activist Robert Francis (Bobby) Garcia bases his essay on his experience of torture as a member of an insurgent guerrilla group fighting the martial law rule of Ferdinand Marcos in the Philippines, as well as subsequently. Whereas most torture narratives focus on the abuses of the state, Garcia's essay addresses the underrepresented issue of torture committed by a political movement against its own members, highlighting issues of personal and political betrayal as well as the difficulty of seeking redress against non-state actors. As a young man, Garcia joined the militarized insurgency led by the Communist Party (CPP) in the Philippines and its armed wing, the New People's Army (NPA). When the CPP–NPA initiated an anti-infiltration operation in Southern Tagalog (similar intra-Party campaigns took place in other regions of the Philippines) in 1988, the danger that members faced in their insurgency against the government suddenly came from within the insurgency itself. Because torture yields false intelligence, the campaign was self-promoting, in that its interrogations produced "information" that increased the number of targeted suspects and the use of torture throughout the Party.

R. F. Garcia (✉)
Peace Advocates for Truth, Healing and Justice (PATH), Q.C., Philippines

One of 55 survivors of the 121 targeted in that particular operation (all of whom were cleared in a later internal investigation), Garcia unsurprisingly left the Party and later told his story in his testimonial To Suffer Thy Comrades: How the Revolution Decimated Its Own *(2001). Its publication led to his work with other survivors nationwide, who allied to form Peace Advocates for Truth, Healing and Justice (PATH) in 2003. Garcia describes here the challenges PATH faced: the reopening of traumatic pasts; an elusive search for justice from a non-state entity; and the difficulty of confronting atrocities within a movement to which survivors had dedicated themselves. The aftermath of the CPP operation has left survivors with deep feelings of betrayal and few avenues for redress, especially as the militarized insurgency against the government and a climate of fear fanned by both sides in the conflict continue. These difficulties, combined with the lack of anti-torture legislation in the Philippines (the Anti-Torture Act, or Republic Act 9745, was only enacted in 2009, and is not retroactive), underscore the ways in which politics and the law can foreclose avenues for justice that survivors seek. Garcia looks internationally for examples of how survivors in other contexts have campaigned for a public accounting of torture and for various forms of redress. He recognizes the survivor-driven work of Torture Abolition and Survivors Support Coalition International (TASSC) as a site where such solidarities may be forged.*

* * *

Pain Revisited

The year was 1979. I was a high school freshman in Manila, a puny boy of twelve, thin and frail but too active and restless for my own good. I still remember how excruciating it was.

Saturday was basketball day. My brother Tony Boy and I were, as usual, back in the cement court, trying to out-dribble, out-pass, and out-shoot our opponents in their home court. It was still sunny and we were sweating, and I somehow believed that the girth I lacked was compensated for by my speed. It was one of those fun days where the boundless energies of youth were spent.

I think our team was slightly ahead on points and the game was proceeding with mid-level intensity. Tony Boy, who had the ball, saw me signaling for an assist and made a quick throw. The bigger boy who was guarding me was reasonably fast, or devious—I couldn't really tell with how quickly it all happened. All I remember is that my legs tangled with his (or he tripped me with extreme prejudice) and I came down hard on the cement. My right arm jerked forward by reflex to deflect the fall, hitting the ground first. The snap was unmistakable and the pain instantaneous. I looked at my right forearm—it was at a strange angle, with a slight bleeding on the underside. My brother looked at it and, horrors, tried to give it a first-aid massage!

For obvious reasons, we cut the game short: dribbling with a broken arm is unheard of in basketball, much less shooting or shaking the hands of the winners. We walked the three blocks back to our house, my twisted arm hanging limply beside me while Jayvee the "tripper" kept saying, "Sorry, Bobby." I barely paid attention to him, as my mind was focused on the stabbing pain that shot up my arm whenever I tried to wiggle my fingers.

When we reached home, my panicked mother quickly brought me to the orthopedic hospital where the doctor, upon inspection, said with complete nonchalance, "*Bali ang buto.*" ("The bone is broken.") After some wait, I was guided to a hospital bed where the medics started working on the injury. I'm still not sure if what they did was standard medical procedure then. While I was lying down, they tied my right fingers with gauze bandage to a horizontal rod above, such that my injured forearm was hung vertically and perpendicular to the upper arm—which was weighted down with a pail of water. This contraption gave the initial "stretch"—apparently to facilitate the setting back of the two fractured bones (the "radius" and the "ulna").

From there the medics started manually pulling my forearm at either end in order to put it back to shape, and… well, no words can describe the pain it delivered. It was so maddeningly severe I wished I would pass out. My screams echoed all over the hospital as I held the hand of my father, who had arrived sometime later. Alas, the procedure was to no avail and the ordeal amounted to nothing, as a piece of flesh was trapped between the breaking points, preventing the alignment of the bones.

It was only much, much later that it occurred to me: couldn't they have used anesthesia? A week later, I went through surgery. My bones were mended and metal implants were screwed into both bones for added strength, and this time, the doctors used anesthesia. I was henceforth called the "bionic man" at school. This injury occurred almost four decades ago, but the memory remains quite vivid. Indeed, certain things in life can never really be forgotten, such as another experience—which happened in totally different circumstances and surpassed the agony of fracture—that came a decade later.

This time, I found myself shackled not with medical gauze but rather with metal chains. The physical pain was not as horrific as extracting your teeth with ineffectual painkillers (another incident I went through as a young adult), but the psychic agony was infinitely worse; indeed, I do not believe I have ever completely recovered. Furthermore, the pain was inflicted not for the purpose of healing a broken bone, but for breaking the will. This intention—the intention behind torture itself—renders all manner of pain nearly unimaginable.

The Horrors of Torture

Let Me Rewind a Bit

I was what we in the Philippines called a "martial law baby." We were the generation who spent our growing-up years under the iron rule of former president Ferdinand Marcos. The martial law Marcos imposed in 1972 drove many youths and students out into the streets and behind the barricades. These so-called "first-quarter storm" activists defied Marcos by the hundreds of thousands, challenging his rule and, for those particularly inclined, waging a revolution against the "US–Marcos dictatorship." We, the martial law babies, followed in their footsteps—waving placards, shouting ourselves hoarse, and meeting in whispers.

My initiation into the world of the underground was not particularly unusual. Like any typical freshie, I entered college wild-eyed and raring for novelty and thrill. That was 1983—a period of political ferment. Opposition leader Benigno "Ninoy" Aquino was assassinated, spontaneous mass movements erupted all over the country, and I found myself in the center of radical political activity. The call to change society was compelling, and the notion of being a "revolutionary" also had its intrinsic romantic appeal. I was still a freshman when I embraced that role. One of revolution's distinguishing characteristics is the level of conviction and commitment it engenders among its followers, and its sense of certainty and the predictability of the future.

Human society, however, evolves in mysterious ways. History did not turn in the way we predicted or for which we worked. Marcos did not fall as a direct result of our armed revolution (though we can take credit for chipping away at his fortified institutions). He was instead deposed through a mass uprising that was led by the most unlikely personalities and forces, of which our movement was a reluctant part. The Marcos aftermath was not exactly the future the movement envisioned; thus, the revolution continued. This explains why, in 1988, I was still a gun-toting guerrilla waging war against the establishment, rather than a college graduate easing his way into a promising future.

Injustice and inequality are the *raison d'être* of dissent. Revolution offers a new order: the antithesis of wrong. But opposites do attract; and if not, they sometimes follow the same direction. One of the most popular activist slogans during our time was: "Those who seek the light must endure the burning." This held a lot of meaning for us because the risks were so real. The threat of being tortured and killed by state forces was always there, and we never lacked for accounts of how comrades suffered various forms of torture or were killed by the military or police.

A guerrilla comrade narrated how his penis was burned by cigarettes when he was in detention. He managed to escape, however, by executing what we called a "tiger jump" (a kind of maneuver where one jumps over an obstacle, lands hands first, rolls forward, and runs) when he got the chance. Unfortunately, much later he was captured again, and this time the military did not give him a second chance: they punctured his back with a soil pick and buried him alive. Such accounts abound in the context of dissent and counter-insurgency. It was not uncommon to read stories of severe beating, water cure, electrocution, sexual abuse, and rape. We had to steel our nerves for such an eventuality, not discounting the possibility that it could happen to us.

And happen to us it did, but with a twist; in fact, my experience of torture, when it was my turn, did not come from the enemy, but rather from closer to home. It happened under the so-called Operation Plan Missing Link (OPML), the anti-infiltration operation launched by the Communist Party of the Philippines (CPP) in Southern Tagalog in 1988, in which a task force was created to lead the arrest of "enemy spies" within the party. The task force arrested a few Party members and even allies of the revolution and began interrogating them. When they got no satisfactory information, they employed torture.

That was when the bodies started to roll. Under pain and terror, the initial suspects were forced to own up to the accusations and say whatever the interrogators wanted to hear. They invented stories and, worse, were compelled to name other comrades. This created a domino effect: more torture bred more victims, spreading like a contagion throughout the movement. It became a vicious cycle that threatened to raze the entire Party machinery, including its top leadership. Worse, the operations included village folk who just happened to be at the wrong place at the wrong time. It was November 1988, at the tail end of the OPML, when I was swept into the whirlpool of violence along with six other guerrillas. By now, OPML officials seemed to have already developed a standard format for interrogation and torture.

One of the worst punishments we endured was the denial of food. We were fed just enough to keep us alive: no more than a teaspoonful of rice at mealtimes; sometimes nothing at all. The rain was partly a blessing, as we could drink from pools of collected water. We became skin and bones in a matter of no time. Some begged the guards for their leftover fish tails and bones. Apart from the starvation, I also suffered a dislocated jaw, head concussions from club beatings, and wounds where the chains rubbed on the skin. In between interrogation and torture sessions, we were chained on makeshift stretchers where our mobility was limited to lying down and sitting up.

Others endured more severe forms of torture: from slapping and punching to the more imaginative "flag ceremony," in which the victim was hung by her wrists for a few hours to a few days. The strain ripped the skin of some, exposing the wrist bones; others' hands became grotesquely swollen and their movement paralyzed. The tormentors slit the skin with a knife or shaved off the captives' eyebrows for fun. They forced the victims' legs apart and sat on their thighs. They seared the skin of their victims with a gas lamp. Some victims were made to witness the execution of their co-detainees, magnifying the terror effect.

The list is long. I could go on and narrate other details, but I guess you now get the picture. The Party leadership—which gave its full blessing to the OPML—finally realized the folly of this exercise, probably because the contagion was reaching the highest levels of the organization. They finally put it to a stop, albeit belatedly: sixty-six comrades had already been killed and only fifty-five of us remained alive. CPP officials' individual review of the cases cleared all victims from the utterly false charges of espionage. A handful of the surviving victims remained active and committed, but most of us left the Party for good—living with the trauma and trying to live down the horrors of being tortured by one's own.

The Aftermath

"At the time of the ordeal, I told myself that should I ever come out of it alive, I should write." This is a passage in my book, *To Suffer Thy Comrades*, which came out thirteen years after the OPML. It was in the process of writing this book that I began to understand the full depth and breadth of the internal "purge" of the Party. That what happened to us in Southern Tagalog was by no means isolated, but a systematic and continuous Communist Party practice all over the Philippines throughout the 1980s. That the casualty figures in OPML represented but a fraction of the total number of victims of the purges, still now being counted. It cannot be fewer than 2000 dead, and most likely far higher. That there was something fundamentally flawed in the movement to which we had committed our lives.

After the book's publication in 2001, many other survivors and families and friends of those killed during the purges started coming out. More stories were shared. Hope was renewed for those with missing kin. We decided to do our work related to the CPP's anti-infiltration campaign more systematically, and formed Peace Advocates for Truth, Healing and Justice (PATH) in 2003.

Negotiating the path back to a difficult past engenders real challenges. We had to take extreme care in reopening old wounds with an eye to closing them properly. Also, the CPP has fragmented into many smaller factions, with Party leaders and operatives found in all these groups; as such, culpability for the crimes has been reduced to finger-pointing.

The justice question is even more circuitous. As I wrote in a previous article:

> All of our members are involved in various other advocacies and campaigns, but find this particular one far harder and fraught with obstacles. Many of us are human rights workers who never tire of hollering against the State's abuses—work that is by no means easy, but pretty much cut and dried. It enjoys the luxury of certitude and 'political correctness.' Furthermore, legal remedies addressing State-perpetrated violations of human rights and international humanitarian law are very much in place. The issue of non-State-perpetrated violations, however, such as the Philippine communist purges, is much more complex and uncertain. For one, we are hard-put to carry this issue to a government audience, knowing full well that the latter has to equally answer for much atrocity in the same vein.[1]

---

[1] Robert Francis B. Garcia, "Not Only the State: Torture by Non-State Actors: Towards Enhanced Protection, Accountability and Effective Remedies," The Redress Trust (May

What adds to the complexity of this issue is that the war is still raging. Given that the end to the violent conflict between the government and the CPP–NPA is nowhere in sight, addressing the issue of past violations inevitably gets mired in political maneuverings. The government uses it as effective propaganda ammunition against the rebels, while dispensing its own counterinsurgency measures that fall way below human rights and international humanitarian law (IHL) standards. Presently, left-wing activists are being summarily executed, while the government in effect is mouthing, "They had it coming," or, "Just like in the past, they are killing their own comrades." In such a situation, the truth suffers, along with justice and accountability.

Bringing up the purge issue remains a dangerous undertaking, simply because the CPP–NPA and other left-wing groups are still armed and active. They have also categorically dismissed any possibility of reopening the issue, claiming that it is already a closed book. The scores of victims' families who do not know what really happened, and the thousands of dead and disappeared, point to the contrary.

Having formed PATH, we have explored various legal options, including the filing of criminal cases against identified lead perpetrators, such as those involved in the OPML. As expected, when faced with uncomfortable truths, the wheels of justice grind to almost a standstill. Gathering evidence of a crime that happened more than a decade back poses a terrible challenge, including the lack of witnesses willing to testify and the blurring of memory through time. The absence of an anti-torture law in the Philippines also poses a limitation; thus, the charges filed are limited to serious physical injuries and illegal detention.

Jesse Marlow Libre is a particular case in point. In November 2005, we at PATH, with the help of forensic scientists and volunteer experts, were able to exhume the remains of Libre's parents, revolutionary couple Jesse and Nida Libre. They were falsely suspected of being spies and killed by the CPP–NPA in Cebu in September 1985. The truth behind the disappearance of the young orphan Libre's parents was withheld from him by the movement (it claimed the military killed them). It was only in 2005 that he learned the disconcerting reality, upon seeing his parents' skeletons buried together in a mountain gravesite, their bodies bearing tell-tale signs of severe torture and violent death. For Libre then, as for many, with the exhumation of truth comes the cry for justice.

2006): 5. http://web.archive.org/web/20160405180227/http://www.redress.org/downloads/publications/Non%20State%20Actors%209%20June%20Final.pdf

What are the legal options available to him? We can barely find witnesses willing to testify. Who is responsible? A whole Party organization was involved. What are the levels of accountability? It was a complex hierarchical setup: there were onlookers, guards, interrogators, torturers, executioners, decision-makers, and Party directives. Truth and justice are simply lost in the labyrinth.

Another quasi-legal option is our call for the creation of a Truth and Justice Commission. Even as we are aware of the extreme difficulty of filing individual court cases, we also know that such commissions have been undertaken successfully in post-conflict situations involving countries in transition to new governments after hostilities have ended (e.g., Chile, South Africa, and Rwanda). We find no precedent of a Truth Commission set up in any country with ongoing conflict, although we are open to setting such a precedent back home.

These are the challenges we continue to face. Through painstaking work, we have been able to exhume a total of nine remains, but that is a miniscule number compared to the thousands of families still looking for their loved ones. It is in the middle of these undertakings that we echo our appeal to the Communist Party of the Philippines, as well as the other armed left-wing groups, to face up to this issue once and for all. If justice for survivors and accountability for perpetrators would prove to be too tedious, the least they can do for now is to make a full accounting of all the nameless victims of the anti-infiltration campaigns, to exert all efforts to find them, and to return the remains to their families for a proper burial.

It is a task that we at PATH have taken on for the moment, while maintaining that such a responsibility rests on the Party that has wreaked the havoc. Other countries have shown that it can be done. The African National Congress (ANC) in South Africa demonstrated that it is possible to make a full accounting of a grievous wrong when it set up the Skweyiya Commission to settle the injustices the Party had done to its own members.[2]

Indeed, international experience shows that there are many ways to deal with torture and its aftermaths in ways befitting human beings.

---

[2] See "Skweyiye Commission Report: Report of the Commission of Enquiry into Complaints by Former African National Congress Prisoners and Detainees," The African National Congress, 1992. http://www.anc.org.za/content/skweyiya-commission-report.

Our TASSC

What is comforting is that our issues and undertakings in the Philippines find resonance in other countries. This is particularly illuminated by our involvement with the Torture Abolition and Survivors Support Coalition International (TASSC), the only international organization with a mission of addressing torture that is also founded and run by survivors, where the broad array of the torture phenomenon is completely evidenced. At TASSC we can see how various abominable acts have been inflicted by repressive governments and violent movements the world over: the death squads of El Salvador, the military regime of Guatemala, the Fujimori government as well as the Sendero Luminoso of Peru, the severing of civilians' limbs by the Revolutionary United Front (RUF) in Sierra Leone, the extrajudicial killings in the Philippines, the waterboarding of the US military, the political persecution and genocide committed by the Saddam Hussein government in Iraq, and so on and so forth.

At TASSC, we campaign from the perspective of those who know by personal experience what it is like to be deliberately hurt. What it is like to have information pried from you by brute force. What it is like to be physically punished, either for what you believe in or for what you are accused of. What it is like to have your will demolished, and to experience the lingering agony of trauma for the rest of your life.

More importantly, at TASSC we fully understand the meaning of solidarity. There is nothing more powerful than a pain that has been shared by all. The collective experience of having survived torture is TASSC's powerful weapon in its battle to end a practice that benefits no one and dehumanizes everyone.

With this struggle, we can ultimately regain our complete humanity.

CHAPTER 4

Translating Trauma, Witnessing Survival

Laurie Ball Cooper

For many years, Laurie Ball Cooper worked as a translator and interpreter for the Torture Abolition and Survivors Support Coalition International (TASSC), interpreting Spanish testimonials into English in individual sessions and public forums. In this essay, she discusses the emotionally and ethically fraught work of interpreting torture survivors' stories. Survivors who wish to testify to their abuse often must rely on interpreters to circulate those stories to a wider audience. In this way, interpreters function as key figures in translingual and global campaigns against torture, and in solidarity and therapy initiatives among survivors. Less often considered are the ethical and emotional facets of interpretation: how, as Ball Cooper explores, translators are at once entrusted by survivors to convey the depth of individual experience and "trespassing" on the intimacy of suffering. She explores the twin challenge of making torture "imaginable" to listeners without usurping the survivor's voice and experience.

Interpreters not only subvert torture's attempt to silence the victim; also crucial, Ball Cooper explains, is the role of interpreters in shaping the responses that stories of torture may elicit and the effects of those responses on survivors. Translators influence listeners' interpretation of the veracity of testimony as well as their emotional response; and they are conduits for

L. B. Cooper (✉)
Ayuda, Falls Church, VA, USA

© The Author(s) 2018
A. S. Moore, E. Swanson (eds.), *Witnessing Torture*, Palgrave Studies in Life Writing, https://doi.org/10.1007/978-3-319-74965-5_4

questions and responses to survivors that range from sympathetic to hurtful and antagonistic. In mediating the confusion or misunderstanding that (mis)translations may generate, Ball Cooper describes the delicate balance of stepping temporarily outside of the role of interpreter to serve as a facilitator in certain contexts, a role that requires shifting between channeling others' voices and inserting her own. She ultimately argues that just as the work of interpretation requires elements of trust and imagination between the speakers, so does the relationship between speakers and the wider listening public, who might work together to oppose torture.

* * *

She sits in front of the room, reading a testimony of torture, suffering, and survival in Peru. Her voice, usually steady as it relays emotions and experiences, begins to quiver as the suffering she speaks of grows more detailed. The tremble in her voice is subtle; perhaps many in the room manage to ignore it by focusing intently on the content of the testimony. Finally, the testimony ends, the panel concludes, and the woman with the quivering voice quietly disappears into the crowd.

I was the woman with the quivering voice on that panel, but the story that I told in that room was not my own; rather, I was reading the English translation of a Peruvian woman's story. The owner of that story sat next to me, having completed her story in Spanish already. She had broken down in tears during her speech before the audience gathered in observance of the United Nations' Day in Support of Victims and Survivors of Torture (June 26). As her interpreter, I experienced the quiver in my voice as a physical manifestation of the intrusion upon her experiences that my work as an interpreter necessitated, as though through my inability to ward off emotions, I was trespassing on not only experiences but also emotions that were not mine to live or to feel.

As an interpreter for survivors of torture with the Torture Abolition and Survivors Support Coalition International (TASSC) for five summers, I struggled with the notion of emotional and experiential trespassing. Much of the annual week-long observance of June 26 revolves around survivors sharing their stories with each other and with "outsiders"—including State Department policy-makers, congressional members and staffers, lawyers, therapists, and others. Torture, as the diversity of voices in this volume sadly attests, is a global scourge and its effects are felt in stories lived and told in myriad languages. As such, the various testimonies of torture and its profoundly personal effects often reach any given audience only through the mediation of at least one interpreter. The most deeply private experiences and emotions that so many seek to convey, and indeed many of those conveyed in this very book, often reach the listener or the reader in a voice that does not belong to the story's owner.

As an interpreter for TASSC's Spanish-speaking members, it was my voice that very often told those stories, despite the fact that they were not my stories and I did not craft their narratives. My role was to be the voice for survivors who trusted me to convey their emotions, memories, stories, ideas, opinions, and meanings. It was a daunting task indeed, one that posed countless professional and personal challenges, but one whose reward was also without limit. Chief among the challenges that I faced has been coping with the sense that I was continually trespassing in a space made sacred by the enormous depth of suffering and the awe-inspiring reach of survival.

Transforming "Unspeakable" to Spoken

I do not remember much about my first year as an interpreter with TASSC, a role I fell into naturally from my position as an intern with the Guatemala Human Rights Commission USA, then a non-governmental organization (NGO) that stewarded TASSC's development into its own independent organization. The words and stories that I would translate during the week were far beyond the reality I had known up until that time; they exceeded the imagination that I had developed prior to my experiences as a TASSC translator. I have clear memories of the people I met during that first year, many of whom became treasured friends I saw each year, but I cannot remember the specific moments and emotions that contributed to what now exists in my memory as an overwhelmed haze.

I do remember, within that barrage of emotions that contributed to a general sense of disorientation, a deep-seated awkwardness. I tried to keep my distance in many ways that year—always trying to sit outside of the circle and to limit my involvement with survivors over meals and free time throughout the week. I was worried that it would seem that I did not know my place as an interpreter rather than participant in the week's events, and was afraid of trespassing further than my work as an interpreter necessitated.

The idea that I could somehow place clear and logical limits on the nature of my trespassing was shattered during my second year working as an interpreter and the first time that I awoke from someone else's nightmare. I lay staring at the ceiling in my apartment, watching specters of terror—small fractions of one survivor's experience—dance hauntingly on the white paint. In that moment, the challenge of making sense of the complex effects of my role as interpreter with survivors of torture stood before me, as it does still today. The lesson I learned, when the cold sweat had dried on my forehead and the nightmare had temporarily faded, was that I could not succeed at keeping an artificial distance between myself and the survivors, whom I was coming to know so well that any such attempt was a well-intentioned, yet ultimately impossible, pretense.

There is a natural distance between myself and those who have survived torture, a distance borne of entirely different experiences and realities, yet my work as an interpreter shortened that natural distance ever so slightly, bringing me next to a trauma so severe that most prefer to maintain whatever natural distance from it they can achieve. Most consider torture's trauma unimaginable, and through their inability or refusal to imagine torture, they are able to maintain not only the natural distance between themselves and torture, but also an additional, unnatural distance that denies the interconnectedness of human existence and, by extension, human trauma.

As an interpreter, I know that in the most basic sense such horrors are indeed speakable, and often they must be spoken. Many survivors have a need so strong that at moments a sense of desperation comes through their voices and eyes. Many survivors were told by their torturers that no one would believe them. Many have held their memories in fear-inspired silence for years, choosing just the right moment to slowly reach out with their story. The survivors who tell their stories find the courage to speak of the experiences and their aftermath; in turn, I must find the words to adequately relay their stories to the English-speaking audience. Sometimes finding the words is more difficult than others, but the truth that translation reveals is that, ultimately, such horrors are speakable if only we are willing to search for the words to speak of them.

SERVING AS AN AGENT OF HEALING AND HURT

Interpretation goes in the other direction as well—interpreters relay not only survivors' stories, but also people's responses to those stories. As an interpreter, I am spared the responsibility of an immediate reaction to the stories that I render in another language. The experiences, emotions, and trauma enter into my thinking as narrated to me by the survivors, and quickly exit my thinking as an English representation of the narrative. The listener(s), however, usually search for some reaction to the story as relayed—a comment, a phrase, a question—some spoken response to a story that the listener finds him- or herself feeling unnaturally close to, if only for a moment.

In many cases, interpretation seems somehow less central during the listener's response to survivors' testimonies of torture than it does during the survivors' narratives, given that much of the substance of most appropriate responses is relayed through body language, eye contact, and a certain sincerity that manifests itself on the listener's face. Of course, as always, an interpreter's accuracy provides the basis for that sincere look to transform itself into a sincere interaction; however, it is unfortunately in the cases of inappropriate reactions or hostile questions that a translator's role becomes all the more crucial.

On more than one occasion, I was horrified by the reactions of those with whom many TASSC members so earnestly shared their experiences. I found myself wishing that I could take that person aside for a moment, explain how their reaction is about to cause hurt or pain or further distrust, and somehow avert the impending damage. Often the comments that cause pain are well intentioned, sometimes they are even comments made among and between survivors themselves that hold the potential for unforeseen hurt. As the interpreter, I was spared the responsibility and denied the opportunity to intervene to interrupt or soften these comments, even when I saw the hurt just beneath the surface. As I interpreted an insensitive question, a well-intentioned but poorly conceived comment, or a thoughtless response, my voice became the agent of hurt. The survivors know better than to blame me for what was said—in their minds, as in reality, I was clearly a vessel for words rather than the crafter of comments or the origins of hurt. But as the words took shape on my lips, I cringed at the hurt that I realized they were likely to cause.

However, sometimes my role as interpreter placed me in a position to deflect hurt through clarifying misunderstandings. Especially in meetings of survivors from all over the world, there are occasional situations that arise from linguistic confusion—now and then due to interpretation inadequacies, but far more frequently through the linguistic chaos of a room with three or four simultaneous working languages. Sometimes it became clear that while someone's words may have been understood or interpreted, their meaning was clearly lost in translation or in inadequate understanding. In those cases, the interpreter is sometimes the only person in the room capable of understanding the root cause of the confusion or hurt, and of rectifying perceived wrongs or mistaken meanings.

On the few occasions when I have stepped forward in an effort to clarify meanings rather than strictly to interpret, I have felt a heightened sense of awkwardness. In these moments the base-level awkwardness inherent in interpreting delicate matters grew larger because I was stepping out of my role as an interpreter to speak in my own voice, crafting my own words and seeking to convey my own meaning rather than relaying another's voice. In those moments, I felt my place inside the room temporarily shifting. In efforts to clarify, another delicate balancing act that interpretation necessitates is clearly illustrated: there is a constant tension between literally serving as someone's voice by accurately interpreting meanings, and coopting someone's voice by presuming meanings. When a conversation is spiraling away from productivity, it is tempting to jump in with "He meant to say…" Yet even when this seems to be the case, as a translator or interpreter in this situation I am stepping even closer to the line between serving as a projector of voice and overtaking the survivor's voice with my own.

In a group of torture survivors discussing something as important and as personal as their experiences with trauma and healing, it is clear that ethical challenges abound. However, my time with TASSC taught me that, at least in the context of the emotionally charged observance of June 26, when interpretating for or working with a group of survivors discussing anything of importance, the ethical challenges are many and often center upon this concept of projecting voice without assuming it. To return to the earlier example about clarifying meanings, instead of asserting what one survivor meant to say, commenting "I think this may be a matter of linguistic confusion" and following that with carefully conceived questions and a general slowing of the conversation can be the most productive approach. This may be best practice in all cases of group dialogue and confusion, yet in the context of facilitating conversation between survivors of torture and across language barriers, the importance of projecting voice while preserving the rightful ownership of voice is all the more crucial.

Beyond Being a Translator: Being a Fellow Human Being

In an earlier passage, I wrote about the fact that as an interpreter, I was often spared the responsibility of an immediate response to stories of trauma, because my responsibility was to interpret rather than to process or respond to the experiences set before me. However, in the personal setting of TASSC's June 26 commemoration, I became a known face and a person across the table at lunch, in addition to being a necessary intruder upon intimate conversations. There are moments in the course of these interactions, in which I was a friend or acquaintance first and an interpreter second, that force a response to the stories I interpreted. More often than not, I found that my non-verbal responses were most important in these interactions. It was the moments in which I shortened the distance between myself and a survivor by taking a hand, extending a smile, or sharing space at a table for lunch as friends, not as survivor and interpreter, when my responses were the most appropriate, even if they never felt or could have been adequate.

It was through seeing survivors as people who have survived torture rather than solely as survivors that I most dramatically shortened the distance between them and myself. The natural distance—the giant gap between our life experiences—would never disappear or lose its importance in limiting my ability to truly understand the experiences and challenges faced by survivors of torture. However, by finding friendship with TASSC's members, I found my greatest reward for my work as interpreter, and perhaps offered the greatest contribution I could to their healing.

This friendship also provided the support I needed to cope with the emotional challenges of interpreting trauma and survival. In the course of my summers interpreting with TASSC, I was approached on numerous occasions by survivors or mental health professionals who work with survivors, concerned about my wellbeing in the face of the emotional intensity of our days together and the stress of translation's responsibilities in this context. Always, I found myself both surprised and slightly uncomfortable with this concern, given the many survivors around me who had lived trauma rather than interpreting it. However, as someone who has awoken from others' nightmares on more than one occasion, there is also a level on which I understand that the effects of interpreting trauma are real, even if they are far indeed from the effects of the primary trauma itself.

One June day, walking along Capitol Hill side by side with a survivor who had become a friend, I was caught off-guard by a conversation about my work's effects on me. She asked me if I felt sad when I left work, and if interpreting the stories of survivors was difficult for me. While there were obvious answers to both of those questions that might have been accurate, I paused for a long moment trying to formulate my answer. I was afraid that this friend would think I saw my relationship with her as a burden, or would feel that I was somehow unaffected by the burden of trauma and survival that she carries every day. As I was thinking carefully about my answer, she took my hand in hers. "You cry when you leave sometimes, don't you?" she asked.

"Yes," I replied slowly, "some days I do." I squeezed her hand gently and smiled at her. "But I am very happy to do this work."

She looked at me with tears in her eyes and offered me the words that have brought comfort and reassurance to me in many trying moments since. "Maybe tonight I will cry a little bit less," she said to me slowly, "because I know that you are crying a little bit for me."

In that moment, both our eyes shining with tears, we were two humans confronting the enormity of torture. One of us has and will confront torture in every moment; every fiber of her life has been affected by torture's reality. As an interpreter rather than a survivor, I was granted the luxury of moments removed from torture's trauma, but also challenged by the combination of responsibilities born of a knowledge of torture more intimate than many possess and the privilege of being far more distant from torture than many have been forced to be.

As someone who has been exposed to the realities of torture far more than many non-survivors have, through my role as an interpreter and the friendships that have resulted from this work, I often find myself in situations and conversations about human rights, torture, and public policy that call to mind my experiences with TASSC. Time and again, I have found myself to be the only one in a room or in a conversation who has known a survivor of torture. While I will never speak for a survivor of torture, I can always speak with a voice that has been informed by survivors' voices and by my relationships with people who have survived torture. In this way, I occupy dual roles, facilitating conversation and, in other settings, bearing witness myself. As an interpreter in a room of torture survivors seeking the space for conversation, my role was to ensure that those who wished to find the words to bear witness and describe their trauma were given the opportunity to make themselves clearly understood by others in the room. As a sometimes-interpreter for survivors of torture in a room of public policy or law students exploring the definition of torture and its potential effects, my role was to bear witness myself to the suffering of torture and its widespread effects, which I have seen through voices entrusted to me by survivors.

A Final Word about Bridging Distances

Ultimately, what has shortened the distance between myself and members of TASSC has been that very trust that they have granted me. My somewhat natural entry into the role of interpreter with TASSC as a college intern resulted in friendships and experiences that have shaped my own understanding of reality and will continue to do so far into the future. However, in part this distance was shortened by a choice I made to accept the trust that the survivors offered to me, to reach out my hand to bridge that distance between our disparate lives for just a moment and to imagine what would be far easier to cast aside as unimaginable.

This book offers each of you as readers that same chance. In the chapters of this volume, survivors have reached out with testimony and analysis, stories of all kinds, in an offering of trust with the hopes that you will do your best to see the world through their eyes. Whether or not reading this book will offer you the chance to see through those eyes, to really hear those voices, largely depends on your own willingness to imagine. If you listen to the voices in this volume and process the stories told to you by human beings in a language that you understand, then you too might find yourself with the discomforting knowledge of torture's effects seen from a seat of privileged comfort. The survivors who are members of TASSC and those who have written in this volume have offered their stories in the hopes that somehow the world will hear their voices, seek to understand their stories, and, by so doing, begin to see torture for what it is: a global scourge whose effects are felt in stories lived and told in myriad languages that cannot be allowed to persist in our world.

Bridging the distance between survivors and non-survivors can be daunting. There is a deeper level on which those of us looking in from outside will never understand the suffering nor the healing which people who have survived torture have known. Yet there is a level on which each of us, if we accept the trust offered to us in these pages, can rid ourselves of the artificial distance that we so often place between ourselves and the very speakable, imaginable, translatable suffering of torture—if only we are willing to translate, imagine, and speak it.

PART II

Witnessing Torture and Recovery: Survivors, Health Professionals, Institutions

In *Human Rights: A Political and Cultural Critique*, Makau Mutua analyzes an all too familiar "metaphor of human rights" that characterizes atrocity in terms of a savage perpetrator, passive and helpless victim, and agentic savior. Mutua argues that the Savage-Victim-Savior (SVS) metaphor is integral to normative human rights stories that secure western hegemonic ethnocentrism. Such ethnocentrism typically posits atrocity elsewhere and provides an alibi for humanitarian intervention as imperialism. The savior in these narratives, according to Mutua, functions as "redeemer, the good angel who protects, vindicates, civilizes, restrains, and safeguards,"[1] indicating that its functionality also depends upon a definition of the victim as passive and immature beneficiary of the savior's expertise and actions. It is easy to see how this metaphor could be transferred to the context of health and recovery, where health-care workers and therapists work with clients to treat the physical and mental damages that torture inflicts. The power imbalance that Mutua identifies is only exacerbated when health professionals dictate and narrate the terms of treatment from the safety of professional distance, and without reflecting on the personal dimensions of their work. The four chapters in this section productively dismantle the SVS metaphor and its rhetorical scaffolding in relation to torture treatment centers. In place of detached professionalism, the chapters reveal and analyze the interpersonal and more broadly social dynamics of recovery, as well as the processes of witnessing that are integral to it. Thus, these chapters respond to the implicit questions: What

---

[1] Makau Mutua, *Human Rights: A Political and Cultural Critique* (Philadelphia: Pennsylvania Studies in Human Rights, University of Pennsylvania Press, 2002), 11.

would it mean to consider health-care professionals and their clients and patients as witnesses to torture's predations? How might we understand communal witnessing as integral to individual recovery? To what extent can life writing open up these questions to better understand torture's hold on those who have suffered it, as opposed to shifting attention away from survivors to health-care practitioners? These questions are all the more compelling as we write at the end of 2017, when the US administration demands "waterboarding and worse," advocates the assassination not only of suspected terrorists but also of their families, assembles a cabinet of pro-torture, conspiracy-minded former military officers, and psychologist James Mitchell, one of the architects of the US torture program at Guantánamo Bay, publishes a book justifying his actions.

All of the chapters in this section emphasize a multimodal approach to healing and recovery that prioritizes the agency of survivors in their relationships with health professionals. Survivors' control over the recovery process may take many forms, including determination of the pace of the disclosure of their suffering and their treatment. In addition, regardless of their disciplinary training, the authors recognize that torture has impacts on psychological and physical health as well as social, political, and legal standing. If recovery and healing include rebuilding the trust between survivors and the world that torture destroys, then health professionals must learn to become active witnesses to survivors' testimony, symptoms, and desires, with a range of approaches for mitigating torture's lasting effects. It is through this process of the recognition of harm and of reciprocity of feeling that the bonds of humanity might begin to re-form.

We begin with Linda A. Piwowarczyk's examination of "The Role of Health Professionals in Torture Treatment." Understanding health professionals as witnesses as much as experts first requires acknowledgment that medical doctors, psychologists, and other health workers are often integral to torture itself (devising torture programs at the limits of what the body can withstand, monitoring victims during torture, etc.). This means that in order to be effective at treating torture survivors, health professionals require self-reflexivity and a willingness to understand how their professional expertise may have been used for harm. Rather than unilaterally determine what the patient needs, Piwowarczyk argues for health professionals to understand themselves as "accompaniers" to the patient's healing, who can use their professional training and personal self-reflection to testify to and advocate for the humanity of the survivor.

The following two chapters, by Orlando P. Tizon and Judy B. Okawa, focus more narrowly on the interpersonal relationships between survivors and their therapists, and the ways those relationships take place within larger social and institutional matrices. In "Assessing the Treatment of Torture: Balancing Quantifiable with Intangible Metrics," Tizon analyses the Torture Abolition and Survivors Support Coalition International (TASSC) from his perspective as both a survivor and an intake coordinator at the organization. Having this dual perspective allows him to understand the delicate balance between institutional and individual needs and goals. Rather than see these perspectives as necessarily oppositional, Tizon frames them both as integral to establishing "communities of healing." Just as torture takes place within a broad network of socio-political relationships, so must healing, a process that involves multiple actors, processes, and resources. Okawa's chapter, "The Little Red Cabinet of Tears: The Impact upon Treatment Providers of Bearing Witness to Torture," considers what Tizon's call for communities of healing might mean from the perspective of a psychologist working in a torture treatment center. Like Piwowarczyk, Okawa demonstrates how envisioning one's role as a health-care professional in terms of witnessing can give space to the forms of discomfort and vicarious traumatization that therapists may experience, without allowing that self-reflection to overtake the work itself or to displace the focus on the client. Complex witnessing does not, then, substitute the therapist's suffering for that of the survivor; rather, it constitutes a means of alleviating the burden survivors regularly bear of having been told repeatedly that no will believe them or care about their experience of torture.

This section concludes with "Beyond Institutional Betrayal: When the Professional Is Personal," Ellen Gerrity's forceful analysis of the troubling position staked out by the American Psychologists Association (APA) after Jane Mayer's 2005 exposé[2] detailing the role of psychologists James Mitchell and Bruce Jessen in designing US torture protocols for the war on terror. As an APA member (who has since withdrawn from the organization), clinician, and academic researcher on the psychological effects of torture, Gerrity witnessed how the APA betrayed its ethical principles that prohibit patient harm by protecting the organization's alliance with the Pentagon and refusing to denounce the torture program. In what is at

---

[2] Jane Mayer, "The Experiment," *The New Yorker*, July 11, 2005, http://www.newyorker.com/magazine/2005/07/11/the-experiment-3

once a personal and institutional examination, Gerrity identifies the choices and paths available both within and outside of the APA to psychologists who wish to resist and condemn torture. Her words resonate powerfully in our current historical moment.

Together these chapters illuminate the ways in which survivors and health-care workers hold multiple positions as individuals and members of institutions, each of which affords the opportunity to make individual choices, as well as to forge relationships against torture and to promote ethical engagement and some degree of restoration.

CHAPTER 5

The Role of Health Professionals in Torture Treatment

Linda A. Piwowarczyk

Licensed psychiatrist Dr. Linda A. Piwowarczyk is co-founder and Director of the Boston Center for Refugee Health and Human Services, where she has worked with hundreds of torture survivors. In this chapter, she provides an overview of the factors that shape the relationship between torture survivors and health professionals. She highlights the need for health professionals to understand survivors' pain or illness as multidimensional—including physical, psychological, social, and spiritual suffering—as well as to recognize the ways in which the behavior and norms of health-care professionals might unwittingly reproduce patients' previous traumatic experiences.

In detailing the complexity of survivor/health professional interactions, Piwowarczyk addresses such difficult topics as: the need to take a medical history while also being sensitive to survivors' reluctance to disclose their torture, as well as to the fact that medical questioning can feel like interrogation; the desire to heal patients while not wielding expertise in a way that negates their understanding of their condition; the need to understand the potential linkages between physical and emotional illness or pain without

L. A. Piwowarczyk (✉)
Boston Center for Refugee Health & Human Rights, Boston, MA, USA
e-mail: piwo@bu.edu

© The Author(s) 2018
A. S. Moore, E. Swanson (eds.), *Witnessing Torture*, Palgrave Studies in Life Writing, https://doi.org/10.1007/978-3-319-74965-5_5

reducing patients solely to their past experiences of torture; and the need to recognize that one's medical opinion may have a legal bearing on patients' petitions for asylum or other protected status.

Piwowarczyk ultimately argues for health professionals to envision their roles not as experts with answers so much as "accompaniers" who can assist survivors with their healing and recovery in their physical, psychological, social, and spiritual dimensions. She also underscores the role of health professionals as advocates who, following the lead of survivors, can testify in specific situations, but who also can work institutionally to increase the legal and medical protections available to torture survivors.

* * *

Introduction

We are living at a time in which basic human rights continue to be violated by governments, and humanitarian crises challenge our commitments to humanitarian law and international conventions. According to Amnesty International, torture and ill treatment are practiced in over 150 countries around the world.[1] There is no greater affront to human dignity than torture, with its explicit intention to mercilessly cause pain and suffering. Moreover, its goals extend to destroying families, terrorizing communities, and silencing their members. Within this frame, it is the intentionality of torture and the defenselessness of its victims that are particularly egregious.

Around the world, what constitutes torture is often "redefined" by governments so as to allow its use under the guise of national security. To maintain their position in power, governments may revert to the use of torture against opposition candidates or their supporters. Today, the "war on terror" singularly challenges governments to continue to observe their responsibilities and obligations under the United Nations' Convention against Torture. Should there be exceptions? Ticking-bomb scenarios have entered the discourse, attempting to frighten and tip public opinion toward allowing coercive interrogation methods. It has been well documented that information received under torture is often not reliable, yet the practice continues.

---

[1] Amnesty International, *Annual Report 2006: The State of the World's Human Rights* (London: Amnesty International, 2006).

Torture can impact the minds, bodies, social capacities, and souls of its victims. Interventions which incorporate these domains of people's lives are necessary to the healing process. Some survivors are resilient to the impact of torture and do not have long-term effects. Others, however, suffer from post-traumatic stress disorder, depression, anxiety, psychotic symptoms, somatic symptoms, and chronic pain, and may also experience changes in self-concept, profound mistrust, feelings of shame, and feelings of being damaged. Many face significant existential dilemmas as they wrestle with why this has happened to them. Some may feel that God helped them through their ordeal, while others wonder how, if God existed, He would allow such cruelty to occur.

As with other kinds of trauma, it can be very difficult for survivors to talk about their experiences. Torturers often tell their victims that no one will believe them and that if they tell anyone they will have more problems or face death. Communities can ostracize survivors because of fear, as can families and neighbors. Remembering the range of such past events can trigger painful feelings for survivors, who often must exert great efforts to avoid anything that reminds them of what they have lived through. Shutting down emotionally as a coping mechanism can secondarily make it difficult to obtain the social support that is important to the healing process.

It can also be difficult for survivors to disclose their past experiences of torture to health professionals. That is why it is important for health professionals to ask if their patients have experienced torture. Risk factors for torture noted by Weinstein et al.[2] include being a refugee or asylum seeker, an opposition leader, or a relative of a survivor; having a history of arrest or detention or having been a prisoner of war; coming from a country where there is a totalitarian or military regime; being a member of a minority group; or coming from a country which has sustained a civil war.

In countries where torture occurs, there can be pressure on health professionals to become involved in the torture machine. This can take the form of monitoring the impact of the torture to assess whether it can continue or if it should stop. The goal of torture is to cause profound damage, not to kill someone, although some people do die from the injuries they have sustained. Physicians also falsify documents, in that they may attribute a death to natural causes or illness rather than reveal the role of government operatives. Behavioral health professionals have also been known to inform

---

[2] H. M. Weinstein, L. Dansky, and V. Iacopino, "Torture and War Trauma Survivors in Primary Care Practice," *Western Journal of Medicine* 165, no. 3 (1996): 112–18.

torturers of specific vulnerabilities so as to have the greatest, directly targeted impact upon their victims. Consequently, talking to a health professional can be potentially emotionally laden and triggering for survivors, who may have lost trust in the medical profession as a result of their experiences. Elements of the physical examination can also be reminiscent of their experiences during detention, which needs to be taken into account when examining patients. It should also be kept in mind that intensive questioning of one's history can potentially be experienced as an interrogation.

What Role Do Health Professionals Have in Treating Survivors?

Health professionals can play a pivotal role in the lives of their patients who are attempting to recover from the effects of torture. A health professional may be the first person to whom someone discloses what they have experienced. It is in the relationship between the torturer and the one tortured that the profound fracture in trust occurs. As such, it is also in the relationship between the survivor and the healer that the restoration of human connection can begin to take place. This process is fostered by the multiple roles that health professionals can play, both traditionally in the context of the Hippocratic function, but also more broadly as healer, accompanier, spiritual guide, and advocate.

It should be noted, however, that as helpful as health providers may be to the process of recovery, it is in solidarity and identification with other survivors where much internal strengthening occurs. It is not uncommon for trauma survivors to feel that they are the only one who has had experiences like theirs. This perception is very isolating. When survivors begin to develop relationships with others who have endured such suffering, hope and strength can be drawn from others' support and example of recovery, thereby moving beyond the torture experience.

Role as Healer

Re-creating a sense of safety is central to work with trauma survivors. The establishment of safety is a prerequisite for treatment and healing to occur. Creating safety is an active process, initiated in part when one recognizes the survivor's basic needs, including food, clothing, and shelter, all of which are often problematic when one comes to a new country. Understanding the potential effects of torture, conditions in the country and region from which the survivor originates, cultural practices, and health beliefs are all significant to helping survivors to feel understood. Survivors frequently experience significant anxiety about how they may be viewed, and whether they will be believed if they share their life stories. Other challenges they face are those related to acculturative stress, which results from being exposed to a culture different than one's own, as well as uncertainty over one's legal circumstances. All these factors must be recognized and taken into account in clinical encounters.

After establishing a sense of safety, psychoeducation is helpful to understand what the person has lived through and its emotional impact, as trauma survivors may not make the connection between their current symptoms and their past. It is important for them to gain a sense of control over their life. Relaxation, meditation, and exercise can help to reduce anxiety and muscle tension. Gathering testimonial information helps to establish the context and chronology of what has occurred. Grounding techniques can be helpful in helping individuals to stay in the present.

The process of working through trauma often involves addressing cognitive beliefs around survivors' perceived sense of responsibility, the phenomenon of survivor guilt, feelings of self-blame or sometimes shame, fear that they will never improve since they have been left irreparably damaged, and crises of hopelessness. Working with nightmares and improving sleep, the cognitive processing of experiences, including de-sensitizing to memories and their effects, and strategies to decrease the client's reliving of the past in the present are helpful to the process of recovery. Psychotropic medication can also play a significant role in reducing distress. Work with the body can help with the fragmentation that torture causes, as the body is used by the torturer to access the person's inner world and soul. Holistic approaches take into account the multiple domains of people's lives that can be affected. Hence, approaches which simultaneously address these facets are necessary in helping to integrate the disparate parts of people's lives that have been fragmented by their experiences.

It is not uncommon for health care to be unavailable to survivors when detained. Many die in jail or after being brought to a hospital too late because they were not given the necessary medical attention. After survivors have fled the scene of their trauma, the residual effects of former injuries, illnesses endemic to the region of origin, ongoing health concerns, and the need for age-appropriate preventive care require evaluation and treatment. Chronic pain is a common problem. Torture, which often involves the use of rape, may result in exposure to HIV: a double burden for the survivor. Ongoing primary care is necessary, as is access to subspecialists. Changes in diet and exercise in a new country frequently contribute to a rising incidence of illnesses more commonly found in the industrial world than perhaps in the client's country of origin.

Survivors may be forced to go into exile and to ask for protection in a new country as an asylum seeker. In the United States, they must file an asylum claim within one year of arriving. Health professionals can play an important role in assessing asylum seekers, specifically as to the effects of torture and persecution. This involves interviewing and examining the patient about their past history prior to torture and persecution, their torture experiences, their life after torture, both in their country of origin and after arriving in the asylum country, the nature of their escape, past medical and psychiatric history and treatment, family history, mental status examination, and physical examination. Not having been witness to the events shared by the patient, the role of health professionals at this stage is to assess whether the symptoms with which they present are consistent with the narrative they have related. In the U.S., affidavits can be prepared and testimony offered to the Bureau of Citizenship and Immigration Services and the Department of Justice. These documents can play a significant role in the survivor's case when they are seeking asylum.[3]

Role as Accompanier

Survivors possess the fundamental voice about the negative effects of torture. They have the most reliable information about the impact of torture on their lives and on those of their families. With the "war on terror" and questions about the true effects of torture, survivors are in the best position to advise and to help others, including policy-makers, to understand its full impact. Being given the opportunity to provide testimony to lawmakers could enhance the national dialogue on interrogation methods and torture. After regaining their physical and emotional strength, some survivors may choose to speak out against torture. Indeed, efforts to use torture in the "war in terror" are vehemently opposed by survivors, who speak of its drastic degradation of human dignity, and also argue from experience that it does not work, as they know at first hand that people will say anything to make torturers stop the infliction of pain. Unfortunately, the survivor voice remains largely missing from the national dialogue about the utility of torture.

[3] Physicians for Human Rights Asylum Network, www.phrusa.org

The health professional accompanies survivors along the road from first being silenced, feeling as though one has no voice, to finding one's voice in the safe setting created in the therapeutic context, to exercising one's voice by sharing one's story. In some cases, survivors may choose to publicly denounce those who have tortured them, the governments who supported that torture, and governments who advocate the use of *any* torture as a military or political tool, and they may seek criminal penalties for torturers, as well as look for reparations.

Role as Spiritual Guide

Health professionals who work with torture survivors come face to face with the most profound and intentional suffering of humanity. In working with survivors, it is necessary to wrestle with facts related to the intentional infliction of suffering on other human beings. In hearing testimonials about extreme cruelty, health providers must reflect on and be cognizant of their own beliefs about evil in the world and the misuse of power, as their belief systems may also change in response to hearing about the infliction of violence on innocent people. A parallel process is undertaken by survivor and health provider to make sense of what one has experienced and to find meaning in the wake of that experience. What happens in the context of torture is an abomination of the dignity of the human connection. Often there are no words to express what has happened. In addition, there are few with whom one can share these experiences. This profound loneliness coupled with unanswered questions about causality can lead to existential despair for the survivor.

It is a humble honor to be invited into the sacred space of the woundedness of another human being, a space often not shared with that person's own family members. How do we honor our patients at these times of despair as they struggle with the most profound questions of their lives? It is by active listening and by holding on to a sense of hope, which at times can feel imperceptible to the survivor. It is also by providing our presence when it is so difficult for our patients to trust another human being. It is by listening with one's heart and helping to bear the pain, which can be bigger than the words which attempt to describe it. It is by remaining present when hearing about atrocities that are unimaginable. By being open to the existential and spiritual questions that such extreme trauma can raise, we can provide a sacred space for them to be examined and re-examined through the healing process.

Throughout the process of recovery, how one understands and relates to the spiritual issues that arise may change. For some survivors, gaining distance from the experience of torture may lead to reflection upon their journey through torture and its survival, and what conditions maintain the torture system.

Role as Advocate

Health professionals are in the unique position of being able to document the physical and emotional effects of torture. The Istanbul Protocol (1999)[4] was formulated by health professionals to serve as a manual to aid in the documentation of human rights violations. This is an effort on a worldwide basis to systematize the assessment of the effects of torture and ill treatment. Torturers increasingly attempt to cause suffering by methods that do not leave physical scars, so as to reduce the risk of discovery, and employ such methods as threats, excessive noise, and forced nudity. Given this, the documentation by health providers who listen to and validate a survivor's testimonial cannot be underestimated. Such documentation that torture is happening in a particular country can be used for the arrest and conviction of perpetrators under the laws of that country as well as international law.

The role of health professionals can also extend beyond individual encounters to act toward addressing issues of concern in the asylum system, including the detrimental effects on daily life of delays in obtaining work authorization. Not being able to apply for work authorization for 150 days after an asylum claim has been made means that the claimant must rely on the generosity of others for basic needs, including food, clothing, and shelter. Health professionals can provide education to the legal community about the effects of torture and also about how the presence of emotional distress and disease influences testimony in a judicial setting. For example, it can be impolite in some cultures to have direct eye contact with authoritative figures, whereas in a western context a lack of direct eye contact can suggest that one is not being truthful, or that one is trying to hide something. The increasing emphasis on documents to

---

[4] UN Office of the High Commissioner for Human Rights (OHCHR), *Manual on the Effective Investigation and Documentation of Torture and Other Cruel, Inhuman or Degrading Treatment or Punishment ("Istanbul Protocol")*, 2004, HR/P/PT/9/Rev.1, available at http://www.refworld.org/docid/4638aca62.html (accessed 3 November 2017).

support one's case does not take into account the circumstances under which some people are forced to flee their countries. Relying purely on documentation that in these contexts would be nearly impossible to obtain is a disservice to survivors, who often face extreme danger at the time of departure and during flight.

Through their work with human remains, forensic scientists help to answer questions after people have been silenced. Via their meticulous work, forensic scientists are frequently able not only to make identifications, giving the opportunity for some form of closure for families, but also to help answer questions of causality. Such questions include: How did my loved one die? When? For what reasons? This work is crucial, as history can at times be written inaccurately by those with the greater power. If there is documentation that human rights violations have occurred, testimony can be provided to international criminal courts to hold people accountable. When a spotlight is placed on human rights violations, perpetrators are more likely to be held accountable for their actions.

What Survivors Have Taught Me

This work highlights the polarity of the human experience: from the depths of cruelty that human beings are capable of inflicting on one another to the heights of the profound dignity of the human spirit. As health professionals, we bear witness to these extreme realities. We see that the torture experience is not the end of people's stories. It does not define who they are, but rather, through the healing process, becomes a part of their interwoven experience. We learn of acts of courage as well as gentle kindnesses bestowed by and among prison inmates. We learn that it is possible to love others even after experiencing the extremes of betrayal by one's countrymen, governments, civil servants, and humanity as a whole. By preserving one's own humanity in the face of torture, one can acknowledge that although for a period of time a survivor's freedom was taken, their human dignity was not destroyed. As a message to all who suffer such indignities and trauma, the health professional is one who can bear witness that the strength of the spirit can rise above efforts to destroy it.

As Martin Luther King, Jr. asserted, the arc of history bends toward justice. Doing this work, however, calls upon health professionals to actively speak out against the impact of torture, rather than being passive witnesses. As providers, we cannot be silent when we see the deleterious effects of torture, even in the face of efforts by torturers to use methods that leave no physical signs. Health professionals have a moral imperative to engage in the prevention of torture, not only to provide care and testimony, but also to work for justice by helping to identify perpetrators; aiding professional organizations to make clear ethical guidelines regarding the complicity of health professionals' involvement in torture; and working for the eradication of torture everywhere by anyone. This is particularly true for these times.

CHAPTER 6

Assessing the Treatment of Torture: Balancing Quantifiable with Intangible Metrics

Orlando P. Tizon✛

Activist, educator, and former priest Orlando P. Tizon was imprisoned and tortured for four years under the regime of President Ferdinand Marcos of the Philippines. In this chapter, Tizon provides an overview of the central mission of the Torture Abolition and Survivors Support Coalition International (TASSC) as a "community of healing," as well as describes his own role within that community. As both a torture survivor and an intake coordinator for TASSC, Tizon negotiated the dual demands of professional support, measurable outcomes, and the perpetual need to secure funding for the organization on the one hand, with the survivors' needs and desires on the other. The central aim of the chapter is to investigate how healing and recovery are evaluated by different stakeholders, and Tizon pursues this investigation through a consideration of what he terms an "institutional ethnography" of TASSC alongside interviews with the organization's clients. He begins by situating TASSC within the field of torture treatment programs. Moving to the specific services TASSC offers, his institutional

✛ Deceased
O. P. Tizon (✉)
Washington, DC, USA

ethnography focuses on "relations of ruling"[1] that arise from and condition survivors' interaction with different facets of the institution.

Tizon starts his institutional history in the 1970s, when Amnesty International launched a program to address the needs of torture survivors in Chile and an international group of medical professionals began to study torture rehabilitation. Accompanying new research and treatment protocols and facilities were new international and domestic legal instruments: first, the Convention against Torture (1984) and then, in the United States, the Torture Victims Relief Act (TVRA, 1998), which, in addition to its legal effects, provided funding to survivor treatment institutions. In doing so, TVRA enhanced the demand for evidence-based, measurable outcomes of programs seeking support. These outcomes for an organization such as TASSC must include measures of medical, psychological, legal, and social assistance. As Tizon points out, the demands of accountability perhaps inevitably shifted authority over the success of programs from those who experienced them to those who evaluate them, in keeping with what Sally Engle Merry refers to in the title of her recent study as The Seduction of Quantification *(2016). For most of TASSC's clients, legal asylum and the legal and psychological protections it affords constitute their most pressing need, and survivors often learn about the other services of the organization only after their initial meetings.*

In an earlier published essay exploring his own initial reluctance to participate in psychotherapy, "Dreams and Other Sketches from a Torture Survivor's Notes," Tizon explores the challenges survivors may face in seeking psychological assistance after torture and in navigating therapy sessions. He locates his own resistance to therapy in his desire to avoid reopening a traumatic past, to wanting to focus on other survivors, and to the sense that his survival had in part resulted from his inner strength. Thus, to seek help would be to acknowledge the vulnerability of that inner self. Reflecting on the successes and failures of his own therapy, Tizon provides a nuanced examination of the client–therapist relationship, which can spill over from the therapy session into everyday life, and can include the ways in which their power dynamic might inadvertently echo that of torture itself. Tizon insists on the necessity of a therapeutic process driven by survivor needs and desires in all their contradictions and complexities. Such an approach rec-

---

[1] Dorothy E. Smith, "Relations of Ruling: A Feminist Inquiry," *Studies in Cultures, Organizations, and Societies* vol. 2, no. 2 (1996).

ognizes the sociality of the survivor and, in doing so, explicitly responds to the way torture works to isolate subjects from their larger social worlds. Just as torture never involves solely what Stephanie Athey has described as the "dyad of torturer and tortured,"[2] Tizon argues that therapy should similarly not be limited to therapist and client, but rather should involve a wide network of social relations, particularly among survivors, as well as attention to post-therapy phases of healing.

In his contribution to this volume, Tizon focuses more explicitly on how survivors engage with TASSC as members of a community. He bases his findings on thirteen extended interviews he conducted from 2000 to 2010, as well as on his experiences with TASSC up until his death in 2016. The interviews as qualitative evidence reveal—perhaps unexpectedly, given that clients most often came to TASSC specifically for professional help with their asylum applications—that what they count as most valuable in their connection with TASSC is the discovery of a community of survivors. That community, moreover, comprises more than camaraderie and understanding based on shared experience, although those are crucial sources of support. It also forms the foundation for survivors' recognition of their own political subjectivity, as well as the possibility of controlling the direction and pace of their healing. Tizon concludes that "experience in TASSC sheds light on the importance of self-healing, the capacity of survivors to heal themselves, and the need to empower themselves for their recovery." These unquantifiable outcomes demand a broad understanding of mental health that extends beyond a purely medical definition, and is firmly rooted in a community of mutual support led by survivors themselves.

* * *

Introduction

I was imprisoned and tortured under the martial law regime of former President Marcos of the Philippines from September 1982 until April 1986. Three months after my release, I came to the United States to visit family members; after giving in to my family's entreaties, I prolonged my

---

[2] Stephanie Athey, "The Torture Device: Debate and Archetype," *Torture: Power, Democracy, and the Human Body*, edited by Shampa Biswas and Zahi Zalloua (Seattle and Walla Walla: Whitman College and University of Washington Press, 2011): 144.

stay and extended my tourist visa, eventually becoming a US resident. It took me years to decide to look for help after my experience of torture, and this was a step that I took entirely on my own, without any consultation with others. From that experience, I gathered strength and resources to take a job as Coordinator of Direct Service Programs at the Torture Abolition and Survivors Support Coalition International (TASSC), a non-profit organization for survivors of torture and political violence.

As coordinator, I was usually the first person in contact with the clients coming to the office. Survivors are typically first referred to TASSC by their lawyer, social worker, or staff from other organizations. Often they get to know the organization through their communities or through other survivors who have been to TASSC; sometimes they learn about the organization through its website. Most are asylum seekers whose main concern is to get their legal status and work permits in the United States.

The first step for survivors in the process of receiving assistance through the organization is to have an intake interview in order to determine whether they are survivors of torture and political violence, then to assess their priority needs, after which they are referred to different staff members or to other agencies. The various services are free of charge, with the exception of some lawyers, who might charge survivors at a reduced rate.

Clients are then assigned a case manager who helps them with the different services to which they are referred; very often they will need an immigration lawyer and a medical doctor. Some might need to see a psychotherapist, but the process is first explained by the case manager to show how it might assist them. It helps when it is explained that the physician and the therapist can provide documentation and expert witness to support an asylum application. TASSC also facilitates the process of gaining health insurance and support for employment and continuing education.

TASSC holds a monthly gathering of survivors to give them an opportunity to get to know each other, to socialize among themselves, and to be informed about different events in the community or the needs of the organization. It is during these meetings that new people introduce themselves to other survivors—often a very emotionally charged time for them and for everybody. They tell what country they come from, when they were arrested, and why; seldom do they give details of their imprisonment and torture, just the bare facts of why they had to leave their country. Sometimes, though, a few might give details of the political violence that they experienced.

Usually a brief lecture and discussion take place in the meeting; for instance, a lawyer might answer questions about the US asylum process, or a survivor might share some news about the situation in her home country. Survivors are always encouraged to come to the office to visit and to join the monthly gatherings as members of TASSC. Those who live in other states are referred to local treatment centers or other survivors living nearby, so that they can form a local community.

Survivors come to Washington, DC once a year to spend a few days in commemoration of Survivors' Week, which includes the June 26 United Nations (UN) International Day in Support of Torture Victims and Survivors. This week has become a general gathering of survivors from all over the United States and indeed the world. TASSC claims to be an alternative survivor treatment center by building what it calls "communities of healing." In its own words:

> TASSC International uses the International Communities of Healing to focus specifically on the rehabilitation of survivors of torture by healing themselves through mutual support, recognition, and validation.
>
> TASSC International Communities of Healing (ICOH) are spaces where survivors gather and work together to help each other heal. Community self-empowerment is an important part of overcoming the experience of torture. TASSC provides a forum to support that process through the International Communities of Healing.

In other words, TASSC relies upon the services of medical doctors, psychologists, and psychiatrists to support survivors, while also emphasizing the importance of processes of survivor self-empowerment in healing the trauma of torture. As Coordinator in this context, I had always to keep in mind the funding requirements of the non-profit organization by referring clients to treatment and rehabilitation services that used "evidence-based practices" and "measurement-based care."

Survivors mostly welcomed various social services such as housing, health insurance, lawyers, and physicians; however, being unfamiliar with mental health services, since most of them came from countries where these services had negative connotations culturally or were rarely available to the general public, they had a more difficult time understanding the services of a psychologist or psychiatrist. Many of them were suspicious of psychotherapy and most did not like taking psychotropic drugs because of their side effects.

Because most of our clients were asylum seekers, my other priorities were to refer them to a lawyer and to prepare them for immigration officer interviews and court hearings. The main objective in this case was to provide evidence of torture and proof of what the US immigration system and asylum court required as a "well-founded fear of persecution" by reason of "race, religion, nationality, membership in a particular social group, or political opinion."[3]

During my work in TASSC, I frequently found myself living in two worlds: in the non-profit organization with its funding requirements, and in the world of the survivors living their lives and working to persevere and to heal from the trauma of torture. The first comprised my identity as a coordinator working in a non-profit organization, ensuring that we were providing care with measurable outcomes; and the second meant being a witness for our clients in their day-to-day work of surviving in a strange, new society. I realized that my efforts to meet the funding requirements of the non-profit organization by providing measurement-based care were not exactly related to the everyday lives of survivors, including myself, seeking to endure and to heal from the trauma of torture.

For most survivors, what was important was to live in a place of safety, to gain legal status, and to be able to work so that they would not be dependent on others. For me as coordinator of services, I had to make sure that our clients received treatment and rehabilitation services that were using "evidenced-based practices," and that eventually they acquired some form of legal status. I often found myself asking, because I was not sure: "How do I know that my clients are healing and recovering from their trauma as a result of such practices? Are these methods the best way for their recovery?" Complicating the issue was managing my own personal history of being a survivor of torture while simultaneously trying to be a detached observer and manager.

This was my problematic. The focus of my research, then, was to find out how survivors of torture understand their healing and recovery from torture trauma as part of their journey with TASSC, particularly in the face of official prescriptions of mental and physical health treatment, as well as

---

[3] Convention Relating to the Status of Refugees, New York, 28 July 1951. United Nations Treaty Series, vol. 189, p. 137. http://www.unhcr.org/en-us/3b66c2aa10 (accessed March 22, 2017).

legal and social services, that are guided by measurement-based care and evidence-based practices. From their own point of view, how did survivors define their healing and recovery?

Methodology

To answer the questions raised in my work with survivors, I have used a method of inquiry called institutional ethnography, which emphasizes and uses people's everyday experience as embodied actors and experts in what they do in their daily lives. It broadens the idea of work from its conventional meaning as "paid labor" to consider people's everyday lives also through the lens of work, or "what people do that requires some effort, that they mean to do, and that involves some required competence."[4] Such inquiry focuses on analyzing the actual doings and discourses of everyday life, especially the use of texts of all types, using these as data to disclose the relations that affect people and influence their daily lives. This method does not start from theory, but rather originates from the experiences of living human beings in space and time, drawing practical and theoretical conclusions from those experiences. As part of my research, then, I examined survivors' TASSC-related work, including keeping appointments with lawyers, meeting with therapists or counselors, looking for a job, or attending a meeting in the TASSC office. I asked them to recount their work of surviving in a new society after having undergone torture and other forms of politically motivated violence.

Another feature of institutional ethnography that sets it apart from other qualitative methods of research is that it does not aim to generalize from a representative sample of data or to describe a population sample by categories based on the data. Rather than aiming to generalize, it emphasizes that what people do in their everyday lives is coordinated by social relations, including by events that have occurred or are occurring in other places and times. Thus, actions that we take for granted every day, such as buying groceries, taking the bus to work, and so on, are part of social relations connected with others located elsewhere and other times. Social organizations are made up of these interconnections of everyday activities and various social relations and temporalities. Central to this coordination is the role of what Dorothy Smith calls texts, which may be written, oral,

---

[4] D. E. Smith, *Institutional Ethnography A: Sociology for People* (Lanham, MD: Alta Mira Press, 2006), 10.

visual, or other forms of language used to communicate and coordinate within specific social contexts. Texts make social relations replicable in many times and places, standardizing and coordinating courses of action. For instance, a nurse's report on a chart coordinates the different actions in a hospital designated for patient care and would be recognized by other nurses in other hospitals when they activate the text.[5]

By activating and engaging the text, the "reader" enters into power relations, or what Smith calls "relations of ruling," whereby those who dominate exercise their power over those in local situations. Thus, the nurse filling in the chart to report on a patient's condition links up to the hospital's administration and structures all the way to the highest levels, organized to coordinate the hospital's mission of health care. As organizations have become more complex in industrial societies, such coordination has become more significant for purposes of efficiency, cost-cutting, and better management of resources. The disadvantage, however, is that the client's needs often get lost or subordinated to the organization's in the process of this text-mediated coordination. The nurse creating the chart may not be conscious of this as she works to complete the hospital's requirements; however, institutional ethnography reveals these systems and allows the researcher to map the social relations they engender, as well as how people in the local situation are affected in their daily lives by such ruling relations.[6]

EVIDENCE-BASED PRACTICE IN TORTURE TREATMENT AND REHABILITATION

Torture treatment and rehabilitation programs use the administrative language of "evidence-based practice" and "measurement-based care," both of which were adopted from the practice of the natural sciences, particularly medicine. Evidence-based medicine was first proposed in 1992, was then adopted in public health settings, and also was implemented in all programs of the National Consortium of Torture Treatment Programs (NCTTP). As its website proclaims, "Providing health, mental health, legal assistance, and/or other support services to victims of torture,

---

[5] Smith, 27.
[6] M. L. Campbell, "Institutional Ethnography and Experience as Data," in *Institutional Ethnography as Practice*, edited by D. E. Smith (Oxford, UK: Rowman & Littlefield, 2004), 36, 91–108.

NCTTP member centers conduct their programs with the highest professional standards. Research into treatment outcomes and evidence based practices is a strong value."[7]

Compared with other organized efforts to treat and rehabilitate victims of disease or abuse, the field of torture trauma treatment and rehabilitation is fairly new, dating to the 1970s, and roughly contemporaneous with a surge of governmental and non-governmental interest in human rights and human rights violations, including torture. Indeed, torture was the focus of the first and most visible international human rights non-governmental organization (NGO), Amnesty International, founded in 1961 by British attorney Peter Benenson, who was appalled at the situation of "prisoners of conscience"—people detained and tortured for peaceful expression of their beliefs. The organization's earliest campaigns brought attention not only to survivors, but also to their various health needs, even though not much was known about the physical or psychosocial effects of torture at that time. In 1974, a group of doctors in Denmark collaborated with health professionals in Chile, Sweden, and Greece to begin work on torture rehabilitation methods, and soon founded the International Rehabilitation Council for Torture Victims, which now maintains affiliations with more than 140 torture treatment centers in 70 countries.[8] Over time, in response to a clearly growing need, torture rehabilitation has become a global movement.

In 1998, the US Congress passed the Torture Victims Relief Act (TVRA), authorizing funding for medical, psychological, legal, and social services for survivors of torture in domestic and international centers, as well as research and training of service providers. The TVRA provides resources and support for the creation of more programs for torture rehabilitation. In the United States several organizations, including TASSC, joined together to form the NCTTP, which in turn became a funding body for member organizations. For the purposes of resource allocation, the TVRA set guidelines—based on the original language of the UN Convention against Torture—to define torture and, thereby, to identify survivors eligible for treatment.

---

[7] National Consortium of Torture Treatment Programs (http://www.ncttp.org/aboutus.html).

[8] "ICRT Marks 40 Years of Anti-Torture Treatment with a Special Event in Copenhagen," World Without Torture Blog, 4 September 2014. https://worldwithouttorture.org/tag/denmark-and-torture/ (accessed March 29, 2015).

This legislation uses the following definition of torture, given in section 2340(1) of title 18, United States Code:

(1) "torture" means an act committed by a person acting under the color of law specifically intended to inflict severe physical or mental pain or suffering (other than pain or suffering incidental to lawful sanctions) upon another person within his custody or physical control;

(2) "severe mental pain or suffering" means the prolonged mental harm caused by or resulting from:

(A) the intentional infliction or threatened infliction of severe physical pain or suffering;
(B) the administration or application, or threatened administration or application, of mind-altering substances or other procedures calculated to disrupt profoundly the senses or the personality;
(C) the threat of imminent death; or
(D) the threat that another person will imminently be subjected to death, severe physical pain or suffering, or the administration or application of mind-altering substances or other procedures calculated to disrupt profoundly the senses or personality.

As used in the TVRA, this definition also includes the use of rape and other forms of sexual violence by a person acting under the color of law, upon another person under his custody, or by physical control.

All services provided through the TVRA and via other funders require treatment outcomes and evidence-based practices in their programs in order to ensure that funds, including public funds, are accounted for and used for their intended purposes. While clearly this objective is crucial, one perhaps unintended consequence of the widespread implementation of such quantitative assessment measures is that it hands power to physicians and other service providers involved in rehabilitation, including judges and lawyers. This distribution of power may contribute to survivors' sense of powerlessness and may not lend itself well to the complex and messy processes of healing—and of "measuring" that healing.

Legal services are an important component of the rehabilitation program for torture survivors, since acquiring legal status and a permit to work are vital to their rehabilitation. Legal services also require evidence-based practices, but, unlike health services, the evidence required in this case inheres in the legal asylum process. Anyone seeking asylum in the United States must first meet with an immigration officer to explain why he or she is seeking asylum. The main evidence that the immigration law seeks is "credible fear of persecution or torture," explained by immigration law in this way:

> An individual will be found to have a credible fear of persecution if he or she establishes that there is a "significant possibility" that he or she could establish in a full hearing before an Immigration Judge that he or she has been persecuted or has a well-founded fear of persecution or harm on account of his or her race, religion, nationality, membership in a particular social group, or political opinion if returned to his or her country.[9]

In this case, the burden of proof is on the asylum seeker to provide evidence and convince the immigration officer that he or she is eligible for asylum or protection in the United States; the judge makes the final decision in a "defensive" asylum process. If the judge is convinced by the evidence, the court is obliged to grant protection according to the Convention against Torture, ratified by the United States in 1984. The evidence is mainly the survivor's testimony, substantiated by expert witnesses and by available documentation, such as medical and mental health evidence of torture. The survivor's lawyer supports the client throughout the process; such representation is crucial, given that the process can be intimidating and adversarial, in the presence of a judge and a government lawyer whose task is to rebut the survivor's arguments. Most survivors originally contact TASSC because they are in need of help with their petitions for asylum.

"I was anxious about applying for asylum and I needed a lawyer," Abner told me. The US asylum process is difficult to navigate, even for someone with a legal background. Most of our clients do not understand its requirements. Azeb, for instance, said that she needed some papers and she got upset when I was not able to provide them for her. Her anxiety was understandable: survivors know that being granted asylum ensures that they will not be deported. Sara explained: "My asylum was important, it has achieved something that I've been struggling [for] for so many

---

[9] "Credible Fear FAQ." United States Citizenship and Immigration Services. http://www.uscis.gov/faq-page/credible-fear-faq#t12831n40090 (accessed November 23, 2015).

years; I was not sure if the court would accept it, now here I am safe." Survivors live with the constant fear of being deported, yet paradoxically there is an added source of fear, because meeting with service providers, and especially facing the judge in the full court, replicates the torture situation where they are placed before persons of authority who have all the power and claim to possess the truth.[10]

Interviewing Survivors of Torture

In order to get at this paradox of fearing service providers—lawyers, social workers, doctors, psychologists—while also needing to engage with them in order to work toward gaining legal status, starting a new life, and even healing from the wounds of torture, I conducted open-ended interviews of thirteen survivors of torture from six countries, eight women and five men. Most were from Africa, except for two from the Middle East and one from Central America. Most live in the Metro DC area, and at the time of the interviews held various legal statuses, from citizens to asylum applicants. I used English for the interviews, except for two cases when the survivors asked for an interpreter/translator to express ideas and feelings better. The interviews took an average of four hours and were conducted face to face or by telephone. The questions centered mainly on their experiences in and relations with TASSC. All names have been changed in order to protect identities.

In most instances, survivors of torture avoided talking about their treatment under the hands of their torturers or their experience in prison. Only one, Abraham, offered information about hearing soldiers torturing a man in a room above his cell, throwing the body inside the cell next to his, and leaving a bloody jacket hanging by the door to his cell. Abraham mentioned this incident after several hours of interviews, during which he told me about breaking down in tears when a staff member in the office asked him directly about his torture. He did not talk at all about what the torturers did to him.

Survivors spoke about *living in the dark, life at an end, keeping quiet and avoiding others, living as if there is a secret inside you, just living day by day.* They generally avoided talking about their torture or the institutions connected with it such as prison, or the guards, or how they managed to get out.

---

[10] See, for instance, Dianna Ortiz, *The Blindfold's Eye: My Journey from Torture to Truth* (New York: Orbis Books, 2002), 31–33.

You feel like there is a secret inside you, you feel guilty, murmured Elsa.

I arrived in the US in 2010, so broken and lonely and scared. I did not want to talk to anyone, I just kept to myself, and just think and think, I felt so hopeless, shared Lidija.

Initially, survivors were reluctant to speak of their experiences, and instead focused upon their current work and life situations. When I asked them what activities in TASSC proved most helpful to them, they described the following as the most important.

Meeting Other Survivors

A common refrain was: *You're not alone! You think that you're the only victim.*

Most survivors remember the first time they came to TASSC. For instance, Helen remembers vividly how she was received and made welcome by a staff member and offered food. It was the first time that she had been treated this way in the United States, and when she recalled this greeting, she exclaimed: *I felt very wonderful.*

All the interviewees articulated that meeting other survivors during TASSC's annual June Survivors' Week and during the monthly gatherings of survivors in the office and other occasions was very important. Hearing the stories of other survivors was especially significant, as shown by their various reactions during the gatherings:

I thought I was the only one.
You're not the only one, you're not alone.
Others suffered worse treatment than I.
Torture happens also in other places of the world, no matter your race.

Sharing meals, ideas, advice, and experiences with others about surviving helped; they especially noted that their voices and opinions were being heard and responded to when they exchanged information about job opportunities, the asylum process, or classes to learn English.

It was consoling, comforting to be with others.
I felt protected.
It felt like being with family, with brothers and sisters.
Same people, same feeling, that is a family, like being with family, Sara emphasized.

Many mentioned working together, teaching each other how to sew and make bags, or instance, as important for relaxing and helping to forget the pain. Survivors shared that such gatherings were different from meeting a therapist individually: *Better than psychotherapy*, Kedir and Abner described the experience.

Sharing Stories

Survivors remember the torturers' warnings:

> *After torture you are told by your torturers not to say anything, not to tell others what happened*, according to Rahel.
> *You feel like there is a secret inside you, you feel guilty.*
> *You're not able to throw out the anger.*

But when they are able to speak out despite and against the torturer's threats, then it is a healing experience for them:

> *When you get it out, you feel free, a sense of relief.*
> *Telling others what happened is like getting out of prison*, Omer described it. *As soon as you get it out, you feel free, like getting out of jail. I am out, the day I fled the country, the day I spoke in public.*

Juan cites the difference when speaking among survivors and other groups:

> *When you speak before survivors, you feel solidarity, when you speak to other groups, you feel happy, hopeful in denouncing torture.*

Speaking in Public

Speaking in public and meeting US citizens and leaders when TASSC members lobbied Congress on the June 26 UN Day against Torture were eye-opening experiences for the survivors. Denouncing torture publicly was especially significant, because it gave them hope and validated their position against their governments—and because usually it had been their acts of speaking out against government repression that had caused them to be detained and tortured. It was for many of them a chance to explain to others why they had been imprisoned and tortured, and thereby to justify themselves against the authorities who had tortured them—and who had often told them that no one would ever know of their torture.

Survivors had been most often arrested for taking a stand and speaking the truth; now it was their chance to make sure that others knew the truth. Sara explained:

People are tortured because they don't want to do what they think is not right, to be a slave and to obey. You speak the truth and you go to prison. Now, here, you speak the truth and feel safe. I am satisfied that others will learn.

Ahmed quoted his torturers telling him: *If you are right, why is the US supporting our government?* Because of these words, he looked for opportunities to talk to ordinary Americans and their leaders about what their support meant to the people in his country. Meeting individual Americans who were shocked at hearing their stories and who sympathized with them gave many survivors a sense of comfort. This was important to their healing, because it proved to them that not all Americans agreed with the support that the United States gave to a government that was responsible for imprisoning and torturing them.

Healing

After torture it's like life is finished, you can't do anything else. Now I can move on. Before I could not talk, I was quiet, kept things inside, Elsa remembers.

Many survivors enjoy volunteering in the office with odd jobs. I have asked some of them to help interpret for new people just arriving whose English is inadequate. One volunteer described this work as her accountability for those who could not speak. Most want to actively do something to stop torture and work for human rights, to make a difference in the lives of others in the United States, and the opportunity to do so through TASSC contributes to their sense of empowerment and healing. Telling others about TASSC and sending them to the office is another common way to help others. Between 2000 and 2010, more than 50% of referrals to the office came from other survivors.

Years ago, a friend told Juan: *You will never forget what happened.* Twenty-eight years later, he could speak without feeling the same anxiety about his torture and the nightmares would not come with the same intensity: *Before, I would always cry when I spoke, and have nightmares afterwards.* Kedir agreed: *I was living from day to day. Now I can make plans. Before, I could not think of tomorrow. I was like someone with Alzheimer's.*

Feeling better, feeling safe, and *hope restored in myself* were other descriptions of survivors' ongoing healing. Other significant signs of healing for survivors included being able to make the decision to attend school, taking steps to apply for a better job, writing their memoir to share with others, and deciding to be open to entering a relationship.

Elias narrated how he was tortured by using electrodes on his genitals for a number of sessions, causing him to be impotent as a result. After many years during which he went to psychotherapy, used herbal medication, and participated in activities at TASSC with other survivors, he gradually regained his potency and decided to get married. He told me during the interview that he and his wife were looking forward to the birth of their baby.

Many survivors still go through ups and downs, but are better able to manage these incidents over time and with connection to survivor communities. Healing from torture trauma is a slow, ongoing process. It takes time and preparation before survivors are ready to speak openly about their torture, either by sharing experiences with other survivors or by speaking to the public.

The passages above are from survivors' own descriptions of how they are recovering from trauma. Their experience at TASSC sheds light on the importance of self-healing, the capacity of survivors to heal themselves in community with other survivors, and the need to empower themselves in order to begin their recovery. Through their work in TASSC communities of healing, they have shown the capacity of survivors to heal themselves through solidarity with others and by empowering themselves, and not solely by depending on therapists, doctors, and psychotropic medication. By listening to and supporting one another, and by speaking out about their torture and against their torturers, they are breaking the torturer's chains and restoring their connections with others, with a safe community, and ultimately, with life itself. Their experiences highlight their capacity to heal themselves with various health and legal providers as support persons, not protagonists, in that healing; their experiences also raise questions about the narrow view on evidence-based health care that emphasizes individual treatment to the neglect of the social and structural causes of and responses to trauma.

As psychologist Ignacio Martin-Baro writes about his experience in treating people caught in the civil war in El Salvador:

Psychosocial trauma [...] constitutes the concrete crystallization in individuals of aberrant and dehumanizing social relations, like those prevalent in the situation of civil war [...] Therefore, as psychologists, we cannot be satisfied with treating post-traumatic stress. This is necessary and especially urgent with children. However, the underlying problem is not a matter of individuals but of the traumatogenic social relations that are part of an oppressive system that has led to war. So it is of primary importance that treatment address itself to relationships between social groups which constitute the 'normal abnormality' that dehumanizes the weak and the powerful, the oppressor and the oppressed, soldier and victim, dominator and dominated alike.[11]

The point here is not to deny the uses and effectiveness of psychotherapy and other performance-based care of torture trauma; in fact, several of the survivors claimed it was of benefit. *Therapy helped. My healing started when I went to Coalition B (a torture treatment center)*, declared Sara. After ten years, Asmara still goes to psychotherapy and receives medication. Most are grateful for the help of their medical doctors, who treated their physical injuries, and for their lawyers, who walked them through the asylum process.

Still, survivors' experiences as shared in their own words can help providers to create expansive, multifaceted, qualitative and quantitative approaches to healing that include the survivor herself as an expert in her own care. This power of self-healing is supported by the work of Dr. Richard Mollica and his staff at the Harvard Program in Refugee Trauma, who found that survivors of political violence and refugees were willing to tell their stories, given a conducive environment; more importantly, they realized that the trauma story was the key to releasing the powers of survivors' own self-healing. Mollica adds: "Doctors often fail to see the patient's innate healing process because they are interested only in the healing generated by their own medical interventions. The patient's efforts become a sideshow to the enormous medical apparatus that the doctor brings to bear."[12] In the future, with the help of doctors, therapists, survivors, and refugees working together, the major role of self-healing will be recognized in the treatment and recovery of traumatized persons.

---

[11] I. Martin-Baro, "War and the Psychosocial Trauma of Salvadoran Children," transl. A. Wallace, in *Writings for a Liberation Psychology*, ed. A. Aron and S. Corne (Cambridge: Harvard University Press, 1994), 125, 135.

[12] Richard Mollica, *Healing Invisible Wounds* (New York: Harcourt, 2006), 10.

Conclusion

I started this essay by describing the problematic that I faced while I was working at TASSC as coordinator of social services, providing services that met the funding requirements of evidence-based and measurement-based care. I realized that my efforts to provide those services were not exactly related to the day-to-day lives of survivors working to survive and heal from the trauma of torture, and I often felt as if we were living in two different worlds. I wanted to find out how survivors of torture lived their lives and were healing from their trauma while they were receiving services from the organization, and how, in turn, I might learn from them about how best to meet their needs and to help them thrive—even if those methods did not always adhere to standard quantitative assessment measures.

Using institutional ethnography to analyze survivors' interviews as data, I looked into their experiences and day-to-day lives of surviving and making a transition in a new society. My interviews and analysis showed that they were capable of healing themselves from trauma. This power of self-healing was unleashed by coming together with other survivors and friends, by listening and speaking, and by sharing a common experience. Their experience calls into question the power of health-care institutions emphasizing evidence-based care and the ongoing medicalization of mental health care today.

CHAPTER 7

The Little Red Cabinet of Tears: The Impact upon Treatment Providers of Bearing Witness to Torture

Judy B. Okawa

Dr. Judy B. Okawa, a licensed clinical psychologist, founded the Program for Survivors of Torture and Severe Trauma (PSTT) in northern Virginia (an area with a high concentration of refugees, asylum seekers, and immigrants, including many torture survivors) in 1998. In addition to her clinical work, she has served as an expert witness in survivors' asylum cases, testifying to survivors' psychological harm and situating it within the cultural contexts in which it took place. In this chapter, she recounts her initial feelings of inadequacy in addressing the needs of survivors, and then charts the complex personal and professional development that shifted her approach to and understanding of her work. In this way, Okawa shows how ethical, professional care can be conceptualized as a form of witnessing, including self-witnessing, through which therapists learn how to lessen the burden past torture exerts on survivors' present lives.

For Okawa, the process of learning to bear witness began with the anguish of hearing about intense suffering and of recognizing both human and state capacities to torture. In order to maintain care for her clients

J. B. Okawa (✉)
Pacific Psychological Services, Honolulu, USA

© The Author(s) 2018
A. S. Moore, E. Swanson (eds.), *Witnessing Torture*, Palgrave Studies in Life Writing, https://doi.org/10.1007/978-3-319-74965-5_7

(and avoid shifting the focus to her own vicarious traumatization), she cultivated support networks with other therapists, drew upon survivors' continued religious faith to resolve her own crisis of belief, and developed protective layers to shield her emotions while still being present for the survivor through a process she calls "cloaking." These strategies underscore the work of therapy as itself socially situated, and the relationship between survivors and their health-care workers as a process of dynamic exchange that shapes them both.

Okawa's work as an expert witness in political asylum cases involves a different form of witnessing. Here her task is to certify whether torture took place or not, and if it did, to place the torture in its social context, which often demands an ethnographic approach to explaining socio-cultural customs to a judge.

These two different forms of witnessing—that which the therapist performs in listening to survivors' stories, and that as an expert witness who translates torture into legally and culturally legible testimony—dismantle any simple binary oppositions between victim and therapist, suffering and health, and pain and the wider medical, legal, and cultural worlds in which it circulates.

* * *

I remember well the first account of torture that was related to me.[1] *An anguished young woman, slight in stature, described being hung by her wrists from the ceiling of a jail cell in Saddam Hussein's Iraq and beaten with a bat so that she swung back and forth, slamming into other prisoners. She described the stench of urine, feces, sweat, and fear in the cell, and brought alive in our therapy room the sounds of people moaning, people screaming, people begging for mercy.*

Although I had had much experience working with people who had suffered many different forms of trauma, including incest, sexual abuse, domestic violence, combat-related trauma, and traumatic experiences as refugees, I was undone by this and her further accounts of torture. I didn't know what to do with the expression on my face. How should I respond? I felt that I had no tools to help this young woman, that nothing I could

---

[1] All cases described are composites, representing forms of torture experienced by countless survivors.

possibly say or do would be adequate to help her heal from the emotional and physical pain she was suffering. Previously not very religious, I found myself putting my head on my desk before her appointments and asking God to please give me words that would help ease her pain. The horror caused by the images of her torture and the enormity of her suffering gave me intense feelings of being deskilled. At that point in my work I had not yet learned the healing power of simply bearing witness to what she had experienced, a critical first step in "walking" with her through her memories.[2] Nor had I enough familiarity with the types of torture she had experienced, which I came to learn were endured by far too many others, to keep me from being overwhelmed by them and to enable me to hold them in the room for this survivor, in whose life they still had a powerful presence.

Shocked by the ineptitude I felt in the face of torture accounts, I decided that perhaps most therapists would have similar reactions. In Washington, DC, there was a clear need for therapists with experience dealing with torture, because of the large population of refugees there from all over the world. I was a psychologist and Clinical Director at the Center for Multicultural Human Services (CMHS) in Falls Church, Virginia, a multicultural mental health center that provided a broad range of services to refugees and immigrants in many languages. CMHS was participating in a training grant that also included psychologists from the Marjorie Kovler Center in Chicago and the Center for Victims of Torture in Minneapolis. After lengthy discussions with these caring, skilled psychologists who worked full time with survivors of torture, I decided to start a torture treatment program within CMHS. With the support of CMHS Director Dr. Dennis Hunt, we applied for funding, and the Program for Survivors of Torture and Severe Trauma (PSTT) was born in 1998.[3]

This chapter is a personal account of my journey as a clinical psychologist, as I learned how to bear witness to the accounts of torture experienced by the survivors with whom I worked, and thus how to be

---

[2] Sister Dianna Ortiz uses the apt term "walking with survivors" to describe the process of the therapist accompanying the survivor on the path toward healing from torture (personal communication). For a powerful personal account of torture and its impact, see her book *The Blindfold's Eyes: My Journey from Torture to Truth*.

[3] PSTT is now within Northern Virginia Family Services in Falls Church, VA.

more effective in helping them heal from their trauma. It is with much trepidation and some shame that I dare to write of my own experiences of pain from exposure to stories of torture. How dare I speak of symptoms of vicarious trauma and secondary traumatic stress when my clients suffered from far more devastating symptoms of post-traumatic stress? Yet one of the purposes of this book is to invite survivors to write from an analytical point of view rather than their usual first-person testimonial voice, and for people who have not suffered torture but are working in the field to write from a personal point of view, to share some of the vulnerability of the "I" voice. Thus, I offer this personal account.

The difficulty I feel in baring my soul gives me an inkling of how painful it must have been for the survivors who have had to do so with me. My heartfelt thanks go to the many survivors of torture who endured great anguish to put into words for me the experiences they had hoped would never have to be exposed to the light of day. They inspired me with their endurance, their faith, and their courage to keep moving forward to find a new life.

The goal of this chapter is to describe the developmental process I went through as I moved from being traumatized by my survivor clients' torture accounts to becoming an effective therapist and expert witness. During the initial stage, which can aptly be entitled *Coming Undone*, I learned a great deal about different types of torture and post-traumatic symptoms, my own and my clients'.

The middle stage, *Learning to Hold the Trauma*, involved a long process of learning and growth, with many challenges to my belief systems and perspectives. Over time I learned how to hold the trauma so that the survivor could tolerate the excruciating process of describing what they had endured. This was quite critical, because if I could not tolerate hearing the story, the survivor could not speak of it. The therapist must provide a safe environment in which the torture is robbed of its overwhelming symptomatic power over the life of the survivor. During this period, I also developed protection against secondary trauma symptoms.

The final stage was one of *Transformation and Resilience*. I found it was possible to learn from my own symptoms of secondary trauma, to transform some of them and make use of them. Indeed, the work itself was transformational. Working with survivors can have deep meaning for the clinician as well as for the client. I found the journey of working with survivors of torture to be profoundly inspirational, one that has blessed me with vicarious resilience after initial vicarious trauma.[4,5,6,7] My hope is that others who work with survivors of torture, whether they be mental health professionals, physicians, judges, attorneys and paralegals, case workers, human rights activists, or interpreters, can have a similar journey, and that they not feel disheartened if they are at the point of feeling "undone." There are many rewards ahead.

Coming Undone

The trauma therapist's process of development involves a journey deep inside with social, emotional, and spiritual consequences, as well as challenges to their worldview.[8] In her seminal work *Trauma and Recovery*, Judith Herman points out that "trauma is contagious" and that the therapist "empathically shares the patient's experience of helplessness."[9] In the earliest days of hearing my clients' stories of their torture, I truly was undone by them. Everything about torture was new to me, and hearing accounts of torture was extremely shocking. I hurt deeply for the survivors who were coming to me for help. When I tried to talk about this to my supervisor, who did not work with torture survivors, he suggested that perhaps I should not work with them because it was too painful for me. This response felt silencing. J. David Kinzie, who also worked with torture survivors, reported that by sharing complicated feelings about working with trauma victims, "one runs the risk that such openness may be misinterpreted as professional

---

[4] Pilar Hernández, David Gangsei, and David Engstrom (2007, p. 237) describe vicarious resilience as therapist resilience that develops as a result of exposure to the resilience of their trauma clients. It is "a unique and positive effect that transforms therapists in response to client trauma survivors' own resilience." In "Vicarious Resilience: A New Concept in Work with Those Who Survive Trauma," *Family Process* 46, no. 2 (2007): 229–41.

[5] David Engstrom, Pilar Hernández, and David Gangsei, "Vicarious Resilience: A Qualitative Investigation into Its Description," *Traumatology* 14, no. 3 (2008): 13–21.

[6] Pilar Hernández, David Engstrom, and David Gangsei, "Exploring the Impact of Trauma on Therapists: Vicarious Resilience and Related Concepts in Training," *Journal of Systemic Therapies* 29, no. 1 (2010): 67–83.

[7] M. Pack, "Vicarious Resilience: A Multilayered Model of Stress and Trauma," *Affilia: Journal of Women and Social Work* 29, no. 1 (2010): 18–29.

[8] Laurie Anne Pearlman and Karen W. Saakvitne, *Trauma and the Therapist: Countertransference and Vicarious Traumatization in Psychotherapy with Incest Survivors* (New York: W. W. Norton, 1995).

[9] Judith Lewis Herman, *Trauma and Recovery: The Aftermath of Violence – from Domestic Abuse to Political Terror* (New York: Basic Books, 1992), 140.

incompetence or personal weakness. This makes it tempting to hide the thoughts."[10,11] I was determined to continue this work, but I now felt that my supervisor might not really understand the issues I was dealing with. The truth was that learning what torturers did was painful for *anyone*. It just took time for me to learn to hold the trauma effectively. The torture itself traumatized me. Danieli, who works with Holocaust survivors, calls this "event countertransference."[12]

I remember reading everything I could to learn how to assist survivors in dealing with the post-traumatic symptoms they suffered on nearly a daily basis. In particular, books published by the International Rehabilitation Council for Torture Victims (IRCT) and the Rehabilitation and Research Centre for Torture Victims in Denmark were difficult to read, because not only was the content traumatizing, but there were pictures of torture, many drawn by survivors, depicting their experiences.[13] *I used to cover all the pictures with my hands, trying to skim the words in the text without absorbing them fully, because the images they conjured up were so abhorrent. I was trying to titrate my dose of torture content.*

I started developing symptoms of some of the hazards well known to clinicians who work with trauma: vicarious traumatization and secondary traumatic stress. Vicarious traumatization (VT) refers to a "transformation in the inner experiences of the therapist that come as a result of empathic engagement with clients' trauma material."[14] According to Pearlman and Mac Ian, VT is an occupational hazard for therapists who work with

---

[10] J. David Kinzie, "Countertransference in the Treatment of Southeast Asian Refugees," in *Countertransference in the Treatment of PTSD*, ed. John P. Wilson and Jacob D. Lindy (New York: Guilford Press, 1994), 253.

[11] Maria Blacque-Belair (2002, 201) spoke of a similar problem working as a relief worker. See "Being Knowledgeable Can Help Enormously," in *Sharing the Front Line and the Back Hills: International Protectors and Providers: Peacekeepers, Humanitarian Aid Workers and the Media in the Midst of Crisis*, ed. Yael Danieli (Amityville, NY: Baywood Publishing Company, Inc., 2002).

[12] Yael Danieli (1994, 373) differentiates between countertransference that is the therapist's reaction to the client's trauma stories (event countertransference) and reactions to the client's behaviors or characteristics (personal countertransference). *See* "Countertransference, Trauma, and Training," in *Countertransference in the Treatment of PTSD*, ed. John P. Wilson and Jacob D. Lindy (New York: Guilford Press, 1994).

[13] Peter Vesti, Finn Somnier, and Marianne Kastrup, *Psychotherapy with Torture Survivors: A Report of Practice from the Rehabilitation and Research Centre for Torture Victims (RCT)* (Copenhagen, Denmark: Copenhagen IRCT, 1992).

[14] Pearlman and Saakvitne, *Trauma and the Therapist*, 31.

trauma survivors and is a normal—rather than a pathological—response to being exposed to trauma material.[15] VT is a gradual process of change in the therapist that affects therapists' relationships with others, their worldview, spirituality, self-capacities, ego resources, aspects of identity, and central psychological needs.[16] A person who suffers from vicarious trauma may suffer from a decreased ability to trust, altered sense of safety, decreased self-esteem, and a loss of control.

Figley developed the theory of compassion fatigue to describe the convergence of secondary traumatic stress and burnout in caregivers who are repeatedly exposed to the trauma of others.[17] Secondary traumatic stress (STS) is also thought to be a normal, universal response to exposure to a client's traumatic experiences, and is not considered to be pathological.[18] STS is primarily symptom based and includes symptoms of post-traumatic stress disorder, such as the re-experiencing of trauma, recurrent dreams similar to the client's trauma, intrusive thoughts of therapy sessions, suddenly recalling a frightening experience, flashbacks connected to a client's trauma, avoidance or numbing feelings, and persistent arousal symptoms.[19] Therapists are not alone in developing these symptoms, as other professionals such as immigration attorneys[20] and immigration judges[21] have been found to suffer them as well.

I developed a number of these symptoms in the beginning of my work.[22] I went through feelings of devastation, feeling completely deskilled, traumatized, overwhelmed, and isolated. I developed a strong

---

[15] Laurie Anne Pearlman and Paula S. Mac Ian, "Vicarious Traumatization: An Empirical Study of the Effects of Trauma Work on Trauma Therapists," *Professional Psychology: Research and Practice* 26, no. 6 (1995): 558.

[16] Anat Ben-Porat and Haya Itzhaky, "Implications of Treating Family Violence for the Therapist: Secondary Traumatization, Vicarious Traumatization, and Growth," *Journal of Family Violence* 24, no. 7 (2009): 507.

[17] Charles R. Figley, *Compassion Fatigue: Coping with Secondary Traumatic Stress Disorder in Those Who Treat the Traumatized* (New York: Brunner/Mazel, 1995), 124. Compassion fatigue is "the natural, predictable, treatable, and preventable consequences of [caregiving]."

[18] Charles R. Figley, *Treating Compassion Fatigue* (New York: Brunner-Routledge, 2002).

[19] Debora Arnold et al., "Vicarious Posttraumatic Growth in Psychotherapy," *Journal of Humanistic Psychology* 45, no. 2 (2005): 242.

[20] Lin Piwowarczyk et al., "Secondary Trauma in Asylum Lawyers," *Bender's Immigration Bulletin* 14, no. 5 (2009): 263–69.

[21] S. L. Lustig et al., *Bender's Immigration Bulletin* 13 (2008): 22–35.

[22] I take comfort that I'm not alone in having developed these symptoms. Arnold et al. (2005, 248) report that 100% of the trauma therapists in their sample reported having nega-

startle response so that whenever anyone came through my door or spoke to me when my back was turned, I would jump. Strong feelings of sadness and anger plagued me that human beings could torture people in such merciless ways. Descriptions of torture frequently ran through my mind and thoughts of torture began to burst out of me at unexpected times.

I remember going to California and meeting my daughter's boyfriend for the first time. We went out to breakfast in a little diner that had miniature jukeboxes at each table. We each put in a quarter for our favorite songs, and I chose "It's a Wonderful World" by Louis Armstrong, a song I've always loved. When Louis began to sing the verse "It's a Wonderful World" during our fun, light-hearted conversation, I suddenly said, "Do you know what? It is NOT a wonderful world. Do you know what they do to political prisoners in Ethiopian prisons???" I started listing off the forms of torture used by Ethiopian torturers. Suddenly I became aware that my daughter and her boyfriend were looking at me with their mouths open, their eyes sad and full of dismay.

I could no longer tolerate seeing violence on television or in movies and had to walk out if torture scenes appeared on screen, because I now knew the reality of torture. (This will never change for me.[23]) The world no longer felt safe. I had nightmares of being tortured and of my family members being hurt. I worried about my clients often.

With my early cases, I had not yet developed any protection against the shock of hearing what happened as a consequence of someone's torture. One situation in particular affected me strongly:

> *The survivor wept as she said that her brother-in-law was imprisoned and tortured over a period of two years. When he was released, he was "a changed man." He flew into rages and sometimes he did to his fifteen-year-old son, her nephew, what had been done to him in prison. Sobbing, she told me that as a result, her nephew had hung himself. I was stunned. I myself had a fifteen-year-old son. Suddenly what flashed through my mind was an image of my husband being imprisoned, tortured, released, and then torturing our son, who subsequently committed suicide. I felt completely devastated after this session. I felt as if a bomb had gone off in my head.*

---

tive responses to trauma work, whether intrusive thoughts and images (90%), emotional (71%), or physical (33%).

[23] This reminds me of a quote by E. Neuffer, who in speaking of the intensity of her wartime experiences said, "I left Bosnia as a reporter three years ago. What I didn't realize then is that Bosnia [...] will never leave me" (quoted in Danieli, *Sharing the Front Line*, 2002, 286).

It was very clear to me in those early days that I had to develop a stronger ability to "hold" the torture accounts I was hearing if I was to be of any help to survivors. As Kinzie writes, calmness and acceptance upon hearing the trauma story are critical qualities for a therapist working with torture survivors.[24] My capacity for empathy was truly my Achilles' heel.[25] Survivors are exquisitely sensitive to the reactions of others at hearing about their torture. A survivor once told me with certitude, pointing to her forehead, that anyone walking down the street could read on her face that she had been raped during her torture. Survivors are attuned to the listener's facial responses and fearful of any sign that the listener might perhaps find them disgusting or repulsive because of what they have endured, or that the listener might not believe them or might not be able to tolerate hearing the truth of their torture experiences. If I were too vulnerable to the story of the torture, the survivor would not be able to tell me about it. How could my survivor clients heal if I could not hear their stories without feeling overwhelmed by what they had endured? There was little possibility for a successful therapy unless I could deal with the torture.[26]

Once I became tearful along with one of my clients when she described the torture she had endured in a jail cell in Cameroon. When she returned the following week, she informed me that she could no longer talk to me about what had happened to her: "Because it bothers you," she said. From that point on, I exerted great efforts to suppress all tears in clients' sessions, no matter how painful the material was. This was to have long-lasting consequences for me that would only be resolved two years later.

Learning to Hold the Trauma

Pearlman and Saakvitne say that trauma survivors will teach the therapist what the therapist needs to know to help them.[27] Certainly exposure to the severity of their trauma challenged me in many ways. The more familiar I became with

---

[24] J. David Kinzie, "Cross-Cultural Treatment of PTSD," *Treating Psychological Trauma and PTSD* (New York: Guilford, 2001), 270.

[25] S. Megan Berthold (2011) points out that it is paradoxical that a therapist's greatest strength, the ability to empathize and create a strong therapeutic relationship with a client, is also the quality that makes him or her the most vulnerable to developing secondary traumatic stress or vicarious trauma symptoms. See *Vicarious Trauma and Resilience* (NetCE, 2017).

[26] Anna B. Baranowsky, "The Silencing Response in Clinical Practice: On the Road to Dialogue," in *Treating Compassion Fatigue*, ed. Charles R. Figley (New York: Brunner-Routledge, 2002): 158.

[27] Pearlman and Saakvitne, *Trauma and the Therapist*, 403.

types of torture over time, the better able I was to hold them for the survivor so we could work on ameliorating the symptoms they caused. The road was rocky in the beginning, but became more even as I learned from my symptoms and grew more experienced. There are some ways in which I experienced an echo of the survivors' post-traumatic symptoms, such as intrusive images of torture.[28]

Early one Saturday morning I was lying in bed, thinking about the enjoyable things I was going to do that day, like going for a run, doing the laundry, and going shopping for a new dress. Suddenly, in the shadows on my ceiling, I saw the image of a naked man hung by his wrists from the ceiling with electric wires hanging from his genitals.

This image was one of the pictures from the IRCT book that I had tried to cover up at the outset of my work with survivors. It had come back to haunt me after a year of work with survivors whose lives were still plagued by their torture. I came to consider this image in my ceiling as a gift. It taught me what it was like to experience a post-traumatic stress symptom called an "intrusive image"; that is, a trauma image that suddenly intrudes into your mind when you're thinking of something unrelated to a traumatic event. I had turned a corner in my reactions to survivors' trauma stories. They no longer traumatized me as much as they taught me.

Facing the reality of torture had significant social and spiritual consequences as well as challenges to my perspectives and beliefs. This was fully consistent with the theory of vicarious traumatization.[29]

Social Consequences

In the beginning, my social life was affected. I began to pull away from others. I didn't have the energy to go out with friends and was too exhausted to talk on the phone. I needed time to heal during the weekends from the trauma content I was exposed to during the week. Working with survivors to process the impact of torture involves very intimate issues and is intense compared with the work of most people I came across outside of work. I began to feel out of place at social events. It was hard to

---

[28] J. Eric Gentry, Anna B. Baranowsky, and Kathleen Dunning (2002, 124) comment that "symptoms of compassion fatigue can mimic, to a lesser degree, those of the traumatized people we are working with." *See* "The Accelerated Recovery Program (ARP) for Compassion Fatigue" in *Treating Compassion Fatigue*, ed. Charles R. Figley (New York: Brunner-Routledge, 2002).

[29] Pearlman and Saakvitne, *Trauma and the Therapist* (1995).

go to places where I was asked about my occupation. People did not know what to say when I told them what I did. The most common reaction was a discomfited facial expression, followed by a change of subject. Topics discussed at parties began to seem trivial and senseless. How could people complain about mundane issues like irritation with a neighbor when torturers in the Houses of Ghosts in the Sudan were burning prisoners with iron plates and pulling out their fingernails?

At work, I was told that other therapists who did not work with survivors didn't really want to hear about torture because it was too painful. This "silencing response"[30] from fellow therapists and the discomfort of friends and people in the community made me feel quite isolated and lonely at times. When PSTT obtained a large grant from the Office of Refugee Resettlement in 2000, we were able to provide a broad range of services to many more survivors of torture, and more staff members started working with them. We instituted weekly two-hour clinical team meetings for our staff, which turned out to be a powerful means of reducing the isolation and other symptoms of secondary trauma elicited by exposure to torture accounts.[31,32] In addition, PSTT therapists had an "open door" policy with each other to counteract isolation, in case any one of us needed a place to just sit or perhaps do some work in the sand tray after a difficult day. (See my example of sand tray work near the end of this chapter.) I took seriously Herman's statement advocating that trauma therapists have a support system: "It cannot be reiterated too often: No one can face trauma alone."[33]

Another gift of the ORR grant was the creation of the National Consortium of Torture Treatment Programs (NCTTP), which brought together representatives of programs from across the country a couple of times a year. For those of us who were directors of centers or programs, this network of colleagues provided us a place where we felt heard, understood on the deepest level, and supported, and where we could learn, have fun, and be joyful in spite of the trauma to which we were constantly

---

[30] Baranowsky (2002) describes the silencing response as a coping mechanism used by a therapist to end discomfort and pain caused by exposure to trauma content in sessions by shutting it down or minimizing it (156).

[31] Danieli (1994) endorsed the use of a support group to address countertransference reactions, encourage mutual support, and enhance self-care (381).

[32] Kinzie (1994) described the power of a strong supportive network of therapists to reduce the sense of loneliness and isolation generated by exposure to torture accounts (261).

[33] Herman, *Trauma and Recovery*, 153.

exposed. It was wonderful! It provided me with friends around the country to contact for questions or to commiserate with when necessary. It gave us all colleagues to create presentations with, which allowed us to learn from each other and teach to others. Our meetings were always times of learning, growth, camaraderie, and great fun—perfect ways to fight secondary trauma.

When ORR came to our center for a site visit and we told them that we had *fun* at the NCTTP institutes, they seemed to see that as a negative. However, the NCTTP institutes were an essential component of programmatic self-care: they provided us with critical information and support, and helped us return reinforced and wiser to our centers to provide renewed strength to our staffs, and to continue our growth and our fight against secondary traumatic stress.

Changed Worldview

My worldview changed as a result of my work with torture survivors, and many of my beliefs were sharply challenged by increasing exposure to torture. At the deepest level, knowledge of the cruelty of torturers affected my basic belief that people were inherently good and trustworthy. To learn that torturers could repeatedly force their victims' heads in barrels of urine, feces, and bloody water until they nearly drowned, or that they could shoot a mother in the face for refusing to have sex with her teenage son, destroyed my belief that people were basically good. I now saw the capacity for evil in others. One day when I saw a man angrily reprimanding a little boy outside my gym, the thought immediately went through my mind that he was abusing that boy at home. What was shocking to me was how certain I was of this thought. Was this a case of distorted perspective because of my work?

Another belief that was challenged by working with torture was that my own government had basically good intentions toward people and did not torture. I had told survivor after survivor that they were safe in the United States because we did not torture people here. And then the Abu Ghraib photographs hit the press, showing the exact same forms of humiliation, subjugation, and terroristic forms of torture to which many of my survivors had been subjected. My government lied about not using torture, saying that waterboarding (a terrifying form of torture that brings a victim repeatedly to the point of asphyxiation) is only "an enhanced interrogation technique."[34] I firmly recommend that Donald Rumsfeld and John Yoo, who I understand advocated for these "enhanced interrogation techniques," try them and then give a considered opinion on whether they are torture or not. I am enraged about my country's duplicitous use of this euphemism for torture.

I came to recognize that this shift in perspective reflected what survivors had learned about the world. I could use my changed perspective to understand their world, their altered ability to trust. But I too had lost my innocence.

Altered Sense of Safety

Now I knew with certainty that there was evil in the world. As a result, my sense of safety at home and elsewhere in the world was greatly affected. I was more afraid in my community than I had been before, and I worried about the lives of my husband and children, particularly when my children traveled on their own. "They torture people there," I told them about country after country that they traveled through. I couldn't relax until they were safely home. Reading the newspaper and watching television news increased my conviction that the world was not safe and that people were not to be trusted. Human beings did unspeakable things to other human beings.

Challenged Spiritual Beliefs

My spiritual beliefs were also affected. I began to pray every night for the people who were being tortured everywhere, in all the places my clients had been tortured, in prison cells, jail cells, caves, and clandestine sites like the Houses of Ghosts in Sudan. Some nights I would be afraid to pray because it meant I'd have to think about all the people being tortured right that very moment with no one to help them. Even now that I'm retired, I'm sometimes afraid of my prayers. Some trauma responses die hard.

I wondered how God could allow these terrible things to happen so often, in so many places, in so many countries around the world. (Although I was originally raised Christian, I came to believe in God as

---

[34] Judy B. Okawa and Ronda Bresnick Hauss, "The Trauma of Politically Motivated Torture," in *Trauma Psychology: Issues in Violence, Disaster, Health, and Illness*, ed. Elizabeth K. Carll (Westport, CT: Praeger Publishers, 2007).

a universal divine force not affiliated with a particular religion.) Where was God when a young Sudanese was forced to watch a man's decapitation as part of his torture? I became very angry with God. In fact, I began to doubt what I had been taught about God, basic beliefs about God being loving, omnipotent, omnipresent.

This spiritual crisis so troubled me that I went to a class in a seminary entitled "What Is Evil?" taught by a Harvard-educated priest. I had hopes that he would listen to my dilemma about where God was when torturers were torturing people just short of death. However, he met each of my questions both during and after class with a brief, rather dismissive comment, changed the subject, and returned to talk about the Book of Job. He did not seem to want to face real evil in the present-day world. I felt embarrassed and silenced and, pondering it later, told myself I was encountering another of my survivor clients' experiences.

It was through many sessions with my survivor clients that this spiritual crisis began to resolve itself. One after another, survivors told me that the way they coped with post-traumatic symptoms, such as nightmares or sleeplessness, was by reading the Bible or the Qur'an. Then one day, when a survivor told me a painful account of the torture she had endured, I asked if it had affected her faith. She shook her head no and reflected quietly that she thought that God had "just been busy right then" and couldn't be with her that particular day. Her faith had an enormous impact on me. I was to hear similar remarks on a number of occasions from others who did not lose faith in their God, despite having endured days, weeks, or months of excruciating and what I thought would have been soul-murdering torture. In fact, the most common remark I heard was that "God saved me." So, hearing about torture *caused* my spiritual crisis, but working with survivors *healed* it.

The Process of Strengthening Myself to Bear Witness to Torture

Over time I became able to hear about many forms of torture without being undone by them, and my symptoms of secondary trauma gradually resolved. The strengthening process occurred so gradually that I'm not sure exactly how it happened. Bit by bit, I seemed to develop a transparent cloak that helped me focus on my survivor clients' pain and kept me from being distracted by the horror of their torture. With each blow of a torture account that struck, I learned to be able to accept the next, similar account, and it fit around me as if it were a soft, transparent layer of protective cloth. As I learned how the torturers inflicted their pain and how the survivor survived it, I was able to hold more of the story, as if wrapped in another layer, until some new and horrifying event came to light that knocked me to my knees again. Then the process began again, and I became familiar with that type of torture so I could hold it for the next person, and so on until I was able to be strong for many people.

These transparent layers of protection did not make me hard or insensitive in any way to the pain my survivor clients suffered. Rather, they enabled me to be fully present for the survivor without being distracted by my own shock over the details of the torture itself.

The more I was capable of holding the torture story in the room, the more I was able to help the survivor weather the powerful emotions that accompanied the memories.[35] It takes courage and significant risk for the survivor to put into words the deeply personal, humiliating things that were done to him in the darkness of the torture cell. As the therapy work deepens and this communication takes place, the connection between the survivor and the therapist becomes profound. I felt that I was entering sacred ground when a survivor opened himself to tell me the details of his torture, which cost him emotionally.[36] I felt deeply honored to be allowed to bear witness to my survivor clients' accounts of such personal travails, told with such dignity.[37]

Strengthening through Learning

Another way I strengthened myself against secondary trauma was by mastering a great deal of information about torture and its sequelae. As a psychologist, I worked with survivors in two different capacities. In one capacity, I worked as a therapist on the issues my clients chose to

---

[35] Danieli (1994), speaks of the need for the therapist to be able to feel the "full life cycle" of the client's emotion—the beginning, middle, and end—without resorting to a defensive countertransference reaction. The therapist has to identify his or her "personal level of comfort ... to hear *anything*" (385).

[36] Pearlman and Saakvitne (1995) describe the process of participating in the transformation of a person's despair as a "life-altering spiritual experience" for the therapist (403).

[37] Kinzie (1994) also describes the sense of honor that the clinician develops in the therapeutic relationship with the survivor of torture as "a profound sense of having the privilege of hearing such extremely private stories" (255).

bring to sessions, addressing the trauma at the pace dictated by the clients. In the other capacity, I was hired by the survivor's attorney to perform a psychological evaluation and prepare an affidavit to submit to immigration court with the survivor's application for political asylum, and also to testify as an expert witness about the contents of my report. I met with each survivor for a total of approximately eight to ten hours, during which time I performed a detailed clinical interview about the experiences that led her to seek asylum in the United States, and administered symptom checklists to assess if and how she might have been affected by the torture she had described.

These psychological evaluations were the source of great learning for me. I learned about the politics in the countries that were resulting in the flight of torture victims to the United States and which political parties were persecuting which other parties. I learned about tribes and tribal languages, which languages my clients spoke and how to pronounce them. I learned about geography, where their countries were located, what their capitals were, and where their universities were (because often the survivors were university students). I learned a great deal about female genital mutilation, because many of my clients had suffered it. I learned about the adversities suffered by women, how little power they had in many countries, and how they were blamed when they were raped.

I also learned some unexpected things related to my cases. I had several voudou cases for which I had to read everything I could in order to testify effectively in court. In one instance, I read a book by an anthropologist about secret societies in French-speaking Africa whose members believe in an ancient tradition that if you drink the blood of a person, you take on their power. Sometimes a case hinges on a psychologist explaining quite unfamiliar customs to a judge who would have no way of understanding them otherwise.

The more I learned, it seemed, the easier it was for my survivor clients to tell their stories. When I gained greater familiarity and comfort with this material, I could provide greater structure to the evaluation sessions, which seemed to help the survivors. I structured the sessions by giving clear information before the evaluation about what we were going to do, and also information afterwards on what the survivor could expect. It seemed to help the survivor when I was familiar with politics and the major cities and regions in her country. Also, I found that having a long session for the survivor to be able to tell her entire story ended up being helpful for her. Survivors told me afterward that it was a relief to know that they could survive the telling of the entire trauma history. Interestingly, many people told me that it was my eyes that helped them through it. I suppose my eyes showed that I had finally become strong enough for us to hold the torture together, to give it space in the room to be mourned, to be respected, to be judged, to be cared for, to begin to be healed.

There was also significant advantage derived from working in a community with a good interpreter. Fabri calls this the "therapeutic triad."[38] I had the good fortune to work often with an outstanding French interpreter, Brigitte Regnier, who, in addition to having sensitive interpretation skills, enhanced the healing environment because of her compassion and expertise working in the therapeutic setting with survivors of torture. Having both the therapist and the interpreter bearing witness to the survivor's story seemed to bring more energy to the room and more strength to the survivor.

After a session that was particularly difficult for one of my French-speaking clients, I taught her and our interpreter a yoga pose called the Warrior Goddess. As the three of us stood together posed in a tight circle, Warrior Goddesses all, we could feel the torture banished from the room by the force of our unity, the strength of our fight together against her trauma. I can still draw back to my mind today the power of that moment.

Transformation and Resilience

My journey from symptoms of secondary trauma to resilience was marked by a number of lessons on how to transform a perceived weakness into a strength.[39] A colleague taught me this lesson on a day I couldn't type certain words about torture.

A survivor described being led into a small cell that contained only a platform on which there was a candle, a match, and scissors. She described how her torturers cut off her underwear with the scissors, burned her vagina with the candle, and then raped her with it. This image haunted me for months. When the affidavit for her asylum claim was due, I was sitting at my dining room table trying to type up the psychological evaluation with the description of the torture she endured. I could not bear to type the words about the rape with the burning candle. I simply could not make my fingers form those words or stand for my eyes to see them.

---

[38] Mary Fabri et al., "Caring for Torture Survivors: The Marjorie Kovler Center," in *The New Humanitarians: Inspiration, Innovations, and Blueprints for Visionaries*, ed. Chris E. Stout (Westport, CT: Praeger Publishers, 2008), 170.

[39] Engstrom, Hernandez, and Gangsei (2008, 17) call this "reframing."

At that moment, a colleague of mine who also worked with survivors happened to call. I told her my dilemma about these particular words. I could hear her struggle to think of what to say that would help. Suddenly she suggested, "What if you think of it as hammering a shield?" In an instant, these words completely transformed the act for me. I hammered out that shield with all the power I could muster.

I personally experienced the transformation of a symptom that had been plaguing me for about two years, a symptom that I wasn't fully aware was one of secondary trauma. The change of this symptom took place as a result of a single experience during sand tray work. By way of background, PSTT had a sand tray room with shelves containing a large collection of objects representing human figures, spiritual figures, animals, plant life, minerals, dwelling places, furniture, modes of transportation, and miscellaneous objects. The person is to choose whichever objects strike him and bring them to the sand tray, which is a wooden box approximately twenty inches by thirty inches by three inches deep and full of sand. The bottom is painted blue. Ruth Amman aptly describes the sand tray as a "soul garden" where a person's "inner and outer life can develop and reveal itself."[40] I often turned to the sand tray as a way to work through emotions or "stuck" places in my work.

The Little Red Cabinet of Tears
I mentioned earlier that I had stopped having any tears in sessions due to a survivor saying to me that she couldn't tell me about her painful experiences because "it bothered [me]." For a number of months, I was strongly aware of blocking painful emotions and tears as they came up when I heard distressing stories of torture. After a while, I no longer felt aware of that blocking feeling. However, I began to have water coming out of my eyes at odd times. I wasn't crying—I did not have the emotions associated with crying. There was just water dripping out of my eyes. In fact, after a while, the water started to come out of only my right eye.

I thought this was quite peculiar, and I didn't know what to make of it. It would happen at unusual times—when I was very happy, when I was excited, when I was feeling sentimental. Water would come out of my right eye. I definitely did not feel like I was crying. Then one day I was working with a teenage child soldier who had suffered the most severe trauma imaginable. When I

---

[40] Barbara Labovitz Boik and E. Anna Goodwin, *Sandplay Therapy: A Step-by-Step Manual for Psychotherapists of Diverse Orientations* (New York: W. W. Norton, 2000), 3.

asked him about depressive symptoms, he insisted that he has never, ever cried. When I looked at him in some disbelief, given the tragedy he had described, he paused and said, "Water comes out of my eyes, but I never cry." This was exactly what was happening to me! Maybe I was really crying and didn't know it.

Shortly after this session with the child soldier, our center brought Dr. Gisela De Domenico, a well-known sand play therapist from the San Francisco area, to provide staff training on sand play. I had attended two of Gisela's previous training sessions and when she asked for a volunteer to be a training subject, I stepped up. I had brought something from my own collection that I wanted to use, although I had no idea that I was going to do a tray with Gisela. It was a little red Chinese cabinet that had doors that opened out, revealing more doors that opened out, revealing still more doors that opened out, and so on. I plopped that little cabinet in the corner in the sand and said, "That's where all the tears are," and then I started to weep. I wept and wept and wept.

As I wept, I created mounds in the sand where I laid out torture scene after torture scene. This is where they hung him from the wall and tortured him with electric wires. This is where they cut off the hand of the prisoner next to him. This is where they forced her to have sex with another prisoner. This is where they burned her breasts after making her give her baby to the woman next to her to hold. And I wept and wept. I dug sand off the bottom of the tray so I could put more victims in the blue water of the bottom, because people are tortured in water too, after all.

Finally, I sat up abruptly and said that all the tears in the little red cabinet were out. It suddenly occurred to me that I could dig a moat through the sand and weave it throughout the tray so that it connected all the victims, who were barely surviving. At that point, I felt completely convinced that the tears were flowing throughout the moat, irrigating all the lands, bringing healing water to everyone in need. This was a transformational experience. It was a black and white experience. Before, I had felt a deep sadness. After I realized that there could be a moat of healing tears and that therefore all the victims were going to survive, I felt healed and strong. I never experienced water coming out of my eyes again.

It is difficult to describe how powerful that single experience in the sand tray was. It completely eradicated a symptom and transformed a feeling. I don't think I will ever forget it. As additional evidence of the power of this non-traditional therapeutic approach, two of my survivor clients who have published books had only one or two sessions each using the sand tray, but they both described these sessions prominently in their books.

Conclusion

Jennie Goldenberg, who studied interviewers of Holocaust survivors, asked where "those stark and savage images" go when the interviewers take them into themselves and how the images changed them.[41] This is certainly a relevant question for me. Indeed, in the initial stage of bearing witness to torture stories, those "stark and savage images" did make me "come undone" to some extent. I experienced symptoms of secondary traumatic stress and vicarious traumatization, which diminished greatly over time and were no longer overwhelming.[42]

During this period of time I was propelled into learning a massive amount of information about torture and its impact on people, survivors, and caregivers alike. I'm now convinced that I needed to go through the "trial by fire" of secondary traumatic stress and vicarious trauma in order to be able to strengthen myself and to learn from my clients. The work was immensely challenging. I felt deeply committed to continuing it, and my experiences with survivors convinced me that the therapeutic process had value. I had a strong sense that the work was meaningful, even when I was struggling to learn how to handle it. I have felt very fortunate to have had work that gave my life a clear sense of purpose. It has always felt like a calling to me.

Accompanying survivors on their path toward healing transformed me in many ways, and my life has been greatly enriched by walking with survivors on their journeys. My experiences are very similar to those spoken of in the literature on vicarious post-traumatic growth and vicarious resilience.

I will always be in awe of the remarkable resilience shown by survivors who are initially so devastated by the traumatic circumstances that forced them to flee their countries, and yet not only manage to survive but often to thrive. Every day in my office there was ample evidence of Stamm's statement that "the human spirit, while clearly breakable, is remarkably resilient."[43] Through our work together I, too, learned how to cope with adversity. I learned to "reframe" things in my own life, to look at the positive side of things, just as

---

[41] Jennie Goldenberg, "The Impact on the Interviewer of Holocaust Survivor Narratives: Vicarious Traumatization or Transformation?" *Traumatology* 8, no. 4 (2002), 216.

[42] Katie A. Splevins et al., "Vicarious Posttraumatic Growth among Interpreters," *Qualitative Health Research* 20, no. 12 (2010), 1710.

[43] Quoted in S. Collins and A. Long, "Working with the Psychological Effects of Trauma: Consequences for Mental Health-Care Workers – a Literature Review," *Journal of Psychiatric and Mental Health Nursing* 10(4) (2003): 422.

I was encouraging my survivor clients to do in therapy.[44] My own problems seemed so tiny in comparison to what survivors had been through. This work puts everything in perspective.

Survivors have given me a deep sensitivity for the suffering of others. They taught me a far deeper understanding of people from other cultures and of the ways in which politics can lead to torture. Pearlman and Saakvitne comment, "A significant reward of doing trauma therapy has been our increased sense of connection with people who suffer everywhere, across time and across cultures."[45] Indeed, I am now aware of torture all over the globe. When there are riots and arrests in Nepal or Indonesia, I pay attention because I know that we will soon be seeing these folks in our US treatment centers.

I feel great gratitude for my good fortune to have been born in a country where we have free speech and the right to criticize the president as loudly as we wish without fear of being arrested, where we have more than one political party, where there are plenty of books and desks in the university, where police cannot raid our universities and arrest students wholesale, where I can walk down the street without being arrested, where people are not routinely tortured in jail.

The injustice of torture was so loud that it mobilized me to speak up. Since beginning to work with survivors, I have become more active politically and socially, participating in protests, marches, testifying on Capitol Hill about torture, speaking out on torture and issues of victimization through the media, and actively training mental health professionals, attorneys, teachers, human rights activists, physicians, and other community professionals on the impact of torture. Both my country (under President George W. Bush) and my professional association of psychologists have grossly disappointed me by not standing up against torture. Once you know about the reality of torture, it is no longer possible to remain silent about it.

I feel so fortunate to have been invited into the hearts of the survivors who shared their stories, their pain, and the retrieving of their lives with me. In the process, they taught me how to live, how to walk through fire, and how to come out on the other side. These are lessons I will not forget.

---

[44] Engstrom, Hernandez, and Gangsei (2008).
[45] Pearlman and Saakvitne (1995), 405.

CHAPTER 8

Beyond Institutional Betrayal: When the Professional Is Personal

Ellen Gerrity

Dr. Ellen Gerrity's career spans clinical work, teaching, research, and policymaking on the psychological effects of traumatic stress. In this chapter, she offers a personal reflection and an analysis of the institutional role of the American Psychological Association (APA) in US torture policy and its implementation. Her essay is both an indictment of the APA's betrayal of bedrock principles against psychological harm, and a personal meditation on the choices we face as individuals and members of institutions in standing against torture.

At the heart of Gerrity's work is the APA's 2005 Report of the Presidential Task Force on Psychological Ethics and National Security. *In that report, written in response to the disclosure that APA members were assisting in designing and carrying out the euphemistically named "enhanced interrogation techniques" for detainees in the war on terror, the organization attempted to carve out a role for psychologists that avoided the language of torture, although not necessarily the relationships and processes that contributed to it. Gerrity places her analysis of the APA's action in a larger institutional context comprising the position statements on behalf of patients' rights to privacy and genuine care released by three groups:*

E. Gerrity (✉)
Department of Psychiatry and Behavioral Sciences,
Duke University School of Medicine, Durham, NC, USA
e-mail: ellen.gerrity@duke.edu

Coalition for an Ethical Psychology, Psychologists for Social Responsibility, and Physicians for Human Rights. She reveals her own sense of professional betrayal by the field's umbrella organization when it responds to public criticism with personal attacks on detractors, as opposed to the kind of self-reflective questioning the author herself undertakes.

The historical context that Gerrity analyzes stretches from 2005 to 2016, against a backdrop of increasingly scathing disclosures of APA psychologists' roles in torture that are revealed in journalistic reports, in the Executive Summary of the Senate Intelligence Committee Study of the Central Intelligence Agency's Detention and Interrogation Program, *and in the APA's refusal to disavow completely its Pentagon contacts and its slow change in leadership.*

Faced with the organization's intransigence, Gerrity concludes her chapter with an examination of the multiple ways she continues to do her work outside of the APA's umbrella. Finding alternative areas in which to work and areas in which to train, she bears witness to unexpected alliances with survivors and other health professionals that provide mutual support as well as opportunities for fresh initiatives. Indeed, it is in joining with survivors and other anti-torture advocates, as opposed to siding with the security concerns of the state, that health professionals find the emotional renewal necessary to be most effective within their fields.

* * *

Listen with your eyes, as if the story
you are hearing is happening right now.
—from "How to Listen," Joyce Sutphen[1]

Introduction

It has been difficult to write this essay. The challenge posed by the editors of this volume was to move away from the "objective" stance of a scientist to talk about my personal experience, my own feelings and thoughts about torture, and about working with and on behalf of torture survivors. For me, this meant that I needed to shift gears to private, vulnerable places, where both my truths and my uncertainties could be understood and expressed. This has

---

[1] Joyce Sutphen, "How to Listen," *First Words: Poems* (Northfield, MN: Red Dragonfly Press, 2010).

been part of my difficulty. Another part is that the topic of torture is itself *soul-searing*, a term put forward by the editors, and it is especially so when facing the reality of torture now being promoted by some as an acceptable part of my profession—psychology—and as an acceptable activity on the part of my country, the United States. What does this mean for me, as a psychologist, as an American, as a human being? The position that my professional organization, the American Psychological Association (APA), has taken for more than a decade in relation to torture and interrogation has left me embroiled in anger, shame, helplessness, and guilt, and this is part of the story that I was asked to tell. Opening up to all of this has shaken the foundations of what I have understood about life. I knew that what was necessary for me to confront this problem was to do what the poet Joyce Sutphen proposes in her poem "How to Listen," which is to "listen with our eyes, as if the story [...] is happening right now." I—*we*—need to engage with all of our senses, to experience what is happening in a way that is as real for each of us as it is for those experiencing torture. In my view, looking away is not an acceptable option. Sutphen further advises, "This is your chance to listen carefully. Your whole life may depend on what you hear."

I have worked as a psychologist since 1983, in multiple capacities as a teacher, researcher, clinician, research administrator, and federal policy advisor. Most of my work has focused on the psychological impact of trauma, including torture, and on helping to advance research and federal policy related to prevention and improving treatment for survivors. Because of these interests, I became very involved in monitoring what was going on with the APA and its support of torture, a process that was and still is hard to understand.

It is wrenching for me to face the reality of torture squarely, to witness the horror of the experience of those who have gone through it, to wrap my own mind around the reality that this is true, that this is something that human beings do to one another. My personal pain is absolutely nothing compared to the physical and emotional wounds experienced by those who have been tortured. It is important to me to emphatically underscore this as a fact in the context of this essay. I stand continuously in awe of those who have taken their own experience of torture and their own pain, fear, and anger, and turned all of it into a fight for what is right, like Sister Dianna Ortiz—herself a torture survivor, author of *The Blindfold's Eye* (2002), and founder and board member of the Torture Abolition and Survivor Support Coalition International (TASSC)—and so many others involved in this volume. I want to be part of this fight, to do something to help, but in my efforts to find my place and to try to do something to help, I often feel lost and powerless.

Elizabeth Swanson described in the opening section of this book the story of the conference that kindled the idea for this collection. In her description, I recognized the experience of being challenged as a "non-survivor" (someone who has not personally experienced torture) about my right to speak about torture. I was similarly confronted once. I was the co-chair of a 1997 multi-agency conference on the "Mental Health Consequences of Torture," sponsored primarily by the National Institute of Mental Health (NIMH), where I worked as the head of the Violence and Traumatic Stress Research Branch. Over 100 participants were invited to discuss many issues related to torture, with a focus on the mental health consequences. As the meeting got underway, a torture survivor stood up and challenged the format and planners of the meeting, angry that survivors were not prominent speakers. In my role as co-chair, and because I was at the podium when this happened, I felt the responsibility to act immediately. What I remember now is that instead of holding tightly to an official role and defensively explaining how survivors had been included in the planning and as presenters, I felt something shift inside me, and I instead responded as a human being. I said, "You are right. More can be done. Let's do something about it right now. We'll take a break to discuss this together, make up a new panel of speakers, and begin with this panel when we return." This is what happened, and it made a critically important difference to the conference, adding an honesty and vulnerability to the discussions about what this experience really means. I believed it was essential for the survivors to know immediately that they had been heard, and to just act, to make the change that was requested. I felt that in the end, if the meeting was not about what survivors needed, then what was it for?

The conference was much better for this change, more honest and productive, and it generated other NIMH activities, one that was launched by a group of South African representatives from the Truth and Reconciliation Commission who had attended the conference. In a follow-up to the conference, they asked NIMH to develop a formal report describing the scientific evidence related to the mental health consequences of torture and related trauma, to refute the views of those who held that there were no such consequences. It was shocking to me at the time that there would be any doubt about the existence of such consequences. Whether the expressed doubt is, in essence, a disingenuous claim on the part of those responsible for torture to avoid the full consequences of their actions, or is related to a need for more education, increased advocacy, or something else, it is hard to determine. Whatever the cause, the request came as part of the legal and political work underway in South Africa at the time. The Director of NIMH agreed to their request, and I co-chaired a workgroup to develop the formal report. The international workgroup included researchers, clinicians, and advocates who had devoted their lives to understanding torture and related trauma and advancing efforts to help people recover. Sister Dianna Ortiz was an essential member of the working group, providing guidance about the needs and experiences of survivors of torture. I believed then, as I do now, that science means nothing if it does not address the real experiences of the human beings it is studying, and that those human beings have a right to have a say about what that science does. Sister Dianna participated fully in the workgroup discussions as a representative of a larger survivor group who were consulted during the process, contributed to the report, and reviewed all of its contents. The report was completed and delivered to the Commission by its deadline, and was subsequently developed as a book,[2] with proceeds used to keep the book more widely accessible through the publisher at that time. As a result of these and other efforts, including the tireless advocacy of the late US Senator Paul Wellstone, NIMH also directed funding through its normal grant award process to study the effects of torture on human beings, an expansion of research in this area long sought by advocates and representatives of torture treatment centers.

Through these experiences—the conference, the working group, the book, and the research funding—I learned many things, two that I believe are especially important to the issues being addressed in this volume. The first is that research and the "objective" reports based on science and analysis, if done right, are critically important, since they are part of the currency by which survivors and advocates make legal cases and medical analyses that advance efforts to end the practice of torture and support survivors in their recovery. Secondly, I became aware of how the scientific process can, and usually does, leave the survivor's own experiences out of such analyses, and can cause further harm and lead to inaccurate conclusions, however well intentioned. A balance is needed.

---

[2] Ellen Gerrity, Terence M. Keane, & Farris Tuma, eds. *The Mental Health Consequences of Torture* (NY: Kluwer Academic/Plenum Publications, 2001).

I brought mind, heart, and soul to these tasks, while feeling on shaky ground as I bridged the world of NIMH research and the world of the torture survivor. I felt confident in the rightness of doing so as I worked with torture survivors and those who supported them in their recovery. But I still often felt a sense of being an outsider, especially when I saw again the same kind of rift between survivors and researchers at another conference some years later. The creative approach that this volume is taking to bring these two worlds together is a good one. I believe it is important for all those who are committed to this issue to work together in the one world in which we live. I believe such collaboration can heal the lack of trust that can rise up even among those who are on the same side of a cause.

I recognized too that because of some of my own life experiences (e.g., having been raised as a Catholic, and then learning of the Church's history of child abuse), I lack faith in institutions and the claims they often issue about doing the right thing in the face of documented wrong-doing. Instead, I have faith only in the goodness and courage that reside in the individual hearts of those who speak the truth, even—especially—when there are personal consequences and costs for doing so. Likewise, wrongs committed on behalf of institutions are in fact made possible by the individuals directly involved, and also by those internally who could take action but do not. When survivors of torture confront the researchers or policy-makers who meet with them, it may not be because they do not have trust in those specific individuals (though they may, in fact, not). Rather, it may be that the meeting itself allows survivors, perhaps for the first time, to raise concerns to the individuals who are *right now* the ones in front of them, ready to listen to what they have to say, and to believe that maybe it will be this person who will act. Who would not take the opportunity to speak the truth when given such a chance, and to hope (if not trust) that they will be heard? I believe that speaking up in such situations is itself a courageous act, given that any trust a survivor may have once had in people, institutions, or the truth was intentionally crushed by torturers and their protectors.

In the end, I believe that trust is built between individuals, and that such trust can lead to action and change. I accept the truth behind Margaret Mead's statement, "Never doubt that a small group of thoughtful, committed citizens can change the world,"[3] and believe that the trust among such citizens

---

[3] Margaret Mead, The Institute for Intercultural Studies, http://www.interculturalstudies.org/faq.html#quote_use (accessed October 2013). Used with permission.

is built over time, through shared experiences of success and failure. For me, deeper trust came from the experiences I had working with Senator Wellstone, a man of intrinsic courage and compassion. A few years after the NIMH conference, I was assigned to work in his Senate office, an arrangement that lasted several years. He always fought for the "little guy," especially those who have no power and no voice. It was his office that had encouraged NIMH to hold the cross-agency conference on torture and to direct funds toward research in this area. Through this work, I had the opportunity to learn how courage can be contagious. I could be braver because of his example, as could many others. While in his office, I was able to work on issues affecting the daily lives of many people: human rights, torture, mental health and addiction treatment and research, suicide prevention, education, child welfare, and veterans' services, and I collaborated with many others who also fought hard on these issues. I now see this time as an inspiring gift for me, a chance to work with those who take personal and professional risks to do what is right and who then take responsibility for the outcomes. I learned what being part of a community can mean when things go right and when they go wrong, both useful experiences for what came later.

Professional Identity and the APA

> I came to explore the wreck.
> The words are purposes.
> The words are maps.
> I came to see the damage that was done
> and the treasures that prevail.
> —from "Diving into the Wreck," Adrienne Rich[4]

It is with these experiences behind me that I learned about the role of psychologists in the interrogation and torture of prisoners at the Guantánamo Bay detention camp. A story in *The New Yorker*[5] revealed that psychologists were involved in the development of extreme interrogation and torture techniques, and were advising interrogators at Guantánamo regarding the use of these techniques upon detainees. Some health organizations (e.g., the American Psychiatric Association and the

---

[4] Adrienne Rich, "Diving into the Wreck," *Diving into the Wreck: Poems 1971–1972* (W.W. Norton & Company, Inc. 1973).

[5] Jane Mayer, "The Experiment," *The New Yorker*, July 11, 2005.

American Medical Association), although initially silent, began to voice clear positions that their members must not take part in such interrogations. The American Psychological Association equivocated, stating in its now infamous *Report of the Presidential Task Force on Psychological Ethics and National Security* (PENS)[6] that psychologists working with interrogators could use information from medical records as part of the interrogation, and could conceal from prisoners their professional identities or relationship with interrogators.[7] Under pressure, the APA released statements claiming that it opposes torture, but I noted that the careful wording it used in its statements was very similar to that of the military interrogators and those who protect them; for instance, parsing the definition of the word "torture" to make it mean what it wanted it to mean, to somehow distinguish it from "extreme interrogation." The APA began early on to differentiate between the participation of psychologists in "torture" versus participation in "interrogation," and claimed that the presence of psychologists could in fact *protect* those being interrogated. It was clear to me that something was very wrong, that further investigation was needed to discover the meaning of these contradictory and ambiguous statements and what lay beneath them. In Adrienne Rich's poem "Diving into the Wreck," she proposes the purposefulness nature of such investigation: "I came to explore the wreck, the words are purposes, the words are maps. I came to see the damage that was done," later specifying that her exploration was of "the wreck and not the story of the wreck." What I hoped to find was the truth, and not the story of the truth.

Feeling white-hot anger upon encountering these early statements, I immediately contacted the President and Executive Director of the APA. In response, I received an email from a lower-level official who noted the imminent release of the PENS report and claimed that it would provide details that would allay my concerns. Instead, I soon learned from many publications and reports of the flaws in the PENS report and in the nature of the Task Force itself, which included several members with strong ties to the military. The PENS Task Force had held secret meetings and rushed through the approval of the report, precipitously establishing the APA position that it was ethically acceptable for psychologists to participate in military interrogations.

[6] American Psychological Association, *Report of the American Psychological Association Presidential Task Force on Psychological Ethics and National Security*, June 2005.
[7] Steven H. Miles, *Oath Betrayed: America's Torture Doctors*, 2nd ed. (Berkeley, CA: University of California Press, 2009).

Soon, several advocates began calling for investigations, gathering information to challenge the position and actions of the APA. Many of the details of the psychologists' involvement in interrogation were documented and disseminated by Steven Miles, who made available 60,000 pages of relevant government documents via his website,[8] as well as through subsequent reports from others described in detail in what follows. In defending itself, the APA claimed that its purpose in supporting military interrogations is to allow psychologists to prevent "behavioral drift," whereby interrogators could veer from their interrogator role into abuse and torture. By asserting that this kind of control is possible in institutions controlled by the military, the APA ignored years of psychological research and many recent examples where the "behavioral drift" was not that of interrogators becoming abusers, but rather of psychologists themselves becoming abusers.[9] Over time, discourse about APA involvement in torture and interrogation expanded from revelations about its position on torture, to defenses by APA leadership, to protests about its actions, and ultimately to numerous efforts by the APA to marginalize and attack opponents. More details were gradually revealed through the persistence and courage of investigative journalists, psychologists involved in the internal discussions, and APA members (and then former members) who launched protests, leading ultimately to the far-reaching report, *Independent Review Relating to APA Ethics Guidelines, National Security Interrogations, and Torture*, by David H. Hoffman et al.,[10] further described below.

As this process unfolded, I was filled with shame and disgust by the behavior of APA officials and what became many years of dissembling on their part. My first impulse was to resign as a member, as loudly and as publicly as I could. Many people did. Award-winning author and psychologist Mary Pipher returned her APA Presidential Citation award, citing that she

> did not want an award from an organization that sanctions its members' participation in the enhanced interrogations at CIA black sites and at

---

[8] "United States Military Medicine in War on Terror Prisons," ed. Steven Miles and Leah Marks, University of Minnesota Law School Human Rights Library, 2007. http://www1.umn.edu/humanrts/OathBetrayed/index.html

[9] Miles, *Oath Betrayed*, 2009.

[10] David H. Hoffman, et al., "Report to the Special Committee of the Board of Directors of the American Psychological Association: Independent Review Relating to APA Ethics Guidelines, National Security Interrogations, and Torture" (Chicago, IL: Sidley Austin LLP, July 2015).

Guantánamo. The presence of psychologists has both educated the interrogation teams in more skillful methods of breaking people down and legitimized the process of torture in defiance of the Geneva Conventions.[11]

Other APA members protested or signed a joint resignation letter via listservs and websites, such as a 2009 website petition that listed seventy-six members who publicly resigned, stating that "the APA has demonstrated such profound ethical failures that we can no longer, in good conscience, remain affiliated with the organization."[12] I was encouraged to retain my membership by colleagues who were also concerned, but who thought that I might be able to do more from the "inside," perhaps because of my prior involvement with the US Congress. As with many others who tried this path, this proved not to be effective. Many journalists, APA members, and other health professionals who were knowledgeable about torture similarly voiced their concerns, only to face strong institutional resistance and personal attacks from APA officials.[13] Many then moved to take actions outside of the APA.

Among other efforts, three organizations were particularly strong and vocal examples of leadership in challenging the APA: the Coalition for an Ethical Psychology, Psychologists for Social Responsibility, and Physicians for Human Rights. The Coalition for an Ethical Psychology[14] was formed in 2006 specifically to "mobilize diverse groups for the removal of psychologists from US programs of torture and other detainee abuse." It was led in its efforts by Stephen Soldz, Steven Reisner, Jean Marie Arrigo, and others. The Coalition issued many public statements and reports, including *All the President's Psychologists*, a report that presented more detailed analyses of the email evidence that described the role of the APA with the Bush administration on its torture program.[15] These findings were further

---

[11] Mary Pipher, "Why I've Returned My Award to the American Psychological Association—Because It Sanctions Torture," *OpEdNews*, August 24, 2007.

[12] Dan Aalbers, "We Resign from the APA," *ipetitions*, http://www.ipetitions.com/petition/aparesignation/

[13] James Risen, "Outside Psychologists Shielded US Torture Program, Report Finds," *The New York Times*, July 10, 2015, http://www.nytimes.com/2015/07/11/us/psychologists-shielded-us-torture-program-report-finds.html?_r=0

[14] Coalition for an Ethical Psychology, http://ethicalpsychology.org/

[15] Stephen Soldz, Nathaniel Raymond, and Steven Reisner, "All the President's Psychologists: The American Psychological Association's Secret Complicity with the White House and US Intelligence Community in Support of the CIA's 'Enhanced' Interrogation Program," https://web-beta.archive.org/web/20150817031854/http://ethicalpsychology.org/materials/All-the-President's-Psychologists-Key-Findings.pdf

cited by James Risen in a significant *New York Times* report on April 30, 2015.[16]

The Psychologists for Social Responsibility (PsySR) organization, launched in 1982, is an engaged community of members and supporters who work to advance peace and social justice through the ethical use of psychological knowledge, research, and practice.[17] Led in its efforts during recent years by Yosef Brody, Stephen Reisner, and others, PsySR issued many statements and reports calling for a public investigation of the APA's involvement in torture in its work with the military.

Physicians for Human Rights[18] repeatedly issued public statements and press releases, many cited in this essay, calling for a governmental investigation of the APA and adding a significant human rights voice to the public dialogue.

In response to these actions, officials at the APA issued many statements and press releases questioning the reputations and motives of those who objected to APA activities and positions, while avoiding addressing the key issues increasingly being raised by APA members and the press. Efforts were made by some APA members to hold the organization accountable, but these were ignored or attacked by APA leaders.[19] Unfortunately, many APA members, denying or ignoring the growing evidence about its role, did nothing or very little to protest the actions of the APA as an institution or to call for an independent investigation. This is hard to understand, given the gravity of the situation, but as I witnessed more and more of this inaction, I tried to analyze it from a broader perspective. One explanation may be found in the expanding significance of the APA in the lives of psychologists over the past several decades. It is a very powerful institution in the educational and career advancement of psychologists, playing major roles in training, fellowships, licensing, publication, continuing education, and much more—including establishing national connections for individuals to high-level task forces, policy leadership groups, and other activities that could have a significant impact on

---

[16] James Risen, "American Psychological Association Bolstered CIA Torture Program, Report Says," *The New York Times*, April 30, 2015, http://www.nytimes.com/2015/05/01/us/report-says-american-psychological-association-collaborated-on-torture-justification.html

[17] Psychologists for Social Responsibility, http://www.psysr.org/

[18] Physicians for Human Rights, http://physiciansforhumanrights.org/

[19] Risen, "Outside Psychologists Shielded US Torture Program, Report Finds," July 10, 2015.

academic and practice careers. Given the APA's public attacks on those who did voice their concerns about its actions, and the potential impact of a backlash on their personal and professional lives, this could have been enough of a barrier for some to hesitate to speak up. This feasibility raises questions about whether there are sufficient "checks and balances" in place to mitigate the influence of the APA in the lives of psychologists. This idea helped me to have a larger context for the situation, though it does not explain why some could overcome these barriers, and others could not. What made the difference is a question to consider.

In 2014, the public awareness of torture reached new heights with the publication of two major reports that established in detail the participation of the government in activities following the terrorist attacks in the United States on September 11, 2001, including the involvement of psychologists and the APA in supporting government-sanctioned torture. The first was the publication of the book *Pay Any Price: Greed, Power, and Endless War* by James Risen,[20] which examined the consequences of the "war on terror" that was launched after the 9/11 attacks. Included in Risen's book are details about the cooperative role of the APA with the Central Intelligence Agency (CIA) and the latter's use of torture in its interrogation program. The information about the APA prompted more questions from APA members and the public. In the aftermath, Physicians for Human Rights called for a Department of Justice investigation into whether the APA and the CIA engaged in unlawful conduct related to this brutal torture program.[21] I became hopeful that Risen's book and related reports and calls for action would make a difference in holding accountable those responsible and preventing such activities from continuing.

The second publication was the December 2014 release of the Executive Summary of the *Senate Intelligence Committee Study of the Central Intelligence Agency's Detention and Interrogation Program*, which included many more details about the involvement of psychologists in developing and implementing torture techniques, and that this involvement provided

---

[20] James Risen, *Pay Any Price: Greed, Power, and Endless War* (NY: Houghton Mifflin Harcourt, 2014).

[21] "PHR Calls for Federal Probe into American Psychological Association's Role in CIA Torture Program," Physicians for Human Rights, October 16, 2014, http://physiciansforhumanrights.org/press/press-releases/phr-calls-for-federal-probe-into-american-psychological-associations-role-in-cia-torture-program.html

"cover" for the administration's torture program.²² Senator Dianne Feinstein acted courageously in combating strong opposition for the release of this report, which established in detail the role of psychologists and the APA in the torture program, including important information about how even agency health professionals inside the CIA were protesting the approaches that the psychologists were promoting. Noting the role of the APA in a related release, Feinstein stated that "[t]his is a stark reminder that torture can corrode every institution it touches, including medical and psychological professions."²³

Under increasing pressure, the APA authorized an "independent review" to be conducted by David Hoffman of the law firm Sidley Austin LLP regarding

> whether there is any factual support for the assertion that APA engaged in activity that would constitute collusion with the Bush administration to promote, support, or facilitate the use of "enhanced" interrogation techniques by the United States in the war on terror.²⁴

While it may not have been the APA's intention, the timing of this announcement (after the Risen book was published and before the Senate Committee report was released) effectively gave the APA a pretext to avoid questions for months after the Senate report became public, doing so by citing the ongoing review. While a genuinely independent review of the APA's activities was to be welcomed, this strategy seemed familiar to me, in that the APA avoided answering questions after the 2005 Mayer article was published, citing the imminent release of the PENS report, which did not in the end address the expressed concerns of members. Watchdog organizations, keeping a sharp eye on these actions, continued to call for a separate full federal investigation into the

---

²² "Senate Intelligence Committee Study on CIA Detention and Interrogation Program," *United States Senator for California Dianne Feinstein*, http://www.feinstein.senate.gov/public/index.cfm?p=senate-intelligence-committee-study-on-cia-detention-and-interrogation-program

²³ "Feinstein on Alleged Link Between APA, CIA Torture Program," *United States Senator for California Dianne Feinstein*, April 30, 2015, http://www.feinstein.senate.gov/public/index.cfm/press-releases?ID=c4164060-080f-4f04-915f-a3b4b46091b3

²⁴ "Statement of APA Board of Directors: Outside Counsel to Conduct Independent Review of Allegations of Support for Torture," American Psychological Association, November 12, 2014, revised November 28, 2014, http://www.apa.org/news/press/releases/2014/11/risen-allegations.aspx

allegations cited in Risen's book[25] and launched a petition for the immediate public release of the Hoffman review, objecting to the APA's original plans for multiple internal reviews prior to its release to the public or APA members.[26]

These reports and APA's reactions provided ample evidence that torture survivors had reason to be distrustful and cautious in their dealings not only with the US government, but also with psychologists whose primary professional association had violated their rights, time and time again. A significant consequence of the actions of the APA was the serious impact on survivors who sought help with recovering from their traumatic experiences. How many torture survivors would be unable to trust mental health professionals because of the positions the APA had taken regarding torture?

Finally, in July 2015, the Hoffman Report was released to the public through the *New York Times*, verifying much of the evidence that had been cited by Risen and by the courageous advocates who had fought for a decade to reveal the truth of the APA's role in the perpetration of torture as part of the "war on terror." The report concluded, among many things, that

> some of the association's top officials, including its ethics director, sought to curry favor with Pentagon officials by seeking to keep the association's ethics policies in line with the Defense Department's interrogation policies, while several prominent outside psychologists took actions that aided the CIA's interrogation program and helped protect it from growing dissent inside the agency.[27]

The report revealed evidence that the APA's own ethics office "prioritized the protection of psychologists—even those who might have engaged in unethical behavior—above the protection of the public."

The report was released while the APA was still conducting its "internal review" and immediately produced widespread outrage from the public

---

[25] "American Psychological Association to Conduct an Independent Review Into its Role in CIA Torture Program," Physicians for Human Rights, November 14, 2014, http://physiciansforhumanrights.org/press/press-releases/american-psychological-association-to-conduct-an-independent-review-into-its-role-in-cia-torture-program.html

[26] Email to the author from Psychologists for Social Responsibility, http://hosted.verticalresponse.com/442001/0b3f918b43/1493529749/6e6d22ca03/

[27] Risen, "Outside Psychologists Shielded US Torture Program, Report Finds," July 10, 2015.

and APA members. In response, at the APA's annual meeting in August 2015, the APA's Council of Representatives held a vote, which passed almost unanimously, on the issue that

> psychologists shall not conduct, supervise, be in the presence of, or otherwise assist any national security interrogations for any military or intelligence entities, including private contractors working on their behalf, nor advise on conditions of confinement insofar as these might facilitate such an interrogation.

This, described as a "ban on torture," was seen as a major victory for advocates and a major shift in APA policy.

I was surprised by my own reaction. Initially very relieved and heartened by the outcome, over time I became angry, increasingly so as I watched APA colleagues who, after a decade of silence or dismissive responses, were now hastily moving to reconciliation, skipping, in my view, an essential accountability step and the need to establish a watchdog stance while actual changes were proposed. My anger grew when some members extended praise to APA for launching the independent review and for emphasizing how important it is to "work from the inside," thereby dismissing the efforts of the courageous members who had no choice but to work from the outside, and without whom the evidence of the APA's complicity with torture would never have come to light. Equally disturbing were the efforts by some APA members to focus on "institutional betrayal," that is, the anguish that members were feeling at this betrayal by their professional organization which they trusted, as if the most serious issue was how *members* were feeling.[28] The latter, thankfully, was countered by Physicians for Human Rights in a statement reminding those who needed reminding that the focus should be on those who had been victimized by the actions of psychologists who promoted torture and by those who protected them.[29]

Whether the APA vote will ultimately make a difference in how the institution operates remains to be seen. Only a few APA leaders among the many cited in the report have been fired or have left under pressure. Early reports are that the vote may not make a difference. It will only matter if

---

[28] http://www.apatraumadivision.org/hoffman.php
[29] Donna McKay, "The Brutal Toll of Psychologists' Role in Torture," Physicians for Human Rights, August 6, 2015, http://physiciansforhumanrights.org/blog/the-brutal-toll-of-psychologists-role-in-torture.html

it is enforced, and the enforcement is controlled by the APA Ethics Office,[30,31] whose actions in recent years have essentially destroyed its credibility. In early 2016, even before any changes were made in the APA's ethics rules to conform to the new policy, the Pentagon began exerting pressure on the APA to drop or weaken the ban on psychologists' involvement with torture, so that they could go on working in military interrogation settings. The APA has agreed to meet with Pentagon officials. It is difficult to determine whether the future will be like the past, marked with deception and denial, or if real change will occur.[32]

Those who fought for the release of this information were essential to this outcome, and because of their work, much has been revealed about the role of the APA and about what has happened to US policy as a result of its stance toward torture. This public disclosure has helped reverse some of the policy and legislative actions that led to the use of torture. For example, on June 16, 2015, Senators Dianne Feinstein and John McCain, with fifteen Senate colleagues, co-sponsored an amendment to "ban the use of torture," proposed as part of the National Defense Authorization Act. The amendment passed in the Senate by 78–21, and was included in the final law (S.1356/PL 114-92; signed on November 25, 2015), a very positive outcome. However, this is not the final word, as the amendment relies on the Army Field Manual, especially its Appendix M, as the standard for interrogations. The Appendix lists the kinds of interrogation techniques that are allowed, eliminating many forms of torture, though not all. Several coercive techniques, such as humiliation, solitary confinement, and sleep deprivation, are still included. In an effort to address this problem, the Senate amendment requires regular revisions to the Manual, and the involvement of the administration's "High Value Detainee Interrogation Group," which relies on interrogation research and emphasizes the use of non-coercive techniques, such as rapport-building and incentives. In the aftermath of the amendment's passage, tensions remain

---

[30] "Key Provisions of the New APA Policy," American Psychological Association, http://www.apa.org/independent-review/key-provisions-policy.aspx

[31] John M. Grohol, "American Psychological Association's New Torture Policy is Unenforceable," PsychCentral, August 18, 2015, http://psychcentral.com/blog/archives/2015/08/18/american-psychological-associations-new-torture-policy-is-unenforceable/

[32] James Risen, "Pentagon Wants Psychologists to End Ban on Interrogation Role," *The New York Times*, January 24, 2016, http://www.nytimes.com/2016/01/25/us/politics/pentagon-wants-psychologists-to-end-ban-on-interrogation-role.html

between those who hold differing approaches to interrogation. Some officials want to continue to be able to use torture techniques, others want them banned. The debate has continued as agencies prepared their first reports to Congress (required by the new law) on revisions to the Manual.[33,34,35] Vigilance and advocacy are still necessary while these and other debates go forward.

As a witness to these events, it is clear to me that many voices are needed to speak out against torture, and that nothing should be assumed about how institutions and individuals respond under personal, political, or professional pressure related to this issue. Throughout these years, I have observed in myself and in others a continuum of responses: courage and fearfulness; integrity and lies; kindness and cruelty; and intelligence and ignorance. I have tried to find my way to help during this time, although compared to others my contributions are very small. In 2007, I was asked by an APA Division, the Society for the Psychological Study of Social Issues (SPSSI), to collaborate in writing a policy statement for it about the APA's position on torture. The statement focused on research that showed the ineffectiveness of torture, the mental health consequences for torture survivors and perpetrators alike, and the national and international laws prohibiting torture, and included a protest regarding the APA's involvement in torture and a call for the APA to end these practices. It made a strong case for ending the involvement of psychologists in interrogation, opening with this statement:

> The United States and its military should immediately ban the use of torture, and psychologists should be expressly prohibited from using their expertise to plan, design, assist, or participate in interrogations that make use of torture and other forms of cruel, inhumane, or degrading treatment. The use of torture as an interrogation device is contrary to ethical standards of conduct for psychologists and is in violation of international law. Torture is ineffective as a means of extracting reliable information, and likely leads to faulty intelligence. Torture has long-term negative consequences for the

---

[33] Kaveh Waddell, "Here's What CIA Interrogators Are Still Allowed to Do," *National Journal*, December 12, 2014, http://www.nationaljournal.com/defense/here-s-what-cia-interrogators-are-still-allowed-to-do-20141212

[34] "US: Support Anti-Torture Legislation," *Human Rights Watch*, June 16, 2015, https://www.hrw.org/news/2015/06/16/us-support-anti-torture-legislation

[35] Ali Watkins, "Obama's Anti-Torture Team Has One Job—and Nobody Wants Them to Do It," *BuzzFeed*, January 20, 2016, http://www.buzzfeed.com/alimwatkins/obamas-anti-torture-team-has-one-job-and-nobody-wants-them-t#.hv9xedKV8

mental health of both survivors and perpetrators of torture. The use of torture has far-reaching consequences for American citizens: it damages the reputation of the United States, creates hostility towards our troops, provides a pretext for cruelty against US soldiers and citizens, places the US in the company of some of the most oppressive regimes in the world, and undermines the credibility of the United States when it argues for international human rights.[36]

This resolution was published on the SPSSI website, and eventually became the basis for an additional in-house publication[37] and a peer-reviewed journal article.[38] I had hoped that the statement would be put up against the APA's position in some internal and perhaps influential way, given the reportedly independent relationship between SPSSI and APA. This did not happen. The 2007 policy position did spark a series of responses in the Analyses of Social Issues and Public Policy (ASAP) journal,[39] which the ASAP editors described as a valuable opportunity to offer "differing views," but they failed to recognize that even presenting the idea that torture is potentially an appropriate tool for interrogation as a "differing view" is taking a position that contradicts principles accepted in international law (e.g., the prohibition of torture), and violates the ethical principles of many professional associations and religions. The forum merely allowed APA officials to continue making their claim that the APA prohibits torture and to deny the actions that it had taken to the contrary, stating that they could not authorize an independent investigation, although in fact they finally did in 2014. Other authors addressed nuanced research issues related to interrogation, many of which begged the question about the ethical involvement of psychologists or Americans more generally in torture.

I was dismayed by the process itself. Elizabeth Swanson notes in her introductory comments that in her view, "it is a massive step backward in the theory and practice (intellectual, activist, legal) of human rights to open a debate about the potential efficacy of torture, as well as about

---

[36] Mark Costanzo, Ellen Gerrity, & M. Brinton Lykes, "Psychologists and the Use of Torture in Interrogations," *Analyses of Social Issues and Public Policy* 7, no. 1 (2007): 7–20.

[37] Costanzo, Gerrity, & Lykes, *Analyses of Social Issues and Public Policy*, 2007.

[38] Mark Costanzo & Ellen Gerrity, "The Effects and Effectiveness of Using Torture as an Interrogation Device: Using Research to Inform the Policy Debate," *Social Issues and Policy Review* 3, no. 1, 2009.

[39] Costanzo, Gerrity, & Lykes, *The Use of Torture and Other Cruel, Inhumane, or Degrading Treatment as Interrogation Devices*, The Society for the Psychological Study of Social Issues, 2007. http://www.spssi.org/index.cfm?fuseaction=page.viewpage&pageid=1460

various forms and methods of torture." I agree with this view, and it seemed to me that the ASAP discussion had been an example of this kind of debate. I feel that a kind of false equivalency is evoked when those who believe that torture has its place and those who do not are presented as arguing opposite sides of the same principle. In this case, I felt that the ASAP editors were taking the safe road of providing another venue for APA officials and their supporters to state that the APA is against torture, while still using ambiguous wording that allowed psychologists to be involved in military interrogation.

Although I had hoped my effort with this statement would make a difference with what was going on at APA, I see now that this was very naïve; to my knowledge, this is the only public action that SPSSI took during this period. I strongly believe that every action, however big or small, can make a difference, sometimes in ways that are unexpected. But in the case of the APA's continued resistance, it was disturbing to think that all of the protests seemed to be making little difference, that so much more was needed to make a change. It is critically important that the Hoffman Report revealed what it did, but what will happen remains to be seen. To regain credibility, the APA will need to make deeper organizational changes. I firmly believe that vigilant oversight will be essential in the future, whatever APA states its position to be going forward, and especially as this relates to its work with the military and with the government.

I tried to do what I could "from the inside," but I am certainly no longer on the inside, probably never was in any practical sense, and what I could do early on felt like precious little, though I signed petitions, donated funds, and added my voice when I could. I am no longer a member of the APA, although I recently joined as an affiliate member the APA Trauma Division, an experimental step I took to see if this Division, with its understanding of trauma, would take this issue seriously as decisions are made, and if I can help as the Division leaders develop their own response to the Hoffman Report. As of this writing, it is uncertain whether the Division or any other APA Divisions will focus on the serious issues related to human rights, torture, and the role of psychologists in a way that will change the larger organization. If not, the outside advocacy organizations cited earlier and other professional associations are places where I and other psychologists and advocates can contribute.

In the meantime, knowing that there are many ways to help, I turned to my own work to try to do more. For the last twelve years, I have been a senior policy official with the National Center for Child Traumatic Stress, the coordinating center for the National Child Traumatic Stress Network (NCTSN),[40] and in that capacity I try to help children and families affected by many forms of traumatic experiences. This initiative was launched by the US Congress, under the leadership of Senator Tom Harkin, Representative Rosa DeLauro, and others (including Sen. Kennedy, Sen. Durbin, Sen. Wellstone, and Sen. Murray) to expand and improve care for children and families exposed to traumatic events. Within its mission, researchers, clinicians, and other service providers are helping children affected by all forms of trauma, including those related to torture, war atrocities, refugee trauma, and other events. More recently, member centers are helping children who are being trafficked for forced sexual activity and labor. Most of my work has been to raise awareness about these issues and to translate what we learn to inform policy change and improve clinical care. This is important work, but I also am aware of the immense scope of the problem and the gaps in my own organization's efforts. We do not do enough about torture, nor about some forms of traumatic events that include institutional collusion. For example, we focus a great deal on children who experience other forms of trauma, including abuse or neglect by parents who are often themselves poor or abused and who become involved with the child welfare system, but less so on children who have been abused by clergy or coaches with the knowledge of the institutions which protect them. We are beginning our work with children who have been forced into slavery (in my view, an accurate term for trafficking) as part of national and international exploitation, but the problem is growing and we need to do more. Our work with refugee families is substantial, though insufficient, and the torture experience as a unique clinical or political issue is not emphasized. We work hard to collaborate equally with survivors of trauma, but we need to remain vigilant on this issue. There is much more that can be done.

I am grateful to the editors, survivors, and other advocates for this volume, which emphasizes the voices of survivors to point a direction for policy, treatment, advocacy, and research, and allows other authors (scholars, activists, advocates, and clinicians involved in this work) to speak more personally. It is my hope that this will be the beginning of many such collaborations and discussions. My own participation, with its requested focus on the personal, was set in the context of political and public debate, and has led me to explore my own fears and what I can do about them to

---

[40] National Child Traumatic Stress Network, www.nctsn.org

find new ways to contribute. I have asked myself questions, some that I had avoided examining too closely. Could I be a therapist working with torture survivors? Am I skilled enough to do forensic interviewing? This is not merely a training question—I wonder if I am strong enough to be of help, to bear witness, to support someone as they recover. If I am too wrapped up in my own internal issues, I will be of no help to anyone else. Will my non-survivor status mean that my contributions are unwelcome or suspect or ineffective? Will this be even more challenging, now that the APA has so severely damaged the reputation of psychologists? If so, what are my responsibilities to help to break down those barriers? It is acutely embarrassing to admit to worrying about my capabilities or my emotions when survivors, who have been through horrific pain and betrayal, can overcome their own despair to speak up on behalf of those who did not survive or who are still in captivity. But if I can recognize such dynamics and thereby resolve my own issues, perhaps I can then see a clearer path forward. This is something I think about all the time, and I want to move my ideas into new action.

WHAT CAN I DO? WHAT CAN I HELP OTHERS DO?

> Never separate the life you live from the words you speak. ("Conscience of a Liberal," Senator Paul Wellstone)

Helping Those Who Help Those who never give up have my deepest respect. When I was at NIMH in the early 1990s, I met regularly with some representatives of the Center for Victims of Torture (CVT, a torture treatment center in Minnesota), who were asking that NIMH do more to study the psychological impact of torture. They succeeded in this effort then, and have not stopped doing what they can to advance many issues. Since that time, CVT has been a leader of an active consortium of torture treatment centers who advocate for more funding for treatment and to end torture.[41] In 2008, CVT led an effort with other organizations to bring together 200 international leaders to sign a declaration to ban torture.[42] This effort was instrumental in encouraging President Obama to

---

[41] National Consortium of Torture Treatment Programs, http://www.ncttp.org/index.html

[42] "Declaration of Principles for a Presidential Executive Order on Prisoner Treatment, Torture, and Cruelty," *cvt.org*, https://web-beta.archive.org/web/20150905113837/

sign an executive order about torture and interrogation in 2009. This kind of action brings together the courage of many people and must overcome many barriers; it is one way that change occurs when people do not give up, and where more help is needed. At this time, legislation for the reauthorization of the Torture Victims Relief Act, which includes language for the continued funding of torture treatment services, has been introduced, but its final passage is still pending. Research is also lagging; despite the targeted funding in 2000, as of 2016, and due in part to the more narrow priorities of NIMH research, only five grants related to torture are funded across the National Institutes of Health. Much more advocacy is needed here.

The organizations involved with torture that I know best are TASSC, CVT, Advocates for Survivors of Torture and Trauma, and the Guatemala Human Rights Commission. These are among the many organizations that provide services for torture survivors, involving volunteers in the process. In Washington, DC, TASSC also coordinates the June 26 annual event to commemorate the United Nations International Day in Support of Victims of Torture. Opportunities with organizations that help torture survivors include assisting with practical matters (driving, food, office work) or more complex issues such as asylum applications, therapy, legal support, or housing. The issue of being a survivor or a non-survivor may arise in some of these interactions, but I see these opportunities as a chance to build trust. I am exploring the work of these and other organizations, and have taken a course sponsored by Physicians for Human Rights on conducting psychological interviews with asylees who have been tortured as one avenue where I would like to contribute. The reality of doing this is still very challenging to me, but I see what others have done, and that helping those who help is one of the clearest paths forward.

The American Psychological Association As already described, the APA's role in supporting the participation of psychologists in torture has been revealed. Some of the individuals involved have been fired or are resigning or retiring, but whether this will lead to real change is unknown. More is needed, and as a psychologist I feel a responsibility to do more about this, though these experiences have resulted in a deeper skepticism

http://www.cvt.org/sites/cvt.org/files/downloads/CTBT_Declaration_of_Principles.pdf. See also http://www.cvt.org/sites/cvt.org/files/u18/Master%20Endorser%20List.pdf

about institutions being able to withstand pressures and stand up to powerful forces. Perhaps for me this is related to a belief that there is a moral order to the world, one that helps form the basis for decisions around right and wrong, just or unjust. What is important is not to let skepticism, the potential result of experiences such as these, lead to inaction, despair, or fear. What has helped me is to spend my time finding other ways to contribute, such as through the Coalition for an Ethical Psychology, which I believe will continue to be a watchdog, and to allow myself to be inspired by these individuals and organizations as a strong counter to the despair I feel when I witness injustice or passivity. The expressed shock of some members in the aftermath of the Hoffman Report's release is astonishing, given the amount of evidence that had been available throughout the past decade, and I often find myself angry over the disingenuous and ongoing denial of many members. But I do recognize the pressures faced by many members, and that, as with other traumatic events such as child abuse, it is difficult sometimes to accept that these things do actually happen and that voices must be raised for change. In the end, of course, it is up to me to do my part. I can further add my voice to those who have been committed to changing the role of the APA and the United States' views and actions about torture, perhaps finding new ways to help through the courageous organizations who lead in these areas. Even within the APA, some of the original protestors are holding important watchdog roles in the organization, and may be able to influence what comes next.

In December 2014, *The New Yorker* investigative journalist Jane Mayer, continuing her watchdog activity about the torture issue, noted that President Obama may have missed an important opportunity when he spoke in the aftermath of the release of the Senate Committee's report about the extent of government-sanctioned torture. In his remarks, instead of speaking honestly about the brutality that had occurred, he instead praised the CIA officer "patriots" who were involved in post–9/11 activities. Mayer suggested the better path he could have taken. Citing David Luban, the author of *Torture, Power, and Law*, she emphasized that there are many forms of accountability for torture, and one of the most meaningful would be to honor the real torture patriots—those who had tried to stop it.[43] The APA itself could learn a lesson from this advice.

[43] Jane Mayer, "The Real Torture Patriots," *The New York Times*, December 13, 2014, http://www.newyorker.com/news/news-desk/real-torture-patriots

Raising Awareness I believe that scientific evidence can help survivors and advocates in their work, and to that end I am exploring the possibility of updating the information that was included in the report and book for the South African Truth and Reconciliation Commission. So much has happened in the last fifteen years, including changes put in place after 9/11, that has made the world we live in one where human rights are questioned and torture has spread. At the same time, our understanding of trauma has advanced dramatically, with many improvements in clinical care. Because of the courage of torture survivors and their involvement in research and advocacy, we know much more about the impact and long-term consequences of torture. The torture information in the original book needs to be updated, as do the related chapters that focused on refugees, rape, veterans, and war trauma, as well as treatment, neurobiological science, and human rights. I think a new edition, or a comparable research collection, could be a valuable resource for survivors, advocates, clinicians, attorneys, and scientists. I am exploring ways to move forward with this idea.

Within the National Child Traumatic Stress Network, programs and resources have been developed that are relevant to many forms of trauma, but a working group that focuses specifically on torture has not yet been established. I would like to spearhead this effort in collaboration with torture survivors, as I believe that this could help consolidate relevant resources that could be of value for torture survivors and those who help them, and could bring torture into the mainstream of NCTSN's work. Such an effort could also help link the resources developed by the NCTSN with the Consortium of Torture Treatment Centers and other organizations involved in the issue.

Further Thoughts

> It's no use waiting for what only appears at a distance. (Barbara Kingsolver, *The Poisonwood Bible*)

In one of my favorite books, *The Poisonwood Bible*, author Barbara Kingsolver thanks her husband in her author's note for teaching her that "it's no use waiting for what only appears at a distance."[44] For me, this was

---

[44] Barbara Kingsolver, *The Poisonwood Bible* (NY: Harper Collins, 1998).

an encouraging and persuasive reminder that just wanting and waiting will not bring what one hopes for any closer. For me, it means that I will need to take action myself, even when it involves overcoming fear and pushing against seemingly insurmountable personal or external obstacles. For many of us, the goal of ending torture seems to appear only at a distance and sometimes, with all the barriers, seems hopeless. For me, even finding a way to contribute has often seemed to be a goal "at a distance," too. Identifying small steps has helped turn an overwhelming challenge into something manageable, as has finding support from colleagues and friends. People like those represented in this volume take their experiences and their pain, and move forward on the path they are on—whether it is recovery from horrific personal experience, or advocacy, research, counseling, refugee services, legal support, investigative journalism, prosecution, or truth-telling. I don't have to look far for examples to provide courage and hope. Working toward a goal is a form of hope, trusting that I can be of use, and moving the fight along on the path I have in front of me.

In my time with Senator Wellstone, he often advised people "Never separate the life you live from the words you speak," meaning: act authentically and live your life according to the values you profess. He lived that way, even when the outcome of a Senate vote was 99–1, and he was the 1. He did not say "Never separate the life you live from the words you speak, *unless you are challenged, or frightened, or it is really hard to do, or you might lose the election, or you may be threatened.*" He knew what each person might be up against in fighting for human rights or justice, but advised us to *do*, as well as to *talk*. I took this to heart, too, and try to do this wherever possible. I believe that this is what so many survivors of torture do as they advocate for change even in the face of grave danger.

Those who are tortured say that they are told again and again that no one cares or will ever care about what has happened to them. Part of the torturer's objective is to isolate and instill despair. Fighting against this is part of survival and recovery, I believe, and those who support survivors in clinical, legal, or other activities are helping to eradicate that part of the torture. The survivor is not alone, nor is the non-survivor advocate. The question is asked whether non-survivors have a right to speak up against torture, to formulate recommendations for policy change, to try to help. I believe that they—*we*—do, yes, but also as with any soul-searing experience, those who have been through it and who are forever changed by the new knowledge of what it is really like have a perspective that is essential to any presentation, dialogue, therapy, or recommendation for change. I think non-survivors may at times be confronted, and perhaps when that happens they are serving as stand-ins for others who were not or could not be confronted, or who were confronted but failed to listen or respond. When challenged, consider that it is best to listen so that survivors can be heard, and to figure things out together. I think in this work, people know that, and even when it is hard, they try to do exactly that. Hence, this book.

Handing Things Along The example of those who have not given up is the model for the future—what else, after all, can we do, but learn "how to save one another" as Gene Knudsen Hoffman suggests, move things along, take the charge from those who fought before us, do what we can, and pass it to those who come after, grateful always that we are not alone on this journey.

> And I am waiting
> For the song
> To swell from a million,
> Million throats
> Because we learned
> How to save one another.
> —from "I Am Waiting," Gene Knudsen Hoffman[45]

---

[45] Gene Knudsen Hoffman, "I Am Waiting," *Poetry of Peace,* edited by David Krieger (Santa Barbara, CA: Capra Press, 2003).

PART III

Disappearance and Torture, Redress and Representation

Whereas the previous two sections consider, first, the roots and contexts of torture and, second, healing and recovery in torture's immediate aftermath, this final section looks further into the future to address the following questions: What does it mean to think of witnessing as collective practice? How can collective witnessing affect law, public discourse, and artistic and cultural representation? How can we understand and analyze witnessing as a potentially ethical practice? How might teaching students to "read between the lines" (the kind of critical reading promoted by the humanities) of narratives about torture cultivate witnesses against torture, even as it invites humanities educators to reflect critically on their pedagogies? And, finally, how might witnessing by survivors, especially when it takes demonstrably artistic and literary (as opposed to humanitarian or legal) forms, open a pathway to living into a future without torture?

As we discuss in our introduction to this volume, Kelly Oliver has argued that witnessing does not simply offer a report, nor does a witness simply seek acknowledgment; rather, witnessing goes "beyond recognition" to initiate an intersubjective relationship with ethical potential. For Oliver, "[s]ubjectivity requires a responsible witness"[1]; therefore, witnessing is a necessary component of any ethical response to torture and enforced disappearance, because both are designed to deny or to destroy the (inter)subjectivity of their victims. Part II examines how witnessing as a form of intersubjectivity and intersubjectification—as a means of reconstituting a generative rather

---

[1] Kelly Oliver, *Witnessing: Beyond Recognition* (Minneapolis: University of Minnesota Press, 2001), 85.

than destructive social matrix—is crucial to survivors' lives in the aftermath of torture. Here we extend Oliver's argument in another direction: rather than focus on primarily interpersonal relationships (e.g., between survivors and health-care providers), we turn to various forms of representation (legal, pedagogical, artistic, and literary) that might stage intersubjective relationships—and the ethical encounters they entail—between survivors, allies, and larger publics. This turn to representation necessarily emphasizes the forms that representation of torture might take and how and by whom those forms are produced, circulated, and consumed (viewed, heard, watched, read). Although we argue that these essays are forms of life writing in and of themselves, they address witnessing in multiple media and genres.

We begin with human rights attorney and survivor Jennifer Harbury, who insists that the temporal urgency of response-ability, of active witnessing, begins at the moment of disappearance (when a victim of torture and disappearance may yet be alive) and extends into the long aftermaths of mass human rights violations. Such urgency might initially offer some measure of protection to the tortured and, later, help to illuminate systemic methods and rhetorics of torture. As Harbury discloses in "Everardo and the CIA's Long-Term Torture Practices," her nightmare began as a human rights monitor during the brutal Guatemalan military government's counter-insurgency programs in the 1980s, and deepened upon the abduction of her husband, Everardo, commander of a Guatemalan rebel group. Aware of US government complicity with Guatemalan repression and rights violations, Harbury used a variety of techniques, from meetings with US State Department and military officials to filing freedom of information requests to, finally, undertaking a series of hunger strikes in Guatemala and the United States, in order to gain information about Everardo's whereabouts. The victim of cover-ups orchestrated by both governments, Harbury later learned that while she was pursuing the exhumation of graves, searching for her husband's remains, the US government was well aware that Everardo was still alive, being interrogated and tortured by the Guatemalan military. Harbury traces this purposeful obfuscation by the US government in order to provide evidence of long-standing US complicity with torture practices globally and at home. She builds her case with the testimonies of survivors from Latin America, all of whom confirm the presence of US agents in their experience of torture. In this way, Harbury situates her own testimony in the context of collective witnessing to torture by survivors from across

North and South America, up to and including detainees in the US-led war on terror. As at once individual and collective (although differentiated) life narratives, the stories Harbury collects reveal patterns of torture methods and personnel repeating across time and place. Such patterns also make visible communities of survivors that can themselves generate a collective retort to the devastating denial by government officials of violations committed with their approval or active support. In other words, Harbury's essay at once discusses and provides an example of how, by recognizing commonalities among their experiences, survivors and their allies can articulate collective responses to torture, in addition to offering singular narratives of personal harm.

The tremendous potential of collective witnessing is demonstrated in our second essay in this section, by the late torture survivor and activist Patricio Rice. Also writing from personal and collective experience, in "Survivors and the Origin of the Convention for the Protection of All Persons from Enforced Disappearance," Rice examines the active participation by survivors in shaping the International Convention for the Protection of All Persons from Enforced Disappearance (CED), which was adopted in 2006 and entered into force in 2010 (it remains unsigned by the United States). His essay documents how a support network can form the foundation for collective witnessing, in that survivors discover not only their shared experiences, but also how those experiences offer a unique perspective on the juridical-political structures that both enable and might respond to enforced disappearance and torture. Through the process that began with witnessing to one another, survivors and their allies were able to develop strategies and goals for mobilizing their experiences toward legal and political ends. If witnessing often serves as a means of galvanizing attention to a particular issue, then collective witnessing in this instance amplifies and tailors evidence from survivors in order to bring into being the legal instruments through which their experiences, and those of others like them, can be understood, redressed, and possibly prevented in the future. In the example of the CED, Rice charts a remarkable process through which the disappeared come to engender a category of survivors as legal persons, and the family members of the disappeared themselves are recognized as survivors of the crime. Rice's essay is a testimonial to the process of birthing an international human rights convention from the collective experiences of survivors, and it underscores how enforced disappearance is intimately related to torture. First, enforced disappearance shares with torture the "*possibility* of annihilation, the *virtual* disappearance of the witness"[2]: whereas torture works toward the impossibility of witnessing through the threat and administration of pain which attempts to annihilate the subject, enforced disappearance does so by eliminating a forum in which witnessing can effectively take place. Second, both torture and enforced disappearance work to terrorize the individual as well as his or her social network, albeit in different registers. Third, as examples such as the CIA's Rendition, Detention, and Interrogation program and Argentina's "Dirty War" make clear, enforced disappearance is rarely anything other than at once terrifying in and of itself and a prelude to other forms of torture.

Our next contributor, Claudia Bernardi, examines the role of memory in both individual and collective responses to torture and enforced disappearance. As an artist who fled Argentina in the midst of the "Dirty War," and who has engaged in forensic and artistic projects in Argentina, Ethiopia, and El Salvador, Bernardi deeply considers the process through which artistic expression—and the invitation it issues to co-creators and observers—emerges from the material evidence of forensic teams and, all too often, the immateriality of the disappeared. In "The Tenacity of Memory: Art in the Aftermath of Atrocity," she describes how collective memory informs these projects and emerges from them, such that artistic expression becomes the means of (re)imagining the community that includes both survivors as well as those who have perished. As a mode of intersubjective, collective witnessing, the formal dimensions of figurative art through which memory gains shape, color, texture, and value do not offer a fixed representation of the past—a kind of closure that might signify healing. Instead, they are the means of particular, dynamic conversations about when and how representation is possible.

Our fourth essay in this section takes us into the classroom as a site of collective witnessing that demands both imagination and intellectual inquiry. In her essay, "Teaching about Torture, or Reading between the Lines in the Humanities," Madelaine Hron reflects on her own pedagogy to argue for the necessity of humanities courses that focus on torture, although, as she asserts, to be successful such courses need to push against academic disciplinary conventions that would separate literary study from other modes of inquiry. Teaching about torture means embracing interdisciplinarity, creating a role

---

[2] Jacques Derrida, "Poetics and Politics of Witnessing," in *Sovereignties in Question: The Poetics of Paul Celan*, ed. Thomas Dutoit and Outi Pasanen (New York: Fordham University Press, 2005), 68. Original emphases.

for emotion in the classroom, and re-evaluating the role of the teacher as interrogator (however Socratic) and disciplinarian. For Hron, teaching students to read literary and cultural representations of torture carefully provides them with the time, space, and means to forge ethical connections with others, to understand how discourse can be manipulated to different ends, and, ultimately, to challenge the argument that torture offers a legitimate political means through which a body can be made to reveal its ostensible truth. As Peter Brooks wrote early in the war on terror, work in the humanities

> is not salvific, it won't necessarily make you a better person, it is not instrumental—it has precisely renounced the instrumental work of language and symbol in favor of something more reflective and mediated. What the interpretative humanities have to offer the public sphere is ultimately and basically a lesson on how to read—with the nuance, complexity, and responsibility that we practice most of the time in our classrooms.[3]

Hron does not take that practice or her own role in it for granted, but investigates what it might mean in the context of literature about torture, and how it might shape students as future witnesses against atrocity.

What forms of witnessing are possible for those who have been forcibly disappeared legally and politically, but who still exist? Our next essay, "Legal Appeal: Habeas Lawyers Narrate Guantánamo Life," by Terri Tomsky, offers an incisive analysis of proxy witnessing and its politics. In her reading of narratives by Guantánamo lawyers of their interactions with their clients and with the military detention system, Tomsky analyzes how the authors navigate strict censorship regulations to bring their clients figuratively from a black site into the public sphere. Together, the narratives in *The Guantánamo Lawyers: Inside a Prison Outside the Law* (2009) do not so much argue any single client's case as attempt to spur a public conversation about the detention center itself through the lens of the attorneys' life writing.

Tomsky's analysis also underscores a central claim of our volume: that witnessing belongs to no single genre and should be evaluated within and against different generic conventions. In this case, Tomsky demonstrates how contributors to *The Guantánamo Lawyers* define a dual role for themselves, on the one hand as proxy witnesses offering a collective portrait of unjust conditions at Guantánamo, and on the other hand as representatives

---

[3] Peter Brooks, "The Humanities as Export Commodity," *Profession* (2008): 35.

of international law, professional standards, and American exceptionalism. The assertion of values such as respect for law and human rights in the face of their obvious absence allows the authors to represent themselves as ethical patriots, even as their clients have been cast outside the laws and rights that make the lawyers' own exceptionalism possible.

Our final essay, "Did We Survive Torture?" by former Guantánamo detainee Mansoor Adayfi, speaks individually and collectively about the role of artistic production and authorship by detainees themselves in maintaining the humanity that torture seeks to destroy. Adayfi explains the material conditions of creative expression in Guantánamo, as well as the psychosocial effects of artistic production from within the walls of the prison on the creators and their fellow detainees. Although Guantánamo artists and writers must weigh their aesthetic choices against a system of "rewards" for basic necessities and tools based on what the authorities term "compliance," Adayfi recounts detainees' passion for the means to creative self-expression, for an emotional outlet, and as way to imagine a conversation with a larger public. He describes harsh restrictions on artistic and writing materials, production time, and distribution imposed by Joint Task Force-GTMO personnel, ostensibly in the name of security; however, as Adayfi expresses it, those restrictions imply less a concern about the security risk of a painting or poem than a desire to regulate creative expression precisely because it reflects the men's larger humanity. As Erin Thompson, co-curator of the recent exhibit of Guantánamo artwork, Ode to the Sea, has written, "the US authorities there were surprised that the artwork they had been scrutinizing so carefully for hidden messages had a unifying one they had missed: that its makers were human beings. Which is precisely the realization the authorities needed to stop the rest of us from having if Guantánamo is to remain open."[4] For Adayfi, the question that propels his essay is whether, even after his release, he can ever be free of Guantánamo.

Together the six essays in this section focus our attention on life writing as a collective as well as a singular endeavor, whose forms animate diverse publics and demand critical inquiry in concert with imaginative, compassionate engagement.

---

[4] Erin Thompson, "What We Can Learn from Art Painted inside Guantánamo," *The Nation* (December 4, 2017). https://www.thenation.com/article/what-we-can-learn-from-art-painted-inside-guantanamo/. Rprted from TomDispatch.com

CHAPTER 9

Everardo and the CIA's Long-Term Torture Practices

Jennifer Harbury

Jennifer Harbury's essay in this volume begins and ends with the images of torture by US forces in Abu Ghraib prison, Iraq, witnessing the similarity of torture techniques revealed in those images to techniques used by the United States in its support of counter-insurgency efforts across Latin America in the latter half of the twentieth century. Combining her own testimonial to the torture and disappearance of her husband in Guatemala with testimonials from other survivors of torture in Latin America, Harbury makes the case that the United States has been a participant in torture and disappearance for decades, and that the use of torture in Abu Ghraib was no aberration by a "few bad apples," but rather central to US policy and strategy in its "war on terror." Author of three books on the subject of torture in the Americas, most recently Torture, Truth, and the American Way: The History and Consequences of US Involvement in Torture *(2005), which tracks American involvement in torture in Latin America, Southeast Asia, and the Middle East, Harbury is one of the strongest voices bearing witness in the public sphere to US complicity with torture and its devastating aftermaths.*

J. Harbury (✉)
Anonymous, USA

After graduating from Harvard Law School in the early 1980s, Harbury went to work in a legal aid bureau on the Texas–Mexico border, where she supported Guatemalans fleeing government violence and repression at home, only to see them turned away by US immigration authorities. This work led her to visit Guatemala in order to witness the situation for herself, whereupon she met her future husband, Everardo, a commander in the Mayan resistance against the brutal Guatemalan military government. In the following essay, Harbury describes witnessing first hand the role of the US military and diplomatic corps in supporting the Guatemalan military government, even when it was US citizens who were killed by its death squad. She then chronicles Everardo's disappearance, her efforts to locate him, and the cover-up of his whereabouts by Guatemalan and US officials. Harbury's voice is both the analytical voice of the advocate and legal scholar who understands the devastating impact of torture upon citizens and, indeed, upon democracy itself, as well as the testimonial voice of a survivor of disappearance (Patricio Rice's essay in this volume examines the contributions of survivors in formulating and advocating for the United Nations Convention against Enforced Disappearance). Understanding the collective nature of the use of torture and disappearance as repressive mechanisms across Central and South America, Harbury reports testimonials from a range of torture survivors so as to reveal patterns of torture methods and repressive strategies across time and space, in order to counter the denial and repression of these practices by government officials at home and abroad. What follows is both testimony to and argument against the use of torture—anywhere, at any time, by any government.

* * *

As the horrifying images of the prisoners flashed across television screens around the world, most Americans reacted with shock and outrage. President Bush himself rushed to assure us that the young soldiers in the photographs were just a "few bad apples" and "Un-American," and that the United States itself would never engage in torture. This we heard again and again, while the young military policemen and -women were quickly court-martialed and imprisoned.

Sadly, as the public outcry grew, there were some of us who felt only a chilling sense of déjà vu. We are members of a small group of torture survivors from all parts of the globe. The disturbing images came as no surprise to us. We ourselves had endured or witnessed precisely the same tortures. Worse yet, US intelligence agents had been present in our cells, teaching those very "interrogation techniques." The low-ranking soldiers at Abu Ghraib were hardly a few bad apples. They were simply carrying out orders and using standard—albeit criminal—methods developed and used by US intelligence networks for many decades. The soldiers were punished, while the intellectual authors who gave the orders remain free of any consequences. If we allow this grave injustice, then what remains of our prized democracy and system of justice?

Guatemala, a Long-Standing Example

The realities of US involvement in torture were brought home to me in a very personal way in Guatemala. I spent years monitoring the government rights violations there during the 1980s, and like everyone else was horrified by what I witnessed. Friends disappeared one by one—from peasant leaders to judges, priests, physicians, and social workers. Most were never seen again, while others were found dead and mutilated, their bodies sprawled in the streets as a public warning. One young woman searching for her missing husband, a university student, helped to form the Grupo de Apoyo Mutuo, only to be raped, tortured, and murdered herself along with her nineteen-year-old brother and her two-year-old son. All three were found with broken necks. Her body bore cigarette burns, bite marks, and other telling injuries. The baby's fingernails were missing. What did the United States have to do with all of this? As later reported in the United Nations' (UN) Truth Commission, far too much.[1]

The troubles began, of course, with the 1954 Central Intelligence Agency (CIA) coup against the democratically elected President Jacobo Arbenz. The reform-oriented era known as "The Ten Years of Spring" came to an abrupt and bloody end. The military ruled with an iron fist for the next many decades, carrying out a campaign of counter-insurgency that earned it the title of worst human rights violator in the western hemisphere. As later determined by the Truth Commission, the Army engaged in genocide against its Mayan citizens. Some 660 villages were massacred, and 200,000 people were either tortured and executed without trial, or "disappeared" forever. The Army was held responsible for 93% of the war crimes, with 4% unknown and only 3% the acts of the largely Mayan resistance forces, or the Guatemalan National Revolutionary Union (URNG).

---

[1] Comisión para el Esclaricimiento Histórico de Guatemala (CEHG), *Guatemala Memoria del Silencio*, 1999.

The Commission harshly criticized the US government for knowingly backing this regime despite the ongoing atrocities.

For those of us on the ground in Guatemala, US involvement was always painfully clear. A standing joke within the human rights community was that "if you want someone turned over to the death squads, just ask for asylum at the US Embassy." The laughs this drew were always rueful. We were only too familiar with the Embassy's rush to "explain" every new atrocity as "unclear," a mere matter of common crime, or perhaps an act of revenge by the guerrillas. Even when American citizens were murdered, Embassy staffers were swift to defend the death squads from accusations by anguished family members. We had seen the obvious gringos riding in jeeps or descending from helicopters, shoulder to shoulder with Army officials. We saw the soldiers rampaging through the streets with their terrifying dogs, "made in the USA" stamps visible on their equipment. We despaired when military aid continued on the grounds that the United States should help "professionalize" the local military.

In the end, I was driven out of Guatemala by the conspicuous men in dark glasses waiting for me every night in my hotel lobby, guns clearly visible under their heavy vests. Back in the United States, I found that I could not put Guatemala behind me while my friends there were still dying. So, I began a book, writing down their life stories and experiences as they had told them to me. I was tired of the silence in the mainstream press, and I was more than tired of the Embassy's deceits.

EVERARDO

As the book, *Bridge of Courage*, neared completion, it became important to include the young Mayan women combatants. I found their stories remarkable and wished to interview them as well. In 1990, after some negotiating, I found myself at a combat base high in the volcanoes of southwest Guatemala. It was there that I met my future husband, Everardo, who was the commander of the region and one of the founding members of the Organización Revolucionaria del Pueblo Armado (ORPA). A Mayan peasant himself, he had starved as a child laborer, learning to read and write when he arrived in the mountains at the age of eighteen. For the next seventeen years he had remained in combat, rising swiftly to the ranks to become a Comandante, and eluding the military time and time again. We met again in Mexico City a year later, moved in together, and married in late 1991. He returned to the front in January 1992, then vanished into thin air a few months later, during a brief skirmish on March 12. He was the only person missing, and his despairing *compañeros* could find no trace of him.

I was, of course, devastated by the news. The Guatemalan Army was claiming that Everardo had died in combat and that he was buried in a grave in the small town of Retalhuleu. If this was true, then he had died a soldier's death, and I thought I could bear it. If not true, then he was being tortured in a secret cell. This I could not carry. Having visited the morgues only too often to reclaim the dead, I knew what it meant, and could not keep the images out of my head. The UN now deems "disappearances" to be a form of psychological torture of the surviving family members. This is the truth.

The Guatemalan government had provided us with a description of the body found at the site of the skirmish, and it matched Everardo feature by feature. Nonetheless, when I tried to exhume the body in Retalhuleu, I was driven out of the cemetery by the Attorney General himself, who arrived in a military plane, and some twenty-five police armed with rifles. It was then that we all knew that something was terribly wrong.

For months, ORPA leadership searched for clues, quietly speaking with witnesses and tracking down leads. Villagers had seen a body carried out in a burlap bag, but were unsure as to whether the person was dead or alive. The search continued, but few of us believed that Everardo could still be alive. Months had passed. No one survived torture for long.

At the end of 1992, a young man named Santiago Cabrera Lopez escaped from a military base and fled into Mexico to find us. He was from Everardo's combat team and had been captured the year before, together with a young *compañera* named Karina. Both had been severely tortured. Santiago had been held in a pit under an officer's desk, beaten with cement blocks until he hemorrhaged, beaten across the feet until his toenails fell out, given electrical shocks to the testicles, and then chained to a bed without a blanket for months. We were amazed to find him alive. In thirty-five years of war, the Army had never presented a single living prisoner of war to any authority or court of law. Santiago explained that the Army had a new program, from Argentina, which they were using on selected prisoners. Most were indeed tortured and swiftly killed, as before. But some were subjected to long-term torture, with the goal of breaking the prisoner psychologically to obtain his or her information. Physicians were on hand to prevent accidental deaths. The goal was to break the prisoners, not to kill them.

Santiago survived by pretending to be broken, identifying the dead, and deciphering old radio codes he knew were no longer in use. He saluted with respect and waited for his chance. The other prisoners had been subdued with threats that their families would be killed if they tried to escape. Santiago's family, however, had already fled the country. He had nothing to lose, and once he sensed that the officers trusted him, he ran for his life across the border into Mexico. A young Mayan peasant with virtually no education had just outwitted the entire intelligence division.

Santiago knew we were looking for Everardo, his own commanding officer and long-time friend, and he found his way through the underground until he made contact. To his horror, he had watched Everardo being dragged into the Santa Ana Berlin military base on March 12, 1992. He had heard the officers laughing about staging the combat death to avoid an international human rights outcry. They wanted to torture Everardo, slowly and for a long time, without interference. Santiago saw Everardo battered repeatedly. On one particularly grim occasion in June, Everardo was chained to a bed frame with an unidentified gas cylinder at his side. Colonel Julio Alpirez was bending over him taking notes. His body was grotesquely swollen, with one arm and leg bandaged as if hemorrhaging, and he was raving. A doctor was nearby to keep him alive. Santiago saw Everardo for the last time a few days later, a uniform covering the bandaged arm and leg. He looked pale and unwell, but he was still alive.

With that knowledge, I rushed to file an emergency complaint with the Inter-American Commission of the Organization of American States (OAS), and paid a visit to a none-too-friendly State Department officer. I also met with the incoming ambassador, Marilyn McAfee, who expressed great concern and promised to help. She was charming, but I expected the worst. I also visited Capitol Hill, and to my surprise received prompt support from both Democrats and Republicans.

Still, I knew that in the end I was on my own, so I returned to Guatemala and forced the exhumation of the Retalhueleu grave. The Guatemalan government had just suffered an internal upheaval and US aid had been briefly suspended by President Clinton. This came as a bit of a shock to local officials who, as a result, were eager to show that this was a new, improved, and democratic Guatemala. And so I fared somewhat better than the last time around. As I filed the requisite papers in the tiny court house, a courageous official signaled me to read through the files. There was the answer. The report gave incredible detail about the body found at the combat site, describing even the person's underwear and the tins of food in his pack. A precise description of Everardo was given again. At the line on the form for scars and other identifying features, though, the author had written "none." Yet Everardo, after seventeen years of combat, had scars all over his body, including a very visible one on his upper lip from a tumble over a cliff. Clearly, the official had never seen Everardo at all. The news photographs showed the man standing over a body, surrounded by soldiers. Not wishing to die, he had wisely written down the false information as ordered. The autopsy report in the file was dated the same day, but described a far younger and smaller man, with very different scars. The youth had been strangled, shot, stabbed, and battered to death. His skull was crushed. There was ink on his fingertip from being printed. This was no combat death.

It was the summer of 1993, and I was fearful of yet another cancellation. There was no time to lose, and so I said nothing at all and waited for the exhumation. An Embassy staffer came with us to observe. The grave was hard to find and we spent the afternoon watching while four different locations were opened. The forensic team handed me plastic buckets filled with decomposing human heads, while officials demanded a reason for why I believed it was not Everardo. None had the crushed skull described in the autopsy report, and none had Everardo's dental patterns. All were in civilian clothing.

Finally, we opened the fourth grave, and found a tiny figure in an olive-green uniform. The skull was crushed beyond recognition. This was the body in the autopsy report, but it was not Everardo. Forensic tests showed the young man to have been fifteen years younger than Everardo. The gold caps on a tooth were another clear indication. Everardo had no funds for dental care, let alone a gold "corona." He had no caps. As we learned years later, the youth we found in the grave had been a young solder named Valentin. He was dragged from the barracks and killed at the riverside as part of the hoax. His friend finally fled the Army, bringing his identification papers and telling us the whole story.

Once again, I returned to the Embassy and met with the Ambassador, who paled and asked that I give her everything in writing. I did so. Once again, she promised to look into the matter immediately and get right back to me with anything she could glean. I did not hold my breath. Instead, I wrote to the growing number of concerned Congresspersons, and met with a delegation of OAS members visiting Guatemala. I even met with the Minister of Defense, General Enriquez, in his luxurious Casa

Crema quarters. He too paled when I cited the evidence, but assured me that they had never captured Everardo, who "must be hiding somewhere." Enriquez also heavily insinuated that my marital problems were not his concern. I responded that if Everardo were presented alive to the courts of law, I would remain quiet, but that otherwise there would be some uproar. He told me to go ahead and make my uproar, and showed me to the door.

The next morning I was sitting in front of the Polytechnica, the fortress-like military intelligence headquarters notorious for its secret torture cells. I announced a one-week hunger strike and sat for seven days drinking water only. After a shocked public silence, the Guatemalans came forth one by one, bringing flowers and photographs of their own missing loved ones.

The uproar in the press brought still more congressional attention, and the members began to pressure the Embassy. They all received the same form letter, stating that there was no information at all about Everardo, and that there was no independent evidence that any secret prisons existed in Guatemala. Meanwhile, I received protective orders from the OAS, which the Guatemalan military ignored, as well as the support of the UN human rights network, which was also ignored.

Then things began to change, ever so discreetly. For more than six months, I was received by Defense Minister Enriquez, as well as other high-level military officers, for quiet conversations. Enriquez would serve me coffee, then bluster that the Army had never taken Everardo prisoner. "All the same," he would ask me smoothly, "just what would you do if we could 'find' Everardo and present him to the courts as a token of respect?" I answered that I would sign a release of all criminal charges against Colonel Alpirez and publicly congratulate the Guatemalan Army for a historic change in its human rights practices. Enriquez would smile broadly and murmur that I was a most intelligent young woman, then slide the coffee pot in my direction. This went on for months.

I reported all of this to Ambassador McAfee, who became quite agitated and told me that these conversations could not have happened. I also reported the discussions to high-level officials in the State Department in Washington. They dourly promised to continue searching for information, but made it clear that Everardo was no doubt dead and that "all kinds of things happen in Guatemala."

The quiet tête-à-têtes halted as abruptly in the spring of 1994, and all doors closed to me in Guatemala. I knew time was running out. The Peace Accords were to be finalized soon, and the Army would no longer need

Everardo's information. Nor would they allow him to live and denounce the tortures he had suffered. In October, I simply sat down in front of the National Palace and declared a hunger strike to the death. My decision was made, and I was at peace. Maybe I would die there, maybe I would survive, but I would never acquiesce. The official reaction was immediate, with an enraged General Enriquez shouting at the press, and the Guatemalans, as always, risking their lives to sit with me, bring flowers, water, and always the photographs of their own disappeared loved ones. Speaking with them, I remembered an older friend who rose every morning at 4 a.m. to iron her son's shirts. He had been missing for twelve years. These are wounds which never heal.

I remained on the hunger strike for thirty-two days and nights, sleeping in the square on a blanket. My left eye closed, my upper lip stiffened, I developed a heart murmur, and I was cold and dizzy at all times. Even in the noonday sun I huddled in sweaters and blankets, chilled to the bone. General Enriquez threatened to have me tossed into a mental institution if I became "suicidal," so I learned to bend over and tie my shoelaces whenever I felt faint so that blood would rush to my head. There was a shooting one night and non-stop death threats. Ambassador McAfee expressed her great concern.

Then suddenly, Mike Wallace aired a program on *60 Minutes* about us. In it he revealed that the Embassy had in fact received a CIA bulletin confirming that Everardo had been captured alive. This was news to the many members of Congress who had long been trying to assist us, as well as to the OAS and numerous human rights organizations. Everyone had received the same State Department letter claiming that there was no information. In the ensuing uproar, I was invited to come to the White House to talk things over with the National Security Advisor, Anthony Lake. It seemed the better option at that point. As I left Guatemala, the police killed a number of demonstrators, including a young law student who often sat with me in the square. His name was Alioto.

Back in Washington, nothing happened. I did indeed meet with Mr. Lake, who assured me that the bulletin described by Mike Wallace was the only document there was, and that they had "scraped the bottom of the barrel." I asked that all files be turned over to me at once, as for obvious reasons I could not trust my own government. He made no promises and I filed my Freedom of Information Act request, seeking expedited disclosures. I received nothing.

Given the situation, I went on my third hunger strike, this time in front of the White House. There was no more time. The State Department left me out there for twelve long days. Then Senator Torricelli came forward with extraordinary disclosures. Everardo was dead. He had been killed upon the orders of Colonel Alpirez, who was in fact a CIA paid informant or "asset." The State Department knew all this, but had withheld the information not only from me but from Congress as well.

Now Congress was truly furious. It was April of 1995. Some three years had been lost in saving a life. Too little and too late, I began to receive US files and hear from new witnesses. I did not like what I heard. Six days after Everardo's capture, the CIA had informed the State Department that he was a very important prisoner and that his death would be falsified in order to better obtain his information. In short, he was to be secretly detained and tortured. There were several more, early CIA bulletins after this, but they have remained secret to this day, no doubt because they reflect payments to Everardo's torturers. When I first called the State Department in early 1993, the Embassy in fact sent someone to investigate the matter, and received a report confirming that Everardo had been captured alive and held at a base called Santa Ana Merlin. Yet the State officials continued to insist to me and to everyone else that they had no information. A later bulletin confirms that Everardo and some 350 other secret prisoners are still alive. This means that when I opened the grave and inspected the four human heads in the plastic buckets, Ambassador McAfee already knew that Everardo was alive and suffering torture at the hands of the United States' own paid informants. She sent a staffer to accompany me, but she never told anyone the truth.

From then on numerous CIA bulletins went to the State Department. They describe Everardo being battered and drugged and held in a full body cast to prevent his escape. They describe the deaths of his many friends, one by one. Some were kept in pits of water so deep they had to hang on to overhead bars to keep from drowning.[2] After torture sessions the prisoners were thrown dead or alive from helicopters into the sea as a way of destroying "evidence."

Somewhat sourly, the bulletins note that everything Everardo said during the "interrogation" sessions turned out to be false. Once he even agreed to take the Army to the long-sought URNG radio station, leading them instead into a ferocious ambush. He never told them anything

---

[2] The "water pit" is being used now by the United States in the war against terror.

"useful," and so finally he was either thrown from a helicopter or dismembered. All of the 350 prisoners were believed to be dead also. From what witnesses tell me, Everardo was alive until the summer of 1994. Had the truth been timely told, his life and the lives of the others could have been saved.

It does not end there. Between eight and twelve of Everardo's torturers were trained at the School of the Americas. Several were on the CIA payroll. Although the United States had earlier cut off military aid to Guatemala, the CIA continued to pay its assets and shield them from any legal or diplomatic consequences. Col. Alpirez himself received $44,000 shortly after he was seen torturing Everardo with a toxic substance. An unnamed CIA agent took the trouble to deliver the funds to a remote rural area in person. Many people tell me that today Alpirez is living in the United States. As one CIA memo noted, he is the keeper of many secrets. Apparently that includes US secrets as well.

There was a Senate Intelligence Committee hearing on the case. We were told that the CIA abuses represented the work of a "few bad apples," that torture was not to be tolerated, and that it would never happen again. A few agents were ceremoniously fired, but later on they were honored.

Since Everardo's death I have worked to help abolish torture, especially by the United States. We brought the Guatemalan government to a full international trial in San Jose, Costa Rica, at the Inter-American Court on Human Rights of the OAS, and received a unanimous landmark decision in our favor in 2000. As for the CIA, I filed suit in 1996 and spent more than eleven years litigating the motion to dismiss, a matter usually resolved within months. Things seemed hopeful for a while, but with the widespread use of torture by the US since September 11, 2001, the courts have been dismissing cases left and right. My days fighting the case in the United States are clearly numbered. I will finish the proceedings, then move on to Spain. The doctrine of universal jurisdiction is a very good part of international jurisprudence.

VOICES OF THE SURVIVORS

As the uproar over Everardo's case died down, I began to hear from other survivors from across Latin America. Few death squad victims ever survived to tell their stories, but now those few began to make contact with me. Fearful of retaliation against themselves or their families, most have asked that their names be kept confidential. But they wished to make one thing perfectly clear: they too were tortured, and they too had had American intelligence agents assisting and advising the torturers. Worse yet, the techniques used on them match those we have seen in the Abu Ghraib photographs and in other documentation.

Sister Dianna Ortiz: A US citizen and an Ursuline nun [and author of the epilogue of this volume], Sister Dianna had been teaching schoolchildren in rural Guatemala. In 1989 she was abducted, raped, and tortured by government agents. Her tortures included more than 100 cigarette burns on her back alone and an attack by a terrifying dog. Both methods are now used by the United States in Iraq and Afghanistan. An obvious American speaking Spanish with a heavy American accent arrived in her cell and demanded her release. He knew where to find her and he had authority. The torturers responded, "Yes, Boss," and turned her over. The man drove her away in his jeep, urging her to forgive her captors because they were fighting communism. She leaped from the vehicle and ran for her life. For many years the US Embassy claimed that Sister Dianna was mentally unstable and that no such American could exist. Yet a photograph of a CIA agent present in Guatemala at the time seems to match her description.

Maria Guardado: In 1980, Maria Guardado was abducted in El Salvador and brutally raped, burned, and tortured. Left for dead, she was able to crawl to safety and eventually flee the country. She has told her story again and again. There was an American in the torture cell. She heard his voice and recognized his accent. He was supervising her torture session. As each Salvadoran agent finished with her, whether breaking her bones, strangling, or burning her, he would say, "Who is next? What method will you use to make her talk?" and then finally, "She's dead, take her away."

"*Daniel*": Daniel was a young man in Guatemala in 1969. He was dragged off the streets by Army death squad agents and severely tortured. He was "waterboarded," held under water until he lost consciousness, a technique he describes as unbearable. He was also strapped to a metal chair and given excruciating electric shocks. An American was present, speaking with an obvious accent. He was telling the torturers where to place the wires to inflict the most pain. These techniques are now being used by the United States in the "war against terror."

"*Anna*": Anna was a young student in Honduras in 1983 when she was abducted and severely tortured by members of the deadly Battalion 316. Her torture included mock drownings or waterboarding. She was suspended by her arms in "stress and duress" positions that permanently damaged her arms and shoulders. She was also terrorized by a ferocious dog. All of these methods are used today by the United States in its war against terror. An American called "Mr. Mike" often arrived to speak with the torturers, give advice, and collect information. He was fully aware of Anna's plight, but never reported her whereabouts to the police or to her desperate family members. One of the torturers later fled the country and confirmed Anna's report about Mr. Mike, who worked for the US government. A secret CIA report further confirmed that Mr. Mike was a CIA agent.

"*Juan*": Juan was a young combatant captured by the Guatemalan military in 1988. His torture included waterboarding, a technique that was used by the CIA in the US "war on terror." According to the Bush administration, this technique does not rise to the level of torture. Juan described it in detail. He began to gag and had severe pain in his head as he swallowed water. He felt that his ear drums would burst. Then he began to vomit in the water and eventually convulsed and lost consciousness. He awoke when his torturers took steps to revive him. This is a slow-motion mock execution, described by Senator McCain as "very exquisite torture," and used by the United States today in the Middle East. The UN has specifically ruled it torture. A North American was ushered into Juan's cell and began to interrogate him about Cuba. He noted all of Juan's injuries, but simply left him to his fate.

Herbert Anaya: Herbert Anaya was a beloved human rights leader in El Salvador. In 1986, he was shopping with his family when government agents dragged him away in broad daylight. He was secretly held in the Policía de Hacienda headquarters. His wife Mirna learned of his location through secret sources and sent her attorney to find him. The lawyer went to the headquarters and demanded entry, only to be told he must wait. To his surprise, an American advisor came to speak with him, and decided that he could see Herbert in a little while. When the lawyer finally was allowed entry, Herbert was seated with a large blanket covering his lap. He was released a few days later, and explained that he had been forced to stand for so long that his feet were too grotesquely swollen to even fit into his shoes. Not wanting the lawyer to see this, they had covered him with a blanket. Anaya was shot dead at his home a year later, while he was placing his children in the car to take them to school. The technique of forced, long-term standing is excruciating, because the lymph builds up in the limbs and terrible swelling results. It is one of the "stress and duress" methods used now by the United States on detainees.

There are many other cases, which I have set forth in detail in my book, *Truth, Torture and the American Way* (Beacon Books, 2005). Together they paint a grim portrait of the longtime realities of US torture practice. The young soldiers at Abu Ghraib did not come up with those horrific techniques by themselves, nor were they just a "few bad apples." Indeed, the now- notorious photograph of the hooded man on the box shows a technique well known to intelligence experts as the "Vietnam Position."

The young soldiers were simply following orders. They were using methods that the CIA had developed and used for decades, and had taught in torture cells across Latin America. At the bottom of one list of permissible torture techniques appears the signature of Donald Rumsfeld himself, and both President George W. Bush and Vice President Dick Cheney are deeply implicated.

Once evidence began to emerge that the United States was using these methods routinely, the Bush administration hurried to claim that such techniques were somehow not quite torture. I leave that to the reader to decide. The law, of course, defines torture as any act that inflicts severe pain. Psychological torture includes any mock execution or threat of serious harm to the prisoner or his or her loved ones. Both are felonies under US criminal law and both are serious violations of international law, including the Geneva Conventions and the Convention against Torture.

Does any of this make the United States more secure? Surely not. While the Iraqi people once threw flowers to its troops, now they throw bombs. Studies show that humiliation, repression, and torture create conditions that inevitably spawn suicide bombers and other acts of terror. This is a matter of common sense. If a foreign army invaded the United States and carried out a broad campaign of "disappearances," torture, and sexual humiliation, there is no doubt as to what the US reaction would be. Never have Americans been more hated or less safe.

What have we done? Perhaps more crucially, what are we going to do about it?

CHAPTER 10

Survivors and the Origin of the Convention for the Protection of All Persons from Enforced Disappearance

Patricio Rice✝

Originally from Ireland, the late Patricio Rice worked as a priest among the poor in Buenos Aires, Argentina, where he was abducted and tortured by the military regime in 1976. After his release, he continued his pastoral mission among the poor, and also became an active voice against human rights violations and an advocate for the disappeared in Latin America. As Executive Secretary of the Executive Latin American Federation of Families of the Disappeared (FEDEFAM) between 1981 and 1987, he was instrumental in helping to craft the United Nations (UN) International Convention for the Protection of All Persons from Enforced Disappearance (CED). In this chapter, Rice reflects on the process of drafting the Convention and shepherding it through the UN to its adoption in 2006. He offers the extraordinary perspective of a "rare survivor" of the disappearances in Argentina's Dirty War, detailing not only his own story, but also how survivors and their families helped to define the core terms and scope of this international legal instrument. His narrative is at once personal and collective in documenting not only his own motivations, but, even more crucially for this book, how witnessing by a collectivity that, significantly, includes survivors can shape the international legal terrain.

✝ Deceased
P. Rice (✉)
FEDEFAM, Ciudad De Buenos Aires, Argentina

> Rice describes how a network comprising international human rights bodies, religious organizations, and coalitions of survivors and their families worked to demonstrate to the international community the need for a legal response to the increasing use of enforced disappearance as a tactic of abusive government. The process required survivors and their families to become knowledgeable about international law and to be willing to share their stories and their losses in order to lobby diplomats, lawyers, and civil servants; and it required those already empowered to effect international law to recognize survivors and their families as experts on the scope and effects of enforced disappearance.
>
> The impact of survivors and their families is evident in the Convention's robust definition of enforced disappearance as an avowedly political crime that sought to remove those targeted from all legal protection. Moreover, in response to the demands of groups such as the Abuelas de Plaza de Mayo, the final Convention recognized family members as victims who, along with any direct survivors, were entitled to reparations and to their genetic identity. Rice's contribution to this volume provides an important reminder of how the law functions not as a set of abstract principles, but as a generative tool to respond to the legal, political, economic, affective, and corporeal suffering of its claimants; and, how, in our current moment, a law may be used to respond vigorously to conditions beyond those from which it sprang. Finally, Rice's work underscores the central role of survivors in shaping and wielding that instrument.

* * *

Considered first an anomalous practice of so-called third world dictators, the practice of "vanishing" political opponents, subversives, or alleged terrorists has since emerged from the darkness of the night as a favorite way to operate repression with minimum cost—even in democratic countries. The outlook for human rights is indeed grim, as this mutating practice seems to have become a tool in the ongoing murky war against global terrorism. But what is this most cruel form of human rights violation?

Enforced disappearance literally means that armed thugs, recruited from security forces, not only get the green light to operate by kidnapping or detaining people, but are provided with secret bases in which to hold and brutally ill-treat their unfortunate victims, who may be men, women, or children, in order to extract data from them to continue the macabre hunt for "subversives," "communists," "terrorists," or whatever label suits state power at the moment. In most cases, when the disappeared person is no longer considered useful, an anonymous perpetrator decrees death. Care is taken that the victim is deceitfully and "humanely" erased with the secret disposal of his or her body. Meanwhile, their properties are plundered and families blackmailed into silence. To public opinion, that person has simply "gone missing," but of course the next of kin know otherwise.

The true stories of the disappeared only slowly emerge from behind the smokescreen of deceit, and then the titanic struggle for the *desaparecidos* begins to play out its inevitable sequence. As in Argentina or Chile, it may take a generation or more for the truth to be revealed and the prosecution of perpetrators to be initiated. Although many will still argue that it was good riddance to "undesirable elements," the majority who turned a blind eye at the time will likely feel remorse and shame at such a deep social wound, a wound that encompasses victims, their loved ones, and the "bystanders" of society at large.

Enforced disappearance was first practiced in the mid-twentieth century by the Nazis in Germany, and was then utilized by Latin American dictatorships starting in the 1970s. Families led by the Madres de Plaza de Mayo in Buenos Aires and friends standing in international solidarity with the *desaparecidos* then organized to demand accountability from governments and from the larger world community.

At first, the response of the international community was inadequate. Denial and incredulity were followed by the exhortation to renew confidence in the available human rights system. "The phenomenon will surely go away," we were told, as if it were a natural, not a human-made, disaster. As we predicted, however, the cruel epidemic continued to spread to regions such as Africa, Asia, and Europe (particularly in the wars in the former Yugoslavia in the 1990s), until people began to stand up and say: "No, this cannot go on any more!" Studies were undertaken at the UN and gaps discovered in human rights law that rendered enforced disappearance difficult to address and to redress. Finally, in 2002 it was unanimously agreed by the UN Commission on Human Rights that a new treaty dedicated exclusively to enforced disappearance was necessary to overcome shortcomings found in the international system. The process culminated with the approval in 2006 of the Convention for the Protection of all Persons from Enforced Disappearance.

This essay is intended to examine the Convention and its origins and content, and the fundamental challenge of making it a fully operative tool for the prevention of enforced disappearances in our world today. I write from the perspective and on behalf of the Latin American Federation of Associations of Families of Disappeared Detainees (FEDEFAM), for which I served as a founding member and as Executive Secretary. As life circumstances would have it, my personal history became tied up with FEDEFAM from its beginnings in the late 1970s, and so I begin there.

The Experience of Enforced Disappearance

I am a rare survivor of enforced disappearance in Argentina. On October 11, 1976, I was literally picked up from the street together with a young church worker—Fatima Cabrera—by armed security agents who had fired shots to intimidate us. We were first taken to the local police station, and were then abducted and delivered to a secret detention center. I was transported in the boot of a car to a torture place in the city of Buenos Aires whose exact locale I do not know to this very day, despite living in that city since 1988. Beyond the evident trauma of torture and suffering, the experience was one of utter hopelessness, of not knowing anything about where I was, about what I was being charged with, or about the final outcome. Would it be life, or would it be death? Fortunately, due to the prompt intervention of Irish Ambassador Wilfred Lennon, I "surfaced" in official custody a few days later, and after almost two months of political imprisonment, in December 1976 I was deported from Argentina. Fatima spent several years in prison, but she too is a survivor, thanks to international solidarity.

FEDEFAM

After this experience, I became absolutely convinced that international solidarity can save lives in the case of disappearances. For that reason, I campaigned for the cause of the Argentine *desaparecidos* in Britain (1977) and the United States (1978–80), where support was readily forthcoming due to the human rights policies of the Carter administration. My own case got to the Inter-American Commission on Human Rights and, after the hearings, the Commission resolved in 1978 that I had been a victim of torture and illegal detention in Argentina. As that decision was to be debated at the General Assembly of the Organization of American States (OAS) in La Paz, Bolivia in October 1979, I then traveled there. Unexpectedly, that venue proved to be a most important occasion for the creation of FEDEFAM: families of the "disappeared" from Argentina, Uruguay, El Salvador, Chile, and of course Bolivia had gathered to lobby the OAS General Assembly; it was there that we met and began to exchange experiences. The need was expressed to deepen bonding links through a more formal meeting, and it was only a year later when a Venezuelan non-governmental organization (NGO), the Foundation for the Social Development of Latin America (FUNDALATIN), led by Reverend Juan Vives Suria, took up the initiative. Together we organized the First Latin American Congress of Families of the Disappeared in San Jose, Costa Rica in January 1981.

THE NEED FOR A CONVENTION

In Costa Rica, families from all over the continent shared their shock and powerlessness at dealing with this repressive practice. Their loved ones had been disappeared and no remedy was working, as habeas corpus recourses were routinely dismissed by the courts. In this way, an impenetrable wall had been constructed, hiding the fate of their loved one behind it. While society was kept in the dark behind the appearance of normality, people were terrorized by "disappearances" happening around them. From this groundswell of shared experiences of social paralysis, indignation, and struggle surged a clear demand for international action. And so, the debate crystallized into the idea of a new international law against enforced disappearance. Of course, the families had to learn about international law; for example, that a convention in this context was not a *meeting* but rather a *treaty*, obliging states to determine practices and observances. But the families of the *desaparecidos* had already learned much about legal matters in their search for truth and justice. They thereby endorsed the need for a convention, but also brought forth the idea of creating a federation of families of the disappeared. The founding FEDEFAM Congress was held in Caracas, Venezuela in November 1981, and the objective of achieving the UN Convention against Enforced Disappearance became its absolute priority.

We moved quickly. In 1982, we approved a "Convention on Enforced Disappearance" drafted under the guidance of renowned

Chilean jurist Eduardo Novoa Monreal for presentation to the UN. That text became our banner for lobbying at the Commission on Human Rights over many years. In hindsight, it must have come as quite a surprise for those professionally involved in international human rights to see an invasion of their sacrosanct precincts in the Palais des Nations, Geneva by despairing mothers, grandmothers, and distraught survivors demanding that something be done, asserting that existing human rights mechanisms were not working and that a new initiative was urgently needed. Eyebrows were raised and foreheads were furrowed, but we had reality on our side. The practice of enforced disappearance was spreading like wildfire, not only in Latin America but around the world.

It took a generation of persuasion, coaxing, and charming of diplomats, lawyers, and international civil servants to make them aware of the complexities of disappearances and of the need for an international Convention. And when the final process began in 2002, FEDEFAM, together with other family federations such as the Asian Federation against Involuntary Disappearances (AFAD), participated actively in its drafting by sending important delegations to Geneva. Out of that crucible of meetings and debates was born the text of the new Convention, but no less important was the achievement of consolidating a consortium of experts—human rights defenders, representatives of international NGOs, and state delegates to the UN—into a group absolutely determined to end enforced disappearances. Not only, then, did the family associations provide the impulse to get the Convention approved, but we can modestly claim that many of its articles have their origin in our movement, as I will demonstrate in what follows, tracing those most important concepts as we see them reflected in the final Convention text.

The Definition of Enforced Disappearance

Families and survivors were involved from the earliest moments in the debate about definitions. FEDEFAM saw enforced disappearance as a new phenomenon that needed to be adequately defined; indeed, that was to be our major concern. The first definition included in our Convention draft of 1982 attempted to define the violation as the action of "forcibly disappearing" someone; that is, it was an active criminal act between those who did the abduction, those running the clandestine detention centers, the perpetrators of torture, and even court officials who did not investigate. It was clearly a state-orchestrated crime that was meticulously and deliberately concealed to guarantee impunity.

We were aware that in attempting this definition we were responding to the traditional position that saw enforced disappearance as simply a form of "privation of liberty." We claimed it was much more than that, as it involved torture, summary executions, clandestine burials, and other gross violations; "a violation of violations," as it has rightly been called. Those facing indictment for enforced disappearance had up to then simply been charged with the crime of "privation of liberty," which in most penal codes was not considered a serious crime, given that the life or integrity of the victim was not viewed as being at risk. The most serious dimensions of the crime of enforced disappearance, then, were conveniently hidden behind the cloak of privation of liberty. That is why we felt so strongly about overcoming the deficiencies of this limited definition.

Our ideas finally came to fruition in the definition of the UN Declaration on Enforced Disappearance (1992) and the Inter-American Convention (1994), which describe the act as a privation of liberty but with the role of the state clearly determined, with an emphasis upon the fact that where no further information is provided on the whereabouts or fate of the victim, that puts them totally beyond the reach of law. A most serious crime indeed!

The clarity of our understanding of the nature of enforced disappearance was a tremendous asset when we began to debate the text for the Convention, but we faced a new challenge from an unexpected quarter: the Rome Statute, which established the International Criminal Court in 1996, had incorporated a definition of enforced disappearance that was totally inadequate from our perspective. It included elements of subjective responsibility; that is, that the perpetrator must have in mind the end result of the crime when he or she participates in some part of it. But above all, it asserted that enforced disappearances are committed equally by both state and non-state actors—the phrase used is "political groups." Many states wanted that definition to be endorsed in the Convention. FEDEFAM adamantly opposed that position.

It was the inclusion of non-state actors that above all motivated debate in the Draft Working Group, as FEDEFAM understood the introduction of non-state actors into the definition as a "privatization" of the crime of enforced disappearance. If this definition were permitted to stand, enforced disappearance would thereby become a non-political crime, a kind of common crime similar to, if not the same as, kidnapping. Many voices emphasized that non-state actors were indeed engaging in enforced disappearance in many countries. We did not challenge those facts, but argued that in order to do so, such groups had constituted themselves into "quasi" state entities with the capacity for clandestine detention, central command, and impunity. If we were to use the definition of the Rome Statute, then all enforced disappearances could be blamed on non-state actors, and there would be no way of ever combating the practice, as States would easily be able to escape their responsibilities and ensure deniability by using paramilitary and other surrogates to conduct disappearances.

The solution reached in the Convention, whereby non-state actors are not included in the definition itself but rather in a separate article, will permit situations where non-state actors are involved in enforced disappearance to be addressed, as the Convention is authorized to address all forms of enforced disappearance, no matter who the authors are.

The other issue in the definitional debate emerged toward the end of the drafting sessions: was putting a person beyond the reach of law inherent to enforced disappearances, or ought it to constitute a separate element in the definition? Those attempting to set that element apart seemed to FEDEFAM to be engaged in the effort to create some kind of legal formality whereby one could somehow become a victim of enforced disappearance, but yet manage to be within the protection of law. We totally rejected that possibility and were also well aware that some states might attempt to use such a loophole in the Convention definition to legalize a form of enforced disappearance. Indeed, this is currently observable in repressive practices used against terrorism suspects, whereby the victims may appear in official custody but only months or even years afterward and often without charge or trial. We believe there can never be any room for a legal "disappearance" of anyone. Defining enforced disappearance is therefore still a key concern for FEDEFAM.

The Right to Know the Truth about the Fate of the Person Disappeared and All Related Circumstances

The intense and endless searching for news of *desaparecidos* is an experience that does not go away, even with the passage of time. Week after week, year after year, generation after generation, distraught families search for the truth of their loved ones' fates. I don't think that anyone could have imagined that this demand would become so overriding as to go from decade to decade and generation to generation, as it has with the

Madres and Abuelas of Plaza de Mayo, and yet it has, forcing change in international human rights policy and law.

From that anguishing search for truth grew the affirmation of the *right to know*, which I believe has become not only a new human right, but the very *leitmotif* for humanitarian movements in the third millennium. If the twentieth century was characterized by successive genocides where anonymity and non-accountability were dominating features, the gigantic effort in the twenty-first century is to pull the curtain aside and discover "who did what, where, why, and how." It is the right to truth. This right to know what happened to one taken into any form of custody is clearly established in the Convention.

The Right of Relatives to Recover the Remains of Their Loved Ones

Relatives naturally wanted their loved ones back alive, but that was seldom possible, as the victims were routinely killed after secret detention and secretly buried, or their remains otherwise disposed of. Families then had to search in all directions. Human remains began to be recovered and identified due to the science of forensic anthropology and innovative medical research making it possible to read DNA identities. With such recovery work, families were given the possibility of organizing a dignified burial for their loved ones. Now it is expressly stipulated in the Convention that families have the right to the remains of their loved ones, which will of necessity revolutionize the way human remains are handled by state authorities—above all when those remains are unidentified.

The Right to Justice for the Families of the Disappeared

This is another chapter in the Convention which reflects how the struggle of families and survivors opened up new possibilities. Here we can see the fruits of the struggle against impunity, with the Convention's affirmation of the practice of enforced disappearances as an ongoing crime and a crime against humanity in certain circumstances. It also endorses some form of universal jurisdiction for its effective prosecution and sanction. While we would have liked to see a total condemnation of any measures of pardon or amnesty in the Convention text, it was not possible to get consensus from governments on that measure. Certainly, we hope to ensure that in the application of the Convention that gap will never be used, covertly or overtly, to tolerate any form of impunity.

A Broad Concept of Victim, Including Relatives and Close Associates

In early discussions, many states wished to restrict enforced disappearance to address solely the experience of the person who is the direct victim; however, by the time the issue was taken up on the floor of the UN General Assembly in 1978, the social ramifications of the phenomenon were already recognized. No other human rights violation so thoroughly affects people close to the direct victim as enforced disappearance. Uncertainty about the fate of a loved one is devastating to humanity; thus, we must regard family members and friends of the disappeared not simply as third parties to a violation, but also as victims of the practice itself. Over the years this fact has been increasingly recognized and affirmed, and so we arrive at the text of the Convention, where the concept of victim is as wide as the effects of enforced disappearance itself.

Multiple Aspects of the Right to Reparation Are Affirmed

From the moment of a person's disappearance, a human drama unfolds which is impossible to handle. Where is the loved one? In prison? But where? Dead or alive? Why was she taken? What can we do to obtain his release? This uncertainty demands immediate responses, with families attempting to rationalize an otherwise irrational situation. Generally, there is resistance to consent to any administrative measure that would entail declaring the presumed death of a loved one, but there may be no other solution in order to solve inheritance and other issues in the aftermath of enforced disappearance. In some countries (Sri Lanka, for example), a provisional death certificate has been created in order to facilitate procedural issues even while a family continues to search for a loved one, and in Argentina, the concept of "absence due to enforced disappearance" instead of "absence with the presumption of death" was introduced in order to address the predicament of families with respect to the legal situation of their loved one. Families are saved from the dilemma of having to sign off on the presumed death of their loved one, thereby closing the case from future investigation.

Of course, reparation covers other aspects of the aftermath, from monetary compensation to prevention and memorial activities, and again, families have been the principal movers in terms of working to meet those demands. For instance, a novel concept for compensation was devised in Argentina whereby the victim was accredited with a salary over a fixed period of time—the number of years of the military dictatorship—and that amount in government bonds was left to the family as his or her inheritance. It is not, strictly speaking, compensation, but rather a way of offsetting some of the hardship endured precisely because of the loss of a breadwinner at home. The Convention includes the right to reparation in all its multiple dimensions.

The Right to Genetic Identity

There is no doubt that the right to identity was the unique contribution of the Abuelas (Grandmothers) de Plaza de Mayo (Argentina) to the Convention and, more broadly, to international human rights law. For over thirty years, the Abuelas have faced the predicament that the babies of their "disappeared" sons and daughters have been disappeared by means of false adoptions. The legal basis for the claim of the Abuelas to restore these children to their biological families is the right of a person to his or her own genetic identity. The falsely adopted children they are looking for are kept totally in the dark with respect to their own true identities. Nevertheless, the Abuelas persevered, and many cases have been unraveled with positive results for all those young people who have had their own identities restored to them (many of whom then organized as the Hijos (Children) de Plaza de Mayo). This proclamation of the right to know one's genetic identity will, of course, have profound consequences in all future adoption laws where the Convention is ratified.

Never Again: The Right Not to Be Subject to Enforced Disappearance

When FEDEFAM began, our founding leadership emphasized that it was a Federation that should never have had reason to exist, and that our greatest achievement would be that enforced disappearances would never occur again. Alas, our vision of eradicating enforced disappearance has not materialized, and over the years we have witnessed the expansion of the practice in Latin America, from military dictatorships to formal democracies like Colombia, Honduras, and Peru, and then to other regions of the world—Africa, Europe, Asia, and the Middle East. And after the terrorist attacks on the United States known as 9/11, forms of "legalized" enforced disappearance—"ghost prisoners," "extraordinary rendition" of suspected terrorists from one country to another, "undisclosed" detention facilities—have become one of the tools used in the global war on terrorism.

Our dearest ambition has always been to stop all disappearances, and we especially celebrate that the right not to be disappeared has been openly proclaimed in the very first article of the Convention. We enthusiastically support all measures toward that goal, such as ending all clandestine detention, publicizing lists of prisoners, strictly limiting "incommunicado" arrest and detention, and giving immediate information to families on the whereabouts and fate of anyone in custody. The establishment by the Convention of the Committee on Enforced Disappearance to investigate all urgent cases as one of its most noted characteristics plays a fundamental role in this preventive task. The Convention has an importance now, in our post–9/11 world, that we could never have imagined when we began this struggle over twenty-five years ago. It points out that the only way for humanity to progress is to fully and always observe and promote human rights. No form of enforced disappearance can ever be justified, even in the so-called "war on terror." Clearly establishing and defending the right not to be disappeared must be our obsession for these troubled times.

CHAPTER 11

The Tenacity of Memory: Art in the Aftermath of Atrocity

Claudia Bernardi

Claudia Bernardi is an Argentinean painter, printmaker, and installation artist who teaches at the California College of the Arts in Oakland and San Francisco and the Center for Latin American Studies at the University of California, Berkeley. Her work is informed by her participation with the Argentinean Forensic Anthropology Team, which was established to investigate and gather evidence of human rights violations in the aftermath of the Proceso de Reorganización Nacional, commonly known as el proceso *or the "Dirty War." Bernardi has participated in Team investigations in Argentina, Ethiopia, Guatemala and El Salvador. Her printmaking and installation work seeks to remember and preserve the memory of human rights violations documented by the Forensic Anthropology Team, while also aspiring to transcend the brutality of those violations. In 2005, in collaboration with the community of Perquin, El Salvador, she initiated the creation of the School of Art/Open Studio of Perquin, designed to facilitate, implement, and teach art and community-based art projects reaching children and adults living in Morazán, El Salvador, site of the El Mozote massacre of 1981.*

C. Bernardi (✉)
California College of the Arts, Oakland, CA, USA
e-mail: cbernardi@cca.edu

In this wide-ranging essay, Bernardi explores personal and artistic responses to state violence, particularly state-sponsored civilian murders, torture, and enforced disappearances. She begins by marking the limits of memory in witnessing the past. How do we reconcile what we remember with what we know to be true? How can we find modes of addressing and representing the past that provide a foundation for ethical engagement in the present and the future? Addressing these questions requires a complex understanding of memory as a mode of reclaiming the disappeared, resistance and militancy, the foundation for consciousness building, and, when transmuted into material forms, a means of witnessing.

As an artist who draws upon forensic research and works on both individual and collective projects, Bernardi conceptualizes artistic creation as fulfilling multiple roles in witnessing and as an exchange that demands both speech and recognition. An artistic response to atrocity, she writes, is a demonstration that we are listening. In turn, that demonstration, especially when it takes place in community-based art, invites both members and observers into the rituals of commemoration. Such rituals can provide the foundation for rebuilding trust and understanding in communities that have been damaged by state violence.

* * *

Empathy

A few years ago, I was standing at a bus stop in Buenos Aires, the crowded, cosmopolitan, densely populated capital of Argentina where I was born. A man's intense look upon me, his gaze deep, dark, and tragic, alerted me, although it did not feel like a threat. Rather, it felt like a distant plea. I tried to ignore him, but finally his insistent scrutiny made me turn around and face him directly as a way to challenge him.

He stepped toward me and, with a voice that seemed more a lament than a question, asked me: "Are you Claudia Bernardi's sister?"

His question startled me.

I answered: "No. I *am* Claudia Bernardi."

He looked at me as if seeing a ghost. In a gesture that conjured sadness and relief, he took my hands, briefly contained himself, trying not to cry, and pronounced softly: "Claudia… I thought you had disappeared."

Argentina is a country where if one has not been seen for some time, years, or perhaps decades, one may be assumed "disappeared."

The man I met at the bus stop had been a student at the National School of Arts, where he and I had studied in the late 1970s. He was one year ahead of me and, indeed, he had not seen me for many years, because I left Argentina in 1979 during the military dictatorship (1976–83). Given the length of my absence, he had assumed over the years that my name had been added to the long list of 30,000 disappeared people, a litany of pain that defines our history.

"My disappearance" had become so tactile to him that when he saw me standing at the bus stop, he could not conclude that his assumption had been wrong. He was looking at a woman he had thought to be a long time dead; the resemblance to the absent one could, then, only be attributed to kinship. The woman standing alive today in this busy city of Buenos Aires could only be "Claudia's sister."

We hugged and laughed and cried and promised each other to call and remain in touch from that moment on.

We never did that.

I suspect that is because we cannot change the assumptions of the past so easily or so willingly. We remain hostages of our own memory, even when—perhaps especially when—what precedes us has taken the shape of a continent of sorrow.

As I remember now this episode that caused me incalculable sadness and fresh fear, I realize the magnitude of the damage caused by the military junta in Argentina. This random encounter with a lost friend at a bus stop catapulted the past into the present with the solid fact that "I" could have been one of the disappeared, eroding the distance between "them" and "me," thinning the frontier between what happened and what could have happened, and showing the tragic absurdity of a methodology of repression.

We have lost "innocence" in Argentina. Learning on purpose or by circumstances of the abuses committed during the military junta, we learn about the organized harm inflicted upon a large proportion of civilians. This awareness, I believe, exceeds the consideration of politics. It becomes—or perhaps, it should become—a consideration of ethics, of a wounded history, and of empathy.

The violations of human rights perpetrated during the military dictatorship against each and every one of the disappeared in Argentina have caused the recognition that we can no longer live in the chosen numbness of everyday life—not when a system of power, namely the self-imposed military junta, constructed a structure of repression based on torture and degradation. And we are all—each one of us to a certain extent—responsible.

That is the success of state terror.

Argentina is a country wounded by state terror.

The military dictatorship in Argentina produced the death of the country. Argentina committed suicide, risked its future, which indeed has since been tarnished, tainted by the unavoidable repercussions of moral, legal, economic, political, and spiritual corruption.

To modify or annul the past is indeed impossible, for its infinite consequences manage to define the present. When talking about "reconstruction," we are facing not the rebuilding of a country, but the naked truth that we are collecting the wreckage of a new Argentina fractured by its past, eroded by the power in the wrong hands that, embarrassingly, lasted eight years. Even if not personally related to the victims or to the perpetrators during this darkest period in our recent history, we as a country have to face the fact that we are partakers of this tragedy, simply by having been alive during those years, by having witnessed, even if we did not fully comprehend what we were looking at, the collapse of democracy and the implanting of terror. A prerequisite to initiating the reconstruction of our fractured society is to admit our complacency, if not our complicity.

There is no amendment, no healing to genocide.

Victims of state terror who undergo torture—unimaginable, denigrating treatment whereby one endures demolishing techniques intended to cause the collapse of human dignity—cannot heal, cannot become the person who existed before. It is precarious, even offensive, to expect "healing." They are amputated of the person they once were.

Their pain becomes our shame.

After a brutal accident, if someone loses a leg, it is not expected that another leg would grow back. The amputated person could walk again, could dance, and could travel the world, but it would always be in the absence of a vital part now remote and abandoned in the past. This truth, painful and monumental, becomes the necessary acceptance upon which to choreograph a future. The damage inflicted by violations of human rights is designed to cause this amputation of the self. Even if the victim survives the tortures of the flesh, they still will have to face unprecedented challenges to live with the memories of the torments. This is true for the victims and it is true for the constituency at large, for we must assume the responsibility that we have witnessed and accepted a system of implanted terror.

Impotence

In the United States today, I see the installing of effective and fraudulent systems of repression similar to those designed and placed in action as a methodology by the military dictatorship in Argentina. The wording has changed: "terrorism/terrorist" has replaced "subversion/subversive." The practice of abuses of civil and human rights is the same. Unlawful new laws are created to justify persecution and prejudice. Perversely, this is advertised as a method of defending democracy. In Buenos Aires, not far from where I live, the main avenue called 9 de Julio intersects with a street that used to be called "Estados Unidos." In 2003, anonymously but efficiently, with hand-painted letters mimicking the font used by the Argentine municipality on street signs, the public voiced its opposition against the US invasion of Iraq. The street once called Estados Unidos was rechristened "Pueblo de Irak"/"People of Iraq," an eloquent testimony as to whose side the Argentine people appear to be on. Subsequently, they have asked: How did this invasion happen? Why?

Manufactured, imposed poverty in Central America adds to the devastation produced by recent wars. Hunger and isolation force the exit of millions of migrating people, who see their lives as survival instead of having the right to discern their own futures. This is a new version of violations of human rights. In Argentina, the profound fear inflicted upon a generation that was persecuted, censured, repressed, and terrorized has migrated from the past into the present. The implanting of the "inconceivable" as a matter of everyday life has produced another success for state terror—perhaps the most damaging one, even beyond the annihilation of a large segment of civilians: the sentiment of nihilism, transferred and deposited into the next generation. There is nothing more convenient for the success of state terror than a young generation underestimated in their capability for analysis and criticism: a tame, isolated mass of young people incapable of connecting with their communities and sedated by the feeling of impotence.

This sort of implanted impotence may also be the reason why we still do not know how many civilians are killed daily in Iraq. Do we know that? Do we care? General Tommy Franks, from US Central Command, phrased a sort of excuse: "We don't do body counts." I consulted on February 8, 2007 the website of "Iraqi Body Count" to find a minimum of 55,890 and a maximum of 61,605 civilians killed since 2003. According to a survey conducted by researchers at the Johns Hopkins Bloomberg School of Public Health, the number of civilians killed in Iraq is 654,965.[1]

> The researchers found that the majority of deaths were attributed to violence, which were primarily the result of military actions by Coalition forces. Most of those killed by Coalition forces were women and children.[2]

We are informed of the numbers of dead US soldiers. It is estimated that over 2700 men and women have died since the invasion of Iraq started in March 2003. Each of those deaths is a loss of indescribable proportions. However, a distinction needs to be made when comparing military men and women and civilian casualties. Men and women who enroll in the military do so voluntarily, measuring the benefits and also the risks.

For civilians, the murder of entire families of men, women, elderly, and children; the amputations, the disfigurations, the destruction of their economic means to survive; the poisoning of their water, the collapse of their sustainability... all are accompanied by yet another catastrophe: the surprise that it happened to them. The question of why it happened to them is never answered. They had no choice, no way to predict the carnage, and now, no alternative to the devastation.

In 1992, taking the testimony of survivors of massacres in El Salvador, countless times I sat in a precarious lodging to converse with the people who had miraculously evaded a massacre, or with those whose relatives and friends had perished. They would talk softly, almost apologetically, naming the long lists of dead people in their families. Because the method used by the Salvadoran army was "scorched earth," meaning that no one and nothing should remain alive after a military operation, the Salvadoran army would kill the people first, then the animals, and lastly they would set fire to the community and the crops. The survivors would identify the exact number of cows, pigs, and chickens, and even how many corn plants had been burned after the massacre.

They would finish their testimony with a question:

Why has this happened to us?

---

[1] Johns Hopkins Bloomberg School of Public Health, "Updated Iraq Survey Affirms Earlier Mortality Estimates," last modified October 11, 2006 (accessed February 8, 2007), http://www.jhsph.edu/news/news-releases/2006/burnham-iraq-2006.html

[2] Johns Hopkins Bloomberg School of Public Health, "Iraqi Civilian Deaths Increase Dramatically after Invasion," last modified October 28, 2004 (accessed February 8, 2007), http://www.jhsph.edu/news/news-releases/2004/burnham-iraq.html

Memory

Memory, personal and collective, becomes militancy in the postwar period. It is a way to reflect upon that which already has managed to change forever our way of interpreting our past and, consequently, our future. It is a way to vindicate people whom we have loved and who are looking at us from the other side of death, leaving us with a painful caress and a question: Why are we still alive?

More than guilt, it is perplexity.

This perplexity screams back to us that "I," too, could have been a disappeared.

The 30,000 disappeared are the success stories of a mandate of annihilation.

The foam of time impregnating the soul.

On a cold afternoon in 1984, I witnessed for the first time an exhumation at the cemetery of Avellaneda, in Buenos Aires. Shortly after the dictatorship had ended and while the country was transiting toward a frail democracy, there was a need to gather proof of violations of human rights perpetrated by the military junta. Mass graves were identified and investigated. My sister Patricia, who was and still is a member of the Argentine Forensic Anthropology Team, warned me of the spectacle that a mass grave could cause. I saw her descend into an open cavity of the earth. When she emerged, she was bringing two shattered craniums. The fractures were the evidence of how they had died, with a gunshot wound inflicted at a very short distance, execution style. The average age of the two individuals whose craniums she was collecting could have been estimated at around twenty-four years.

That is how old I was when I left Argentina in 1979.

Memory is not a privilege of only a few, but the militancy of many.

The practice of memory as a way to accomplish consciousness which attempts to accept the errors of the past to avoid worse calamities in the future remains one of the most demanding and challenging episodes in the evolution of a culture.

In recent years, buildings that once functioned as clandestine centers of detention and extermination during the military dictatorship in Argentina have been reclaimed by the relatives of the disappeared, by people who survived the imprisonment, by non-governmental human rights agencies, by poets, writers, and artists. The buildings are open to the public as centers of memory. Their open doors welcome a visitation that produces simultaneously empathy and nausea.

In 2002, I visited "el Pozo de Rosario"/"the Hole of Rosario," which had operated inside the Police Department, *la Jefatura*, centrally located in one of the busiest and most densely populated cities of the Republic. It is estimated that more than 3000 people were taken to this camp, of whom very few survived.

The building occupies the entirety of the block. There are several doors and accesses from the street into the building. Two large iron doors have been identified by the few survivors as the aperture through which trucks full of people, mostly young, would cross the frontier between outside and inside "el Pozo." Between life and torment.

I had to walk several meters inside the building until I faced the entrance of a particular catacomb, a space opening downward where the blindfolded prisoners were deposited for unpredictable lengths of time. They were tortured regularly, they were mortified at all times, and eventually groups of people were selected to be "transported," a euphemism that always meant execution.

I walked down the stairs, which were weak as if the weight of many men and women had caused a fragility that was dangerous. The space was uneven. Peculiarly shaped rooms opened to nowhere. There were blind entrances and doors that led to narrow passages. It appeared that the place was staged to produce confusion. I sat in a corner of one of the main rooms, looking around without fully comprehending what it could have been like to be a prisoner there, to hear the daily screams of the tortured inmates, to be the one tortured to the point of agony.

I reclined my back on the wall and I wept.

When I helped myself to stand up, placing my hand on the wall behind me, I noticed a thumbprint exactly in the location where my own thumb, by total coincidence, had landed. The thumbprint was almost unnoticeable until I discovered it, and then it became all that I could look at for a long time. I noticed other handprints, soft, quiet, and elusive. One of those handprints had a scratch next to it, probably done with the indentation of a nail on plaster. I could read the message: "I was here."

I was here.

I was also here, years after this person unknown to me until now was becoming part of me forever.

My hand over the disintegrating handprint of someone whose tragedy I cannot start imagining or measuring. These places of memory are places of consciousness.

The absent bodies of the disappeared are an immense archive of information preserved from degradation through the collective act of memory. Their unknown bodies have become private and public entities. Documents, photographs, literature, and art narrate the history of the *disappeared*, allowing a sculpted liaison between the vacant generation and us all, standing on this side of the abyss.

Memory is a tool to build consciousness.

We remember the disappeared. They march silently but not unnoticed. They whisper their testimonies to the realm of the living.

Art may be the only apt language for addressing genocide.

Art is a communal tool for listening.

We are listening.

Truth

The first time that I participated in an exhumation was not in Argentina. It was in El Salvador, in a distant hamlet located in the north of Morazan, where there had been a massacre in 1981. Only one survivor provided testimony. Her recounting is filled with details. Rufina Amaya Márquez, the sole survivor of the massacre at El Mozote, saw her community being divided into groups: men, women, younger women, and children. She identified a shallow hill, "Cerro de la Cruz," where the Atlacatl Battalion took the pubescent girls and young women of El Mozote to rape them, kill them, and, ultimately, burn them. Rufina saw her husband being decapitated and could identify the voices and screams of her own children before they were shot.

No one survived at El Mozote. Only Rufina, under circumstances that are nothing short of a miracle, was left to bring the truth of the inconceivable massacre of a civilian population to us. Over 1000 people perished in the massacre at El Mozote on December 11, 1981. The exhumation took place in 1992 inside a thirty-five-square-meter building known as "The Convent." The exhumations confirmed the allegation of mass murder against civilians by identifying the presence of human remains of 143 individuals, of whom 136 were children under the age of twelve, with an average age of six.

As part of the investigation and exhumations performed by the Argentine Forensic Anthropology Team in the case of the massacre at El Mozote, I created the archeological maps identifying the locations of the human remains, associated objects, and ballistic evidence found.

Until then, I had never exhumed the remains of children. Some of their bones were so frail that they resembled the bones of a small bird. Because of the young age of the victims and their multiple fractures, the remains became a fine powder, a tender sawdust at the moment they were collected from inside the tiny garments where they had been nestled quietly for more than a decade. The trace of existence would evaporate forever, and with it the last presence of this child robbed of life and future.

Memory, consciousness, the truth.

The last victim of genocide is truth.

Killing truth is not a final act.

It transcends history.

Facing truth is an act of responsibility.

The past cannot be modified. Its infinite consequences may, gently, embroider a possible future.

Art

I am an artist. My art is born from memory and loss.

I design and facilitate art in community projects in locations where there has been an armed conflict and which are transiting into the postwar period.

My art lives in the intersection of art and war.

Four kilometers away from the massacre place at El Mozote, in a small community called Perquin, in 2005, in collaboration and partnership with the community, I created the School of Art and Open Studio of Perquin, serving children, youth, adults, and the elderly. It is a community-based project that uses the strategies of art to rebuild a devastated region where the legacy of the Salvadoran civil war, 1980–92, is being followed by social, institutional, and economic collapse in the postwar period.

The School of Art and Open Studio of Perquin welcomes everyone and all members of the community, regardless of their political or religious affiliation. The curricula and public art projects are debated and designed by the community. The most popular public art interventions have taken the form of murals that narrate, like open history books, the lives and memories of the people of the north of Morazan.

It is not easy to achieve collegiality among people who have been pulled apart by local politics, by the damaging legacies of the war, and by the recent and unprecedented poverty that has been imposed as a result of the erosion of agriculture and the destruction of national industry. While the

Salvadoran currency has been the US dollar since 2001, the everyday reality shows that an average of 450 Salvadorans each day become exiles, resigned to undergo unimaginable personal and legal risks in order to find work in foreign lands, mostly in the United States.[3] The School of Art and Open Studio of Perquin is affected by the poverty and the limitations of the region. We utilize the skills of artmaking to reconstruct and to build the community. It would be imprudent to think that art can remedy tragedies. It would be untrue to suggest that art can amend conflicts; however, art as "a net of gazing eyes" may prove to be a pivotal tool to exercise and to re-establish trust among the survivors.

"Art" and "genocide" belong to fundamentally opposite paradigms. "Genocide" (*geno*, Greek: kind; *cide*, Latin: destruction) is the purposeful and effective praxis of destruction, annihilation in its most successful form. "Art" means generating from nothingness. Art exists through the conviction, praxis, and determination of the maker. Art is a tender caress of remembrance, fatigue, loss, pain, and hope, finding in the proposition of beauty its vindication. Art may not necessarily mean an improvement, but art will assist in the recapitulation of the suffering endured, transformed, and finally rebirthed as a communal proposition.

Endurable peace will never be achieved if the past is not remembered with a sense of communal responsibility that can only occur through the practice of justice. Art adds to the effort in the difficult journey of recovering memory while rebuilding a community like El Mozote, where no one (but one) survived the massacre.

One of the community leaders in El Mozote, Don Florentin, told me:

> *Aqui nos han matado la tierra. Les agradecemos a los artistas por ayudarnos a que la tierra viva otra vez.*
> Here they have killed the land. We are thankful to the artists for helping make the earth be alive again.

We painted a mural at El Mozote on the church adjacent to the convent where more than 136 children perished in 1981. The community shared dozens of meetings, diplomatic negotiations from which the collegial idea for the theme of the mural emerged. They agreed that the carnage of the

---

[3] Dorian Merina, "LA's Busy Immigration Courts Could Swell under Trump," *Take Two 89.3KPCC*, December 27, 2016 (accessed March 28, 2017), http://www.scpr.org/programs/take-two/2016/12/27/54010/la-s-busy-immigration-courts-could-swell-under-tru/

massacre would not be depicted. That was not the message to be preserved in this unique history book. The mural would represent the hamlet of El Mozote as it once was: a prosperous community of civilians who planted and harvested coffee, maguey, and corn. They made drawings of the original church and convent of a community that had lived in harmony as far back as people remembered. They had been poor, as most rural *campesinos* are, but they had not known what devastation meant until they were attacked and killed by the US-trained Atlacatl Battalion.

In El Mozote, there are people who want to remember what happened and many who would rather forget (as if one could). But they all seemed to agree that the names of the massacred children were to be preserved, together with their ages. There were over 400 children identified as victims. The names of these children and their ages, from three days to twelve years, were etched on ceramic tails that crown the south-wall mural of the church.

On December 9, 2006, during the celebration of the twenty-fifth anniversary of the massacre at El Mozote, each of the children alive today chose a name to recite, to name, and never to forget, to bring from the anonymity of death into the realm of the present.

Most people in Morazan are survivors of massacres or relatives of the victims. They would like to forget, but they know they cannot. They know they must not.

Quique was a combatant during the war. He is small and silent. He lost relatives during the war, including his son, aged eighteen, two months before the Peace Accords were signed. Quique was one of the FMLN[4] combatants identifying FMLN who entered El Mozote to bury "pieces of people" after the massacre. There were halves of bodies decomposing; it was impossible to calculate how many. Children he did not see. The ones he saw were hanging from trees, with slit throats. There were others who had been chopped up. The slaughter was brutal and the collecting of the remaining parts scattered all over the hamlet an indescribable task.

Quique has become a textile artist since the art school opened in 2005.

---

[4] The Farabundo Martí National Liberation Front (FMLN) is the guerilla organization (now a political party) that opposed the US-backed Salvadoran government during the Salvadoran Civil War.

In a recent conversation, with the caution that he always exercises, he told me: "I once changed the *cuma*[5] for an M16. Now I am changing a rifle for a loom."

The sadness of the past will never be forgotten. No one can. No one will. No one wants to do that.

There is no amendment for genocide.

Genocide needs to be stopped at all costs.

To count dead civilians in the aftermath of massacres comprises a moral, legal, political, and spiritual catastrophe.

Epilogue

The soul of the world, ephemeral and resilient, is a tender tapestry in which each thread is a voice, a hand, a song, and a memory of someone who has the right to live in dignity. On this fabric, communally, we may deposit the breath of hope.

No one deserves poverty and isolation.

No one should be unassisted when in need.

No one should be a lonely beholder of a tragic memory.

No one should carry sorrows like a wing of stone.

If we are alert enough to detect how to contribute, even in a small way, to remedying someone's misery and it is in our power to do it, we ought to try.

We simply ought to try.

---

[5] *Cuma*: a machete used for agriculture in El Salvador.

CHAPTER 12

Teaching about Torture, or, Reading between the Lines in the Humanities

Madelaine Hron

Author of Translating Pain: Immigrant Suffering in Literature and Culture *(2008), Madelaine Hron is a Professor of English and Cultural Studies at Wilfred Laurier University, Waterloo, Canada. She has published extensively on representations of human rights violations and human rights pedagogy. She is currently completing two projects on cultural representations of post-genocide Rwanda and of children in African literature and culture. In the essay that follows, Hron examines both content and pedagogy in university courses on the representation of torture in public discourse, social media, literature, and film. She argues for fostering students' imaginative, intellectual, and empathic capacities to actively and ethically witness representations of torture, and to analyze how those representations may be formulated and mobilized toward particular political ends.*

If, as Hron evinces, the failure to heed testimony is linked to the failure of imagination, then pedagogies that work against the acceptance and normalization of torture must, first, cultivate students' willingness and ability to move beyond compassion fatigue and/or simple demonstrations of sympathy and, second, must challenge popularized portrayals of the body as a reservoir of truth that may be broken open by force. To accomplish these

M. Hron (✉)
Wilfrid Laurier University, Waterloo, ON, Canada

aims, she advocates several key components of courses on literary and cultural representations of torture. Her first recommendation is for teachers to set novels, poems, plays, television shows, and other representations of torture into their institutional, historical, and cultural contexts. Close attention to context helps students to understand how torture has been a political choice, used primarily against the already disenfranchised. Second, Hron argues for a cross-genre and multimedia approach to representation, to enable students to recognize and analyze how different forms of representation shape our understanding of torture. Especially when students have the opportunity to trace representations within a single form or medium over an historical period, they can see clearly how depictions of torture relate to other ideological and political patterns.

A third recommendation is to teach challenging texts that represent torture graphically and through culturally specific symbols. Such texts ask students to learn to read how cultures create symbols; how the unfamiliar raises questions about aesthetic versus other forms of resistance to torture; how spectacularization functions in both the violence of torture and resistance to that violence; and about the ethics of reading. To balance depictions of torture that are overtly unreal, surreal, or hyperreal, Hron's fourth recommendation is for teachers to consider incorporating an activist element into their classes. Service-learning or community-based inquiry components present unique pedagogical challenges for humanities teachers accustomed to working solely with "text"; however, they also provide students with the opportunity to understand how narrative forms shape our lives.[1] Exploring diverse pedagogies is crucial, Hron concludes, if educators want to avoid invoking the specter of interrogation in their own classrooms.

* * *

It is both an honor and a daunting challenge for me—a professor in the fields of literature, film, and culture—to be invited to participate in this collection, which draws together many survivors of torture and activists

---

[1] For a compelling examination of the role of service learning and how to develop it in such contexts, the editors recommend Marike Janzen's "Experiencing Form: Service Learning in the Literature of Human Rights Classroom," *Teaching Human Rights in Literary and Cultural Studies*, ed. Alexandra Schultheis Moore and Elizabeth Swanson Goldberg (New York: Modern Language Association, 2015): 284–93.

against torture. I know that many of the pieces in this volume were not easy to write, but, rather, were born of profound pain and attest to great courage. I am fully aware that, unlike witnesses to or victims of torture who have experienced torture at first hand, I must rely on my cognitive, affective, and imaginative faculties to move beyond my position of unknowing.

Being part of this collection thus challenges me to be courageous as well. It dares me to get personal, emotional, meaningful, and even, perhaps, provocative. In other words, it urges me to move beyond bookish knowledge and secure critical distance, which are often the refuge of academics, into a more of a "stress position"—be it the space of private confession or that of public, ethical struggle. Therefore, in order to do justice to this collection, I have decided to explore the following, rather broad, yet critically important question: What does it mean for me personally, and for academics in the humanities more generally, to study or "teach [about] torture"—specifically in the fields of literature, film, and cultural studies?

The Academic as Intellectual

For me, being an academic means being a public intellectual. This belief is unquestionably shaped by my personal background: I grew up in the shadow of communism, specifically in the context of the former Czechoslovakia. The communist regime recognized that higher education was political, and, as a result, its policy was to deny any non-conforming or "suspicious" persons entry into universities, especially in the fields of the arts, humanities, or social sciences. My grandfather was a dissident, an anti-communist writer; therefore, in order to obtain a post-secondary education, my mother had to study theoretical physics, and my aunt, puppetry. For them, even these studies were political, and such maneuvering was clearly an act of resistance. I know of countless persons who studied such esoteric languages as Sumerian or Icelandic, or such disciplines as costume design or bookbinding, in order to gain entry into the arts and humanities. In his novel *Katyně*, for instance, Pavel Kohout recounts the situation of a young woman who entered the unpopular, male-dominated field of "execution studies"—or how to be an executioner—merely to pursue some form of higher education. While Kohout's example may seem extreme or unbelievable, the fact remains that in many parts of the world, university education is still inordinately valuable, if not rare, for most of its citizens—and politically charged, even dangerous, for the authorities. Yet in the West, and North America especially, post-secondary education is a rite of passage, and seems a commodity as generic as fries at McDonald's. In my classes, however, I constantly stress to my students that less than 10% of people in the world graduate with a bachelor's degree: it is thus a privilege, and even a responsibility, to be educated. I point out that so many of the persons who suffer human rights violations, such as censorship, imprisonment, or torture, are those who are educated, or intellectuals.

INTER-LEGERE AS IMAGINATION

The literary or cultural critic perhaps draws closest to what it means to be an intellectual; literally, "one who reads between the lines." As scholars, we read between the lines of fiction and reality, or between the "real world" and an imagined one. Such reading demands that we deploy our imaginations, or at least allow ourselves to be open to a space of imagination. Any thinking is an intellectual exercise which demands a leap of imagination. Making that leap means letting go of bearings, of comfort zones. I often tell my students that if they are confused, that is very good: it means that they are learning.

Similarly, I would argue that we, as scholars, should be uncomfortable, disturbed even; it too means that we are thinking—or rather, theorizing—in a space of imagination. It is only in our imaginations that we can conceive of the fictions that we read, or the other worlds and experiences that we encounter, as potentially real. It is only in this receptive and yet disquieting, self-effacing and yet vastly open, potential space of our imaginations that we can engage with the other, be it the survivor of torture or the perpetrator of atrocities. Allowing ourselves to imagine demands humility; it requires us to let go of, or at least admit to, our biases, our "comfort zones," and our errors in reasoning. Entering into this imaginative space does not preclude dismissing the partiality of the other's perspective, nor does it imply wholly dispelling our own doubt or credulity. Yet it does engage us in entertaining the possibility of another reality or an other's reality. When imagining the experiences of a survivor of torture, we are drawn into the aporetic space of atrocity, of that-which-could-have-been. In the same vein, the space of imagination allows us to conceive that-which-could-be: potential, possibilities, ideals—such as those of human rights—or future actions, including as-yet-unrealized activism.

Indeed, I am one of those optimists who believe that literature and culture can change the world. Again, my belief is shaped by my background: I have witnessed the fall of the Berlin Wall and the end of apartheid South Africa. I have seen formerly imprisoned political dissidents such as Václav Havel or Nelson Mandela become presidents. I am profoundly saddened when I consider my students' current position—will they ever see the end of the "war on terror"? Yet, even my students can observe contemporary cultural icons and activists changing the world, be it Malala Yousafzai or Craig Kielburger.

Failures of Imagination

In order to manifest the radically transformative potential of literature and culture in the sphere of lived experience and human rights, it is key to be able to imagine another reality by momentarily suspending disbelief—along with personal comfort, bias, and investment. Failures of history have been shaped by failures of imagination. In 1942, Jan Karski was smuggled into the Warsaw Ghetto and extermination camps in Belzec. He informed the British and US authorities, including President Franklin D. Roosevelt, of the mass murder he witnessed there, and the genocide that was taking place. No one he spoke to—neither government leaders, clergy of various denominations, the media, nor even Hollywood filmmakers—believed his testimony (published in 1944 as *Story of a Secret State*). Each of Karski's interlocutors lacked the imagination necessary to conceive that his testimony may have been true, and instead dismissed it as exaggeration or propaganda. Similarly, in 1947, Victor Kravtchenko published his autobiography, *I Choose Freedom*, where he described the exploitation, slave labor, and concentration camps he had witnessed in the Soviet Union. Again, his testimonial was dismissed as propaganda. In the case of Kravtchenko, skeptics lacked the imagination to consider his account because they were holding fast to their beliefs about communism. In France in particular, leading intellectuals such as Louis Aragon, François Mauriac, and other members of the *Lettres françaises* group preferred to cling to their theories and ideals, rather than to conceive of the dystopic reality disclosed by Kravtchenko.

We need not go back half a century, before the 1948 Universal Declaration of Human Rights, to witness such failures of imagination. On January 6, 1994, General Romeo Dallaire sent a fax to the United Nations (UN) Secretary-General in which he detailed his awareness of plans for a forthcoming genocide of Tutsi by Hutu extremists. Although Dallaire's observations were corroborated by an Africa Human Rights Watch report about ethnic cleansing campaigns in 1990–93, again international governmental officials dismissed the testimonial of the Force Commander in the field, and the extermination of 800,000 Tutsi and moderate Hutu in Rwanda ensued four months later.

Responding to "the testimony of one's own eyes and ears"

Today, we (ordinary citizens of a globalized, media-consumerist world) are flooded with images, reports, and testimonial accounts of suffering that might defy our imagination—if only we let them. As human rights theorist Michael Ignatieff succinctly put it, in our contemporary age, "[m]oral life is the struggle to see—a struggle against the desire to deny the testimony of one's own eyes and ears."[2]

For my students, images of suffering pose a particular problem. Numerous media theorists have pointed to the fact that human suffering has become a commodity in current global mass media: we are bombarded with a plethora of images of pain, cruelty, violence, disasters, or war, to the point that we become "voyeurs of the suffering of others, tourists in their landscapes of anguish."[3] As a result, some theorists, such as Susan Moeller, posit that as viewers we suffer from "compassion fatigue," and that our "moral fatigue and exhausted empathy is, in some degree, a survival mechanism."[4] In the light of so many shocking images, it has been argued that our cognitive processes suffer from "information overload, input overload or saturation" that trains our brains to "filter" or "tune" out disturbing images.[5] More problematically, because of the quantity of suffering we observe daily, certain forms of suffering may become "normalized" or "routine," just as we may be become increasingly "desensitized" or "psychically numbed" to certain forms of suffering.[6] As Stanley Cohen

---

[2] Michael Ignatieff, *The Warrior's Honor: Ethnic War and the Modern Conscience* (New York: Henry Holt and Company, 1997), 29.

[3] Ibid., 11.

[4] Susan D. Moeller, *Compassion Fatigue: How the Media Sell Disease, Famine, War and Death* (New York: Routledge, 1999), 53.

[5] Stanley Cohen, *States of Denial: Knowing about Atrocities and Suffering* (Cambridge: Polity, 2001), 187.

[6] Ibid., 189; 191.

notes in his seminal work on collective denial of human suffering, we are not unaware of the truth, "we are just tired of the truth."[7]

In *States of Denial*, however, Cohen also disputes many of the claims underlying the popular thesis of compassion fatigue, such as information overload, normalization, or de-sensitization. He argues that the excess of suffering in the contemporary media speaks more of "media fatigue"[8] and "compassion avoidance"[9] than it does of compassion fatigue. He argues that "the problem with multiple images of distant suffering is not their multiplicity but their psychological and moral distance."[10] Such "psychological and moral distance" may be defined as viewers' lack of identification with suffering victims, disaffection with the injustice of their plight, or inability to imagine themselves in that position.

As thinkers from Aristotle to Luc Boltanski have argued, it is only by recognizing the other as equally important to ourselves, and their sufferings as being as serious as our own, that we can cultivate an empathic response to suffering, whether shock, disgust, compassion, sentimentalism, accusation, or indignation.[11] For instance, Aristotle theorized that the feeling of compassion is aroused when: (1) we believe that a serious misfortune has befallen an other; (2) we deem this other as important as ourselves; (3) we judge that this other individual was not entirely responsible for their plight; and lastly, when (4) we apprehend that we too are vulnerable to this type of misfortune.[12] Aristotle's formulation invites us to ponder: Does our "compassion avoidance" stem from "information overload" or "media fatigue"? Or rather, does it reflect our dismissal of the other as unimportant? Or of their misfortune as insignificant? In another vein, do we (consciously or not) deem the other as responsible for their misfortune? In so doing, do we dismiss our own responsibility and complicity in relation to their hardship? Finally, and perhaps most importantly, can we imagine ourselves as vulnerable to the same types of misfortunes as those of others represented in the media?

Some two millennia ago, Aristotle posited that dramatic representations, tragedies in particular, offered a potent way to cultivate our emotions

---

[7] Ibid., 187.
[8] Ibid., 192.
[9] Ibid., 193.
[10] Ibid., 194.
[11] Boltanski, Luc. *Distant Suffering: Morality, Media and Politics.* Cambridge University Press, 1999.
[12] Aristotle. *Rhetoric.* Trans. Rhys Roberts. Internet Classics Archive.

and, as a result, our affective responses to others. Tragedies in ancient times delved into and developed diverse forms of suffering, elaborating in detailed performances the human experience of the sufferer. Audiences of these dramatic performances would learn to identify with kings and paupers alike, while coming to better understand the motivations and complexities of tragedies as grievous as parricide or infanticide. Because they identified with both victims and their hardships—in a performance that enabled them to vicariously share in their stories—audiences would be emotionally affected and socially sensitized. Of course, theater today has lost its celebrated place in the public forum; instead, television and the internet are flooded with still photos of suffering or brief news reports about others' misfortune, but rarely do we take the time to vicariously share in the experience of others, albeit in our imagination.

In line with Aristotle, Cohen suggests that, in order to curb the effects of compassion avoidance, the viewer must get closer to subjects in pain—by learning more about their stories.[13] Similarly, Ignatieff posits that the minimal requirement to engage with others' suffering is to spend time with them, to have "enough time to pierce the carapace of self-absorption and estrangement that separates us from the moral world of others."[14] Ignatieff suggests that, instead of merely switching channels or skipping over the headline, we literally need to take time to listen to the testimonies of others, or even work to learn more about their situation. Taken on a figurative level, Ignatieff's exhortation invites us to spend time thinking about the situation of others, visualizing it and experiencing it, in the space of our imaginations.

Seeing critically, reading carefully, writing thoughtfully, or thinking reflectively—in all, spending time imagining the experience of others—can thus perhaps lead us to greater understanding of and concern for their life experiences. When reading in particular, we spend time with the suffering subject; we learn of the many sources and circumstances of their condition. In our imaginations, we are invited to share vicariously in their trials and to feel their pain. Therein perhaps lies the ethical value of literature: it offers an intimate, inventive way of sharing the imagined life of another human being, and so may lead us to greater consciousness and responsiveness to social concerns around us. When reading, we are invited to conceive of others' experiences and others' worldviews, as well as of the

---

[13] Ibid., 196.
[14] Ignatieff, *The Warrior's Honor*, 29.

conditions that shape their lives. The imaginative process of reading fiction therefore increases our historical and cultural knowledge, as well as nuancing our preconceived moral standards, by exposing us to ethical ambiguities and complexities. Finally, reading—or vicariously experiencing the world of others in the realm of fiction—encourages us to reconsider our relationship, response, or even responsibility toward others in the "real world."

FAILURES OF IMAGINATION IN THE ACADEMY

For me, as a teacher and scholar of literature and culture, disciplinary and pedagogical constraints pose a particular problem when I attempt to teach my students to "read between the lines," or when I study human rights in the humanities in my research. Academic units in the university such as the French department or Cinema Studies are often more interested in national, linguistic, or disciplinary boundaries, or accepted canons, genres, current theories, or aesthetics, than they are in shaping ethical values, developing imaginations, or critically reflecting on "real-life" issues, as manifested in current cultural production. I cite but one example of such a failure of imagination: once, in an English job interview, I was asked to point to a "torture text" that I might use in class. I made the mistake of referring to Dostoyevsky's *The Brothers Karamazov*. In this literary classic, hero Ivan asks his brother Aloysha whether he would torture one small child if it would result in the restoration of eternal happiness on earth. In my reply I referred to some of the ethical issues that Ivan's question raises, issues that Chilean writer and human rights activist Ariel Dorfman himself recently engaged in an op-ed entitled "Are There Times When We Have to Accept Torture?" My interviewers were not impressed—did I expect English students to read a long Russian novel in translation? Or a newspaper column by a South American critic? Was I suggesting that my class would engage with ethics? Or "just the moral question of torture"? Clearly, my interlocutors lacked a certain imagination; just as they were not able to picture English students reading a Russian novel or learning from a Chilean activist, similarly, they were unable to conceive of the deeper social justice implications raised by a text, because they were so concerned by its aesthetic value or its pedagogical role in the British literary canon. Rather, more resembling interrogators, they were only interested in certain truths—truths that legitimate and perpetuate the existing order—be it reigning theories, canonical texts, or, more conventionally, the disciplinary order of things.

Bookstores are brimming with testimonials and documentaries which could challenge my students' imaginations as much as Karski's or Kravtchenko's accounts (e.g., Jean Hatzfeld's *Machete Season*, which contains his interviews with Rwandan genocidal killers; Anna Politkovskaya's *A Small Corner of Hell*, about Chechnya; Francis Bok's *Escape from Slavery*, about modern slaves; or Jen Marlowe, Aisha Bain, and Adam Shapiro's *Darfur Diaries*, which showcases testimonials by survivors of the genocide in Darfur). Similarly, films, television, and the internet abound with videos and images of torture, testimonials and affidavits by survivors, as well as numerous legal documents which directly comment on the aesthetics, practices, and institutionalization of torture in contemporary culture. However, these texts would be easily dismissed in, for example, a traditional English department, as they do not strictly reflect the parameters attached to canonical English literature as "practiced" in the contemporary English department—limited to texts written in English; to literature, privileging fiction in particular, the genre of the novel especially (as opposed to other literary, cultural, or media forms); or reflecting current literary theories, such as postcolonialism. Sadly, students graduating from such a traditional English department would likely never put any such literary works into their virtual shopping cart, nor would they have the necessary frameworks to analyze these testimonial, non-fiction, documentary, or "pop culture" examples critically in "real life."

Engaging with such topics as torture in current cultural production therefore demands that one transcend the disciplinary rigidity and scholarly comfort zones that reflect the failure of imagination in certain institutions of higher learning today. Such study demands interdisciplinary scholarship; it requires an unmooring of generic categories; and it calls for an interpolation of diverse theoretical frameworks. Such scholarship should necessarily relate to and engage with "real-life" issues, and thus should prompt, if not encourage, diverse forms of activism. In so doing, it also invites difficult questions, often with complex ethical implications, which relate to both the institutionalization and the praxis of torture, as well as discourses and practices within the academic institution.

TORTURE AND TEACHING AS INSTITUTIONALIZED PRAXES

It is thought-provoking to compare the practices of teaching and torture. Fundamentally, both of these practices are institutional praxes, meaning that they are applications of knowledge performed within established institutions of power. In so doing, both may serve power, they may reproduce or reflect discourses of power, they may operate to maintain and affirm the status quo, or they may function to legitimize and sanction particular abuses of power. As teachers, we should perhaps ask ourselves: To what extent do our curricula or syllabi serve power? Do we work to replicate and perpetuate dominant discourse, or do we, even if unwittingly, preserve the status quo? How might we in fact be enabling abuses of power, either explicitly or implicitly?

Moreover, both of these praxes operate by disciplining the body and mind to be docile, compliant, and conformist, so as to be—ironically—as productive, efficient, and useful as possible within the social order. I like to remind my students that in the nineteenth century, when schooling became mandatory, schools largely functioned to prepare children for shift work in factories. The main purpose of obligatory elementary schooling was to train children's bodies to sit quietly for hours on end, to teach children to respond positively to authority figures, directives, and regulations—in all, to socialize the young to accept an environment of bells, breaks, supervision, automated movements, and rote repetition, so as to more effectively prepare them for their future role as compliant and productive factory workers. In light of this institutional history, it behooves us to ask: What has changed in our contemporary educational system? What role, for instance, is there for the body, instinct, or emotions in the classroom? Is the teacher–student relationship one of blind obedience to authority? Do current schools operate on a model of expediency, efficiency, and productivity? Are contemporary schools merely a training ground for future passive conformity, regulated automation, and deference to institutionalized power?

Manifestly, since I have been allowed to both study and teach such eclectic topics as torture at universities that either I have attended or have employed me (University of Michigan, Carnegie Mellon University, Wilfrid Laurier University), my experience gives evidence to the fact that pedagogy has evolved since the nineteenth century, and that not all educational institutions are concerned with conformity, efficiency, and productivity. Currently, I work in an English and Film department where I am largely free to teach on topics, texts, and scholarly values of my choosing, including courses on torture.

What differentiates my department from others? Most basically, I am fortunate to be in a department where I am valued as an individual, respected as a scholar and a teacher, and listened to and trusted, even when I was still a junior colleague. When I proposed a course on torture, under the rubric of human rights, there was some discussion as to the enrollment in such a course, its structure and thematics, and its function and value in terms of the discipline and curriculum of Literary/Film Studies. Yet, despite their initial reservations, my superiors decided to take a risk and run the course as a "special topic" course. In other words, the administration risked failure: that the course would be under-enrolled; that students would drop out; that they would be dissatisfied; or that they would learn nothing of merit within the current landscape of literary studies. In the end, however, the course was a success. Students found it both valuable in terms of Literary/Film Studies and meaningful in terms of their personal development, as attested by their student evaluations. To again credit my current institution, the administration then heeded these student evaluations, and allowed me to "regularize" this special topic course—to make it a regular offering. That being said, the course description is appended with the caveat: "note: some of the texts may be in translation or subtitled," which highlights my course's non-conformity with other courses in my monolingual English and Film department.

Based on this brief history, let us consider some of the paradigms that are key to changing established institutional practices within an academic context. First, we note the administration's respect of the individual, the capacity of its members to listen to non-conforming points of view, and their ability to imagine other ways of doing things. Second, we observe these same administrators' ability to take a leap of faith and to risk failure, and so to set aside ideals of progress, utility, productivity, or efficiency. Finally, we see that, ultimately, they both recognize *and* take seriously the community they serve.

By contrast, none of these paradigms is present when we consider the institutionalization and praxis of torture. Under an administration that practices torture, there is manifestly no respect of the tortured individual, nor any place for dissenting opinions, differing worldviews, or other *modus operandi*. Rather, every suspect is mistrusted, deemed a threat, and part of a larger menacing system or worldview. Wherever torture is practiced, everything works according to "standard operating procedures" under the pretext of efficiency, utility, and necessity in support of spurious ideals of progress. Torture procedures are deployed, we are told, precisely as measures to minimize risk to ("legitimate") citizens—risks of bombs, attacks, and other life-threatening maneuvers—and to prevent and circumvent the failures of other, more benign, disciplinary institutions, such as those of legal courts or the prison system. Just as administrations which institutionalize torture show no respect for the individual, they completely dismiss the voice of the community whom they purport to serve. If the public voices its opposition to torture, all too often democracy and its ideals do not prevail.

Torture as a Historical and Cultural Praxis

Let us now turn from the institution to the classroom, and from institutional failures to teaching possibilities. In so doing, let us consider some of the potential modules and outcomes of teaching about torture in Literature, Film, or Cultural Studies. What may be some of the lessons that students learn in humanities courses devoted specifically to the subject of torture?

The primary objective of such a course on torture is manifestly to make students aware of the multiple manifestations of torture, as an established practice, throughout the world and throughout history—both in material terms and in contemporary cultural representations. Most students beginning my class have a fuzzy understanding of torture as socio-cultural or historical praxis. When I initially ask what "torture" connotes to them, they immediately refer to medieval torture instruments, the electric chair, or "waterboarding"—in other words, they associate torture with the *techne* or apparatus of torture. Interestingly, when I ask them to cite instances of torture in literature or film, their answers are markedly similar: they recall particularly memorable torture techniques, such as Daniel Craig's carpet torture in *Casino Royale* (2006) or George Clooney's fingernail torture in *Syriana* (2005). In these initial discussions, my students' responses reflect the representation of torture in Hollywood films or on cable TV,[15] where many of them have gleaned most of their understanding about torture. Most of these representations focus on the encounter between an individual torturer and the individual he is torturing, emphasize the information extracted (or not) as the only "context" for the act of torture, and celebrate the instrument or method of torture in achieving one's goals. In other words, like the majority of mainstream media, students rarely contemplate the institutionalization of torture by different regimes of power; they rarely evoke the purpose of torture in different

---

[15] Throughout this essay I make various remarks about torture in current Hollywood films. For more elaboration, see my article "Torture Goes Pop!" in *Peace Review* 20, no. 1 (Spring 2008): 22–30.

historical, political, or cultural contexts; and they rarely draw attention to the terror of victims under torture or the trauma of survivors after torture. Finally, they rarely make apt correlations between "real-life" torture and fictional representations of torture. Yet all of these dimensions are ones that I then further develop and elaborate on in my classes on torture.

Even when I teach torture as a unit in a broader course on human rights, I provide my students with a sound understanding of the historico-cultural evolution of torture. Concomitantly, I also draw parallels, often anachronistic ones, to current cultural representations of torture. For instance, I refer back to the use of torture in the Roman Empire, where torture was not only legal, but a customary part of juridical procedures. In the case of slaves and non-Roman citizens, only testimony obtained under torture was considered valid in court. Yet already in Roman times there were opponents to such uses of torture: Cicero, for instance, eloquently argued that since under torture anyone would confess to anything, confessions arrived at under torture were most likely fallacious (e.g., *Pro Cluentio*). More importantly, in ancient Rome we see that torture operated according to differentials of class, gender, and ethno-nationality: only slaves, women, and foreigners could be tortured, while Roman citizens could not.

It is interesting to note that these differentials still hold fast two millennia later, as reflected in current media representations of torture. For example, we are not surprised that it is the Chinese who torture Jack Bauer in *24*. It is as generic as the North Koreans who torture James Bond in *Die Another Day*, the Cardassian and Borg who torture Jean-Luc Picard in *Star Trek*, or the Nazi dentist torturer in *Marathon Man*. As for female torture victims, we can turn to whole film genres, such as 1930s–1950s Hollywood films about Asians, horror films (*Death-Proof*, *Captivity*, *Turistas*), and television crime series such as *CSI*, *Law and Order*, and *Criminal Minds*, which regularly depict the torture, death, and maiming of nubile young women, as was the custom from ancient Rome to the witch-hunts of the Inquisition and the Puritans.

In the Middle Ages, we see another shift in the interpretation and practice of torture. During the Inquisition, the purpose of torture was not merely to gather evidence for juridical proceedings—it also became a means of attaining existential truths about faith, and of testing a believer's acts of repentance, conversion, and redemption. Tortured individuals had to repent and renounce all of their previous false beliefs and then affirm a new set of beliefs, beliefs that supposedly would assure them everlasting salvation. This conversion, or transformation, took place through a prescribed form of inquiry—the interrogation session—which was based on the question (*questio*) and the confession (*confessio*). This "epistemology of discovery"[16] aimed to arrive, ultimately, at the truth—the truth of who God was, whether Catholic or Protestant, whether one was saved or one was damned, and whether God was, or was not, on the side of institutionalized power. In the Catholic Inquisition, truth was thus equated with torture, and torture with conversion or transformation, wherein heretics would confess the one true faith and be saved for eternity.

Again, we see these outdated cultural assumptions reflected in contemporary representations of torture. The climactic fifteen minutes of current TV crime shows almost always culminate in a successful confession from the "bad guy." On television and in film, interrogation therefore almost always works; it operates as an effective, expedient procedure to gather information and arrive at the truth. Moreover, the torture of a "good guy" is often portrayed as a transformational, if not educational, experience wherein he gains added power and insight; his faith and mettle are tested, and he emerges unscathed, if not strengthened, by the ordeal of torture. Again, this brings us back to outdated representations of torture; for instance, in medieval plays a saint would not renounce her faith, even under torture. To exemplify: in the tenth-century play by German-born nun Hrotsvitha of Gandersheim, *Sapientia; or, The Martyrdom of the Holy Virgins Faith, Hope, and Charity*, three faithful and chaste virgins remain physically and emotionally unscathed by the tortures they suffer; on the contrary, their faith and resilience are only strengthened by their torturous agonies, which include boiling pitch and wax. Likewise, in current media, heroes such as James Bond, Jack Bauer, and Jason Bourne, or heroines such as Sydney Bristow from *Alias*, Stella Bonasera from *CSI: NY*, or Olivia Benson from *Law & Order: Special Victims Unit*, are all tougher and smarter because of the torture, captivity, and abuse they have endured. And none of them "confessed." In TV or films, confession is reserved for the "bad guys" who have erroneous cultural or political beliefs, or for "weak guys" who betray their beliefs through their confession.

---

[16] Hansen, 54.

Exposing the Secret: Torture Today in Fact, Language, and Representation

Manifestly, one of the main objectives in a class on torture is to reveal the secret torture practices perpetrated today. The practice of contemporary torture relies on secrecy and invisibility, on its ambiguous position both within and outside the law. Even in the barbaric medieval past, when official torture was routinely practiced, torture manuals insisted on the secrecy of torture procedures (such as in the *Malleus Maleficarum*, one of the best-known manuals for hunting witches). In our "enlightened" contemporary age, torturers are similarly specifically trained to inflict pain without leaving any proof of their crimes (as in the *KUBARK Manual*, the 1963 Central Intelligence Agency [CIA] interrogation training manual). Although today torture is officially illegal in most countries—since 132 countries have ratified the United Nations Convention against Torture (1984)—in 2016 alone, Amnesty International documented cases of torture in 122 countries worldwide.[17] In the United States, of course, torture surreptitiously became legalized and legitimated by crude instrumentalist and utilitarian theories as a routine "state of exception" under the auspices of the "war on terror."[18]

In my classes, I seek to expose current torture practices as violations of national and international law, as well as ethical and moral failures; in so doing, I also impel my students to examine the not-so-secret justifications, institutionalized rationales, and socio-cultural assumptions that enable torture to continue to be practiced in both democratic and undemocratic societies today. In so doing, we critically analyze representations of torture in various cultural forms, from legal documents to fictional narratives, so as to investigate both the functions and the effects of various contemporary discourses of torture.

Evidence of torture pervades contemporary cultural representations. Just as the practice of torture takes place throughout the world—in sites such as Bagram, Guantánamo, Khaim, Evin, Camp 22, and countless

---

[17] Amnesty International, *Amnesty International Report 2015/16: The State of the World's Human Rights* (London: Amnesty International Ltd., 2016), available online at https://www.amnesty.org/en/latest/research/2016/02/annual-report-201516/

[18] For instance, at the time of writing, American Republican nominee Donald Trump is advocating returning to waterboarding and inventing torture techniques that are "worse than waterboarding" to fight the "war on terror." Trevor Timm, "Donald Trump's Anti-Terror Policies Sound a Lot Like War Crimes," *The Guardian,* July 1, 2016.

unnamed cells and prisons—representations of it can be found in fiction, art, films, documentaries, weblogs, legal reports, and formal memos. Therefore, in creating my course, I seek to expose my students to the broadest range of torture texts possible—including, for instance, canonical literary novels (Orwell's *1984*, Coetzee's *Waiting for the Barbarians*), lesser-known plays (Alleg's *La Question*, Pinter's *Mountain Language*), Hollywood films (*V for Vendetta*, *Death and the Maiden*), art (Goya's or Botero's paintings), TV shows (*24*, *Boston Legal*), documentaries (*The Road to Guantánamo*), affidavits (B'tselem, Khulumani Support Group), legal documents (United Nations Convention against Torture, or UNCAT), as well as, of course, testimonials (Ortiz's *Blindfold's Eyes*, Partnoy's *Little School*, Begg's *Enemy Combatant*). In so doing, I not only want to challenge my students to understand torture in different geographical, historical, and cultural contexts, but also—particularly salient in a humanities classroom—to compel students to think about the ways in which genre, language, and aesthetics shape, limit, or challenge our understanding of torture.

As I teach in a literature department, my classes focus heavily on language: we explore how language may serve to enable or to disable the praxis of torture. For instance, my students are exposed to legal language, which is often dismissed or glossed over in traditional literary studies. By studying legal documents, memos, or speeches, students learn to discern how torture may be concealed and justified by legal jargon or by political rhetoric, just as it can be revealed and resisted in declarations or manifestos by activists. Through examining legal affidavits by torture survivors, perpetrators, and medical personnel—which stress facts, events, actions—students come to understand how torture can be stripped of its painful affective dimensions, just as through analyzing the language of torturers—characterized by neologisms, euphemisms, litotes, or ellipses—they learn how torture can be inveigled, distorted, and authorized in language.

Many of our class discussions revolve around the translation of torture—a language of pain and emotions—into the language of words, stories, or images. In order to better understand how the terrorizing event of torture or its lingering trauma may be communicated, we analyze a variety of texts—interviews, documentaries, testimonials, fiction, poetry, essays, art—by survivors of torture, as well as by writers, artists, and activists against torture (much like the diverse selection represented in this book). As Elaine Scarry has powerfully argued in her seminal study *The Body in Pain: The Making and Unmaking of the World*, the excruciating pain of torture resists language itself. Moreover, as she explains, those who have experienced the pain of torture are certain of their experiences; those who have not, however, are in doubt, and therefore must be convinced of the pain of torture. Thus, evoking torture always necessitates some form of persuasion, or rhetoric, which is conveyed either with linguistic devices, narrative patterns, or visual imagery. In class, therefore, we examine some of the more generic rhetorical and narrative models of representing torture—for instance, we delve into the genre of the interrogation or the confession—while also trying to understand more individual, artistic, or cultural representations of torture. We spend much time deliberating how torture can be fictionalized, either in literature, on film, or in visual representations. In the end, however, I work to bring all of our analyses of fiction back into the real world: we critically analyze the rhetoric, import, effect, and potential of these texts in relation to current events, popular culture, and, most importantly perhaps, in the light of collective and personal activism.

TORTURE CULTURE, AMERICAN STYLE

Given the current institutionalization of torture in the United States, it is also now more crucial than ever for me to teach my students how to read "between the lines"; that is, to learn to critically recognize the institutionalization of torture in American popular culture. Alas, such "low" or pop cultural texts are sometimes also dismissed in humanities classrooms or relegated to the domain of "cultural studies." Yet pop culture examples demonstrate most clearly that torture has long been part of the American imaginary and popular discourse.

Photographs released in April 2014 from Abu Ghraib prison in Iraq perhaps best demonstrate the intimate link between "real-life torture" and "pop culture." I remember when the photos were first made public on television,[19] in newspapers,[20] and on websites worldwide—many people were shocked by these images of naked Iraqi prisoners in demeaning sexual positions or garbed in wires and hoods, and of triumphant American soldiers posing near corpses. At the time, I helped with the "Inconvenient Evidence" installation at the Warhol Museum, which exhibited these

[19] The Abu Ghraib photographs first aired on April 28, 2004 on CBS's *60 Minutes II*.
[20] For example, new photos from Abu Ghraib appeared in *The New Yorker* (May 10, 2004: 42) and *The Washington Post* (May 21, 2004: A01; June 11, 2004: A01).

photographs. Many visitors expressed their shock and outrage at seeing them—yet, more often they were horrified by their graphic sexual imagery than they were indignant about what they signified. Moreover, since some of the perpetrators were from Pennsylvania, some viewers refused to acknowledge the "torture" in these images (like George W. Bush, they called it "abuse" by a "few bad apples") or they found excuses for these crimes.

The Abu Ghraib images were indeed shocking—in their symbolic value. For the first time, exhibited publicly, flaunted for the entire world to see, was incontrovertible visual evidence of torture. As I have mentioned, torture is an art usually practiced in secret. Perpetrators have never before publicly circulated visual evidence of their crimes. Yet these images provided overwhelming irrefutable evidence of torture by the American government, a practice deemed illegal by the United States when it ratified UNCAT. More suggestively, these images offered irrefutable visual evidence of secret practices of torture that human rights scholars and activists had been condemning for decades—be it in Latin America, in Israel, or at the School of the Americas in Fort Benning, Georgia.[21]

Yet when considered in the context of popular culture, the Abu Ghraib photographs are perhaps not as shocking. Sexual in nature, they remind us more of amateur internet pornography than they do of crimes, matters of state, or interrogational proceedings. When we contemplate why these photo-trophies were circulated, we cannot but think of "happy slapping," the practice of recording assaults by camera phone, so that they can later be watched and disseminated for entertainment. We cannot help but compare these images to the torture we may see on screen, in films, and on TV.

Torture is, after all, a commodity, if not a cliché, in contemporary popular culture. Porn websites are laden with sexualized images of torture, as are mainstream films. In horror films such as *The Texas Chainsaw Massacre*, *Saw III*, and others, torture loses its political connotations, and becomes pure fear, commodity, and spectacle. The horror movie *Hostel* makes this point clear: it revolves around customers on vacation who pay to torture people to death—torture has become sheer entertainment and "fun." As

---

[21] Renamed the Western Hemisphere Institute for Security Cooperation, the SOA had trained nearly 60,000 graduates in torture, execution, and extortion techniques, including such dictators as Manuel Noriega and Omar Torrijos of Panama, Leopoldo Galtieri and Roberto Viola of Argentina, Juan Velasco Alvarado of Peru, Guillermo Rodriguez of Ecuador, and Hugo Banzer Suarez of Bolivia.

this film figuratively suggests, participating in torture—albeit vicariously in our imagination as viewers—has today become a form of enjoyment, leisure, or recreational activity. As the flurry of such films attest (*Hostel I–IV*, *Hard Candy*, *Death Proof*, *Turistas*, *Captivity*), the torture horror-porn or "torture chic" genre has most certainly become a mainstream, desirable commodity.

Manifestly, this "torture chic" genre hardly reflects real political torture, characterized by the fact that in order to "rise to the level of torture," acts of brutality must be performed "in an official capacity" (UNCAT). Yet its gore, and its trivialization and the sexualization of torture, clearly relates to Abu Ghraib. What is more perturbing, political torture has also become somewhat of a cliché in current media representations. In certain cases, political torture represents a convention, if not a stereotype, of the genre. In the action film genre, for instance, such as James Bond movies, torture is almost a necessary part of the plot. We are thus not surprised that, in *Die Another Day* (2002), Bond is tortured during the opening credits as we munch on our popcorn: in the action genre, torture is precisely as lackluster a requirement *as* the credits.

It is salient to explore the ways in which political torture has been redefined in popular culture since Abu Ghraib—or since torture has been normalized in US political discourse. In older films and television shows (e.g., *Marathon Man*, *Death and the Maiden*, *Star Trek: Next Generation*), it is clear, for instance, that torture is always performed by the "bad guy," and that torture never leads to any information, confession, or truth. However, more recently, TV "good guys," those "all-American heroes," have taken up torture as a legitimate form of action (e.g., *Law and Order* Detective Joe Fontana, *Alias*'s Jack Bristow, *24*'s Jack Bauer). Notably, most of the award-winning show *24* centers around the "ticking bomb" theory, which rationalizes torture as a necessary evil given impending danger and limited time constraints. What is more, as I have already mentioned, on today's TV shows, torture almost always works; torture is depicted as an expeditious and efficient means of gaining information, confessions, and sometimes even justice. The film *V for Vendetta* goes a step further: it suggests that the heroine *must* herself experience torture in order to achieve an inner transformation and gain an unrivaled power of resistance as a revolutionary. In so doing, much like the tortured "good guy" heroes in today's blockbuster films and TV shows, this film, purportedly about activist resistance, also returns us to medieval notions of torture as "conversion" and "truth." Sadly, only a few of these popular representations are concerned with the human rights dimensions of torture. As Denny Crane quips in *Boston Legal*'s "Guantanamo by the Bay" episode: "This is America. Human rights are so yesterday here."

Imagining More

A class about torture, of course, involves more than teaching students about the ways in which cultural representations reflect, reproduce, or critique discourses about torture. Rather, it seeks to challenge or resist the reigning status quo about torture, and about those involved in it—be it as perpetrators, victims, bystanders, or activists—by cultivating students' imaginations. Students are invited to imagine more—by opening themselves to larger ethical questions, broader human rights concerns, other cultures, new aesthetics, and perhaps even novel forms of activism.

For instance, the aforementioned passage in Dostoyevsky's *The Brothers Karamazov* compels students to consider under what conditions they might torture an innocent human being, just as the rat scene in Orwell's *1984* urges them to think about what would make them break under torture.[22] Similarly, reviewing the UN Human Development Report or UNCAT definitions of torture might lead to a discussion about the relationship between torture and other forms of violence, such as rape or domestic abuse, just as reading Edwidge Danticat's *The Dew Breaker* might incite a reflection between torture and socio-economic or cultural human rights violations.

For me, a teacher of literature and culture, what is perhaps most perturbing about torture is the cultural destruction it implies: destruction perpetrated *upon* and *by using* the language, values, and bodies—often gendered, racially, or ethnically marked bodies—of "others." When viewing the images from Abu Ghraib, for example, I am deeply disturbed by the use of nudity, sexuality, or sodomy; these practices clearly counter traditional Islamic values. The use of dogs or prisoners-on-leashes-as-dogs is similarly deeply degrading in Arab Muslim societies, where dogs are

---

[22] In the climactic scene of *1984*, Winston is tortured by what he fears most—in his case, rats. Moreover, during his torture session, he develops a twisted relationship with his torturer O'Brien, and thus betrays his love, Julia. In class, this scene can be used to ask students a number of thought-provoking questions: about what their possible behavior in a totalitarian system might be; about their fears, loyalties, and beliefs; about the dynamics of the tortured/torturer, or about the dependency/betrayal that a torture session educes.

considered *haram*, unclean and defiled. Clearly, American oppressors are employing cultural values and signifiers to destroy their victims here.

It is perhaps not surprising that torturers are well trained to understand the cultural contexts of their victims—paradoxically, so as to destroy them. After all, the ultimate purpose of torture is to shatter the very essence of what it means to be human. Culture, in many ways, shapes our humanness, our worldviews, and our relationships to others, as community. Therefore, cultural destruction is one of the central paradigms of torture, since it enables the destruction of the essence of the human within.

Reading texts from disparate cultures, however, often draws attention to the powerful potential of creative languages of resistance against such cultural destruction. Nowhere is such resistance more evident than in Réza Barahéni's *Les Saisons en enfer du jeune Ayyâz* [*The Infernal Days of Aghaye Ayyaz*] or Gérard Étienne's *Le Nègre Crucifié* [*The Crucified Negro*], perhaps two of the most graphic of contemporary torture texts, and both written by survivors of torture. Alas, neither of these texts is readily available in English translation, perhaps because of their violent aesthetics and complicated cultural symbolism.[23] In his Joycean opus, Barahéni employs the historical and mythical figure of Ayyaz to both resist and reveal the cultural domination and depravity of theocratic totalitarian Iran under the Shah. Similarly, in *The Crucified Negro*, Étienne deploys the cultural language of Haitian voudou to counter the neo-colonial violence of the Duvalier regime. Both of these texts prove very difficult for my students to read—both because of the complex cultural translation they must perform and the torturous position they must inhabit; that is, the position of the resistant torture victim expressed in a violent, if not grisly, stream-of-consciousness style. However, engaging with such difficult, uncomfortable texts compels students to think about the possibilities and limits of aesthetic, cultural, and even violent resistance. Some questions these texts may raise in class include: What is cultural resistance? And aesthetic resistance? Are these forms of resistance inextricably linked? When does resistance become violence? When are forms of resistance effective? When, on the contrary, might they serve to obfuscate, or even conceal or subvert, the issue at hand? What role must we as readers, or critics, take on to learn to better understand cultural, aesthetic, or violent forms of

---

[23] Barahéni's Persian text has only been translated into French; however, an English chapter from his book "The Dismemberment" can be found in *God's Spies*, ed. Albert Manguel (Toronto: Macfarlane Walter & Ross, 1999).

resistance? What ethics of reading must we, as individuals, espouse when addressing texts about torture?

I never fail to stress to my students the power of individuals (e.g., Dr. Inge Genefke, Sergeant Joseph Darby, and many writers and activists, including those in this collection) and of communal action (e.g., PEN, World Organization Against Torture [OMCT], Amnesty International) to incite change, as far as the practices and legitimacy of torture are concerned. In the humanities, for instance, it is crucial to note that one of the most influential, widely circulated contemporary academic discourses—postcolonial studies—was largely founded on the work of Frantz Fanon. Fanon's canonized classics (*Black Skin, White Masks*; *The Wretched of the Earth*) were largely written in response to his experiences as a psychiatrist in Algeria, where he treated victims of torture—mostly Algerian independence fighters, but, significantly, also their French torturers. Many of the notions circulated in contemporary academic discourse, therefore—from "internalized oppression" to "decolonization"—stem from Fanon's observations of the traumatic *sequelae* of torture. In the "real world" outside the bounds of the academy, Fanon's works have inspired anti-colonial liberation movements in Africa and all over the world for more than four decades.

Most of my classes, then, include the opportunity for students to participate in some form of activism, be it individual or group projects, wherein they draw upon their class knowledge to engage in "real-life" applications. In the past, students' projects have included art or photography displays, awareness-raising videos, information kiosks, surveys, interactive online sites, and even concerts, theater performances, demonstrations, and sit-ins. For instance, one student created a "choose-your-own-adventure website," which then analyzed each participant's character and the type of activism most suited to them. In another class, students staged a "Gitmo show" on the university's main concourse, in which they filmed students' reactions to the performance and urged them to sign petitions and letters to stop the practices of torture perpetrated there.

Academic Praxis and Torture?

Finally, as I myself have attempted to demonstrate in this reflection, my classes also invite my students to consider possible connections between the praxis of torture and that of academic scholarship. If we open our imaginations, we realize that perhaps there are many intimate, revealing, and complex links between the reality of torture and the fictions we choose to believe, be it in books and films, or in scholarship and pedagogy. Throughout this essay, I have alluded to various such links between torture and teaching as institutional praxes, between torture in cultural forms and political processes, or even between narrative tropes, like the confessional or the interrogation, in fiction and in real-life applications of torture. However, many further links are possible, if only we engage our imaginations, and read between the lines.

Torture, like academic discourse, is a modern exercise.[24] As such, it claims to serve a purpose. From ancient to contemporary times, we are told that "torture is the inquiry after truth by means of torment,"[25] it serves "to elicit truth,"[26] "to gather evidence for juridical proceedings," or "to extract information in matters of state."[27] When we stretch our imaginations a little, to consider the *telos* of torture in the light of academic discourse, we might reflect on the following: What is the purpose of academic research? Or pedagogy? What "information" or "truths" do we seek to gain in the university environment?

More specifically, the alleged purpose or *telos* of torture is to gather "intelligence," information, or the "truth," as efficiently as possible. If the tortured subject does indeed confess to such information, such knowledge only incriminates him or her, and can serve to justify further punishment. Though the correspondences may be tenuous, we, as teachers, should perhaps nonetheless ask ourselves: Does punishment or self-incrimination play any role in our classroom? How do we gather information in our classrooms—do we attempt to arrive at answers as quickly and efficiently as possible? What information or truth do we, as teachers, seek in our classrooms? In our curricula? How, in fact, do we define "intelligence"? Does an intelligent response merely reproduce established facts, anticipated answers, or correct interpretations? Or does intelligence entail "reading between the lines," in ambiguities, in complexities, in the space of imagination and invention, or even in as-of-yet-unformulated thought or action?

---

[24] For more, see Michel Foucault's *Discipline and Punish: The Birth of the Prison* (New York: Pantheon Books, 1977).

[25] Azo, thirteenth century CE, quoted in Barry Allen, *Truth in Philosophy* (Cambridge, MA: Harvard University Press, 1993), 21.

[26] Ulpian, third century CE, quoted in Edward Peters, *Torture* (Philadelphia, PA: University of Pennsylvania Press, 1985), 55.

[27] Ibid., 3.

In contrast to teaching, of course, the praxis of torture utilizes the *techne* of physical pain, punishment, interrogation, censorship, social isolation, and a wide variety of reprehensible disciplinary and corrective measures that violate human dignity to force the individual to comply with figures in authority and discourses of power. While hopefully such measures are never deployed in a classroom, still we might ask ourselves if we might not see some correspondences. For instance, as teachers, we might consider what role we grant "pain" in the classroom: How do we, as teachers, deal with negative emotions that may arise in class, such as discomfort, anger, or anguish? What punitive measures do we take when attempting to establish order, correct students, or discipline those who do not heed the rules? Do our class discussions ever sound like interrogation sessions—do we expect a particular answer to our questions? Or do we censor non-conformist responses? Or, in confessional mode, do we wait for students to confess their lack of knowledge or their disregard of established rules?

More pertinently perhaps, torture, like academic discourse, revolves around language. Torturers inflict severe pain on the victim in an effort to force them to divulge information—to confess, to betray their own language, or to disown the language of their community—and thus to surrender to the language of the authorities. Again, we may ask: What is the role of language in academic discourse? Does it serve to censor and betray one's personal experience or the communal language of an "other"? Or does it serve to conform or to perform, by circulating theories, institutional categories, or pedagogical practices? Bringing my argument back to communism, I cannot help but wonder: Does academic criticism enable democracy? Or rather, with its focus on established disciplines, curricula, and theoretical currency, does it censor difference? Does it replicate totalitarian structures under the auspices of rationalism, efficiency, and ideas about learning?

Discursively, both torture and academic discourse function according to the most basic of dialogical principles—the question and the answer. The question serves to test, to dispute, and often, ultimately, to destroy. The answer: to belie, to betray, and, ultimately, to condemn. Again, we may ask: What types of dialogical relationships do we create in our classrooms or in our research with our students, our colleagues, or the "real world"? How do we frame the research questions we pose—do they merely serve to deconstruct, criticize, or condemn? Or do they seek to connect, create, affirm?

Torture also involves feeling, or the manipulation of feeling. In the torture room, the victim of torture, subjected to excruciating pain, is reduced to pure sensation. After the torture session and then years later, the traumatized survivor continues to experience numerous conflicting emotions. Torture activists are motivated by affect as well, ranging from sympathy to indignation. Yet ironically, the practice and legalization of torture rely on the anesthetization or elimination of feeling. Today's torture victims are exposed to "sensory deprivation"—rendered extraordinarily sensitive to temperature changes and light or noise exposure. According to US policies during the "war on terror,"[28] the only pain deemed "severe" enough to be considered torture is manifestly "organ failure, death, loss of significant body function"—in other words, the inability to feel anything at all. Discursively, the pain of torture is supplanted with the need for critical "information" or "confessions"; the sensorial experience of torment is rationalized away with "ticking bomb theories" or "exceptional circumstances," "the state of war [on terror] or the threat of war [terrorism]."[29] We, the public, witness to repeated acts of torture, are asked to embrace these rational, logical arguments—instrumentality, necessity, or expediency—rather than to rely on our natural feelings toward human suffering, which might lead us to react against the authorities, as activists.

And in the academy, what role does feeling play? What function does affect have in academic criticism or in the university classroom? In many ways, academic discourse stifles feeling in favor of critical distance and objective rationalization. Students new to my classes are sometimes disconcerted by a question I often ask: "How did the text make you feel?" While my students are quick to cleverly point out the ways the text relates to such-and-such theory or such-and-such style, sadly they often do not know how to identify or describe the emotions they feel, let alone begin to theorize them. Academic theory still lacks the critical vocabulary to discuss the emotions we so often experience when reading or viewing texts; approaching texts with any "reader-response" framework is largely undervalued in the critical discourse of the humanities. Ironically, scholars persistently

---

[28] US Department of Justice Office of Legal Counsel, "Memorandum for Alberto R. Gonzales Counsel to the President, Re: Standards of Conduct for Interrogation under 18 U.S.C. §§ 2340–2340A," August 1, 2002, available online at https://nsarchive2.gwu.edu//NSAEBB/NSAEBB127/02.08.01.pdf

[29] UN General Assembly, *Convention against Torture and Other Cruel, Inhuman or Degrading Treatment or Punishment*, December 10, 1984.

theorize such concepts such as "compassion fatigue," "information overload," or "psychic numbing"—and yet, we still remember best those books and films that move us the most. As numerous theorists have pointed out, the feelings stimulated by books, theater, art, or film—be they feelings of sympathy or indignation—may have the power to compel us to action, often beneficial action that ameliorates the lives of others.[30]

IMAGINING HUMAN RIGHTS AS MAINSTREAM

As a teacher and scholar of human rights, I must conclude with optimism. After all, that is what my job, and my position as an intellectual, demands: I imagine the potential of more. My optimism is fueled by the recent interest in human rights in the humanities, torture included, as manifested in special issues in various journals,[31] and in the publication of edited collections such as this one. I firmly hope that the essays and testimonials contained within this collection will be circulated in humanities classrooms, that they will bring new insights into academic research, and even that the feelings they provoke will serve to incite change in the real world. Therein lies the challenge for me—to include collections such as these, as mainstream texts, in humanities classrooms so as to teach and study torture, as a mainstream topic, in humanities curricula. Only then do human rights stand a chance of becoming a mainstream practice in our world today.

---

[30] See, for instance, Luc Boltanski's *Distant Suffering: Morality, Media and Politics*, trans. Graham Burchell (Cambridge: Cambridge University Press, 1999), or chapters 6–8 in Martha C. Nussbaum's *Upheavals of Thought: The Intelligence of Emotions* (Cambridge: Cambridge University Press, 2001), or her widely circulated article "Cosmopolitan Emotions," in *New Humanist: The Bimonthly Journal of the Rationalist Press Association* 116, no. 4 (2001). Or going back to the 1670s, Gotthold Ephraim Lessing, a major dramatist of the German Enlightenment, developed a theory of "tragic pity" [*tragisches Mitleid*], in which he argued that the goal of tragedy was to transform "passions into virtuous capacities" (quoted in H. B. Nisbet, *Gotthold Ephraim Lessing: His Life, Works, and Thought* [Oxford: Oxford University Press, 2013], 402).

[31] *See*, for instance, *PMLA*'s Special Issue on Human Rights 121, no. 5 (Fall 2006); the *South Central Review*'s Special Issue on Torture 24, no. 1 (Spring 2007); or the *Peace Review* issue on Human Rights in Literature and Film 20, no. 1 (Spring 2008).

CHAPTER 13

Legal Appeal: Habeas Lawyers Narrate Guantánamo Life

Terri Tomsky

Terri Tomsky, Assistant Professor of English and Film Studies at the University of Alberta, focuses her current research on the figure of the enemy combatant in contemporary narratives of global terrorism. In her contribution to this volume, she looks specifically at the role of habeas corpus attorneys for detainees at the US Guantánamo Bay Naval Base. In addition to providing legal representation for detainees who argued against their unlawful detention, the lawyers functioned as proxy witnesses by providing first-person accounts of detainees whose identities and voices were otherwise largely barred from the public sphere by government security guidelines. Reading the lawyers' writings in the edited collection The Guantánamo Lawyers: Inside a Prison Outside the Law (2009), Tomsky considers their work as proxy witnesses in the narrative context of autobiography and lawyerly professionalism.

This chapter commences with an overview of the popularity of personal narratives among the reading public and the role of those narratives in human rights advocacy. Although the Guantánamo lawyers produced such personal narratives in place of advocacy efforts on behalf of specific clients,

T. Tomsky (✉)
Department of English & Film Studies, University of Alberta,
Edmonton, AB, USA
e-mail: tomsky@ualberta.ca

the lawyers frame their own and their clients' stories with broader questions of international jurisprudence and the search for justice. More specifically, attorneys' reference to the centuries-old habeas legal tradition situates their concerns in the law's longue durée, thereby calling upon juridical tradition and professional values in order to depoliticize their contemporary arguments. Tomsky further suggests that by addressing readers as citizens through a moral appeal to the principles of law and justice, the lawyers, perhaps surprisingly, reassert US leadership in human rights causes.

The lawyers' testimonies constitute a public defense of their work as well as a peek behind the curtain purposefully drawn by the US government to obscure such questionable detention facilities as Guantánamo and other "black sites" around the world. The Guantánamo Lawyers *includes short revelations of detainees' lives, and those revelations emerge from within the regime of censorship that governs all speech produced at Guantánamo (GTMO). Analyzing these depictions, Tomsky identifies three ways in which the book functions as form of non-legal witnessing: (1) it represents the detainees as material and legal subjects who should have the right of habeas corpus, in the context of the state's denial or obstruction of that right; (2) it depicts the material conditions of detainees in language that skirts GTMO's censorship regime; and (3) it presents the authors' own legal work as contributing to rather than in opposition to US patriotism. With close attention to the rhetorical and literary strategies the lawyers employ, Tomsky demonstrates how these first-person accounts provide a moral and abstractly legal critique of the conditions of detainees. The focus on morality and justice creates space for the assertion of the lawyers' own professional conduct within a sphere of American "values," thereby lamenting the lapse of those values at Guantánamo Bay without addressing the political will that made it possible.*

* * *

Life narratives—in both their act of witnessing and their circulation—have belatedly become an important resource in the constitution of knowledge about the detention camps established at the US Naval Base in Guantánamo Bay, Cuba, in January 2002. I say belated because, for the first two years after the camps opened, such narratives were simply not available. Like the identities of the prisoners, the writings were considered classified information by the US authorities, viewed as integral to national security.[1] Until such writings began to surface, the dominant narratives about the Guantánamo experience were filtered through the official channels of the George W. Bush administration (2001–2009). From a legal perspective, the incarcerated individuals were deemed "unlawful enemy combatants," who could be held indefinitely without charge, let alone trial. This designation allowed US authorities to argue that the Geneva Conventions did not apply, that these alleged "armed non-state actors," captured in Afghanistan or Pakistan, engaged in terrorist activities against the United States.[2] Alongside legal discourse, White House officials strove to represent these figures in their public speeches. President Bush described them as "bad men" and Secretary of Defense Donald Rumsfeld called them the "worst of the worst."[3] Media images from the early years of Camp Delta and Camp X-Ray appeared to support that script. Telephoto lenses which captured distant images of orange-jumpsuited men surrounded by chain-linked fences, razor wire, and large numbers of security personnel remained for some time the only images of what quickly became the world's most infamous prison. The prisoners' simultaneous high visibility and inaccessibility encapsulated the exceptionalist logic that authorized the detention of so-called hardened terrorists within the new war declared against "terror."

This hegemonic representation of enemy combatants was eventually contested by the emergence of witness testimonies, life narratives, prison memoirs, and poems produced by or on behalf of these prisoners.[4] Marc D. Falkoff, a criminal lawyer and a Professor of Law at Northern Illinois

---

[1] In his anthology, Falkoff writes: "many of the detainees' poems were destroyed or confiscated before they could be shared with the authors' lawyers. The military, for instance, confiscated nearly all twenty-five thousand lines of poetry composed by Shaikh Abdurraheem Muslim Dost" (*Poems*, 4). Additionally, most poems cleared by the Pentagon were English translations only, since the "original Arabic or Pashto versions represent[ed] an enhanced security risk" (ibid., 5).

[2] Anicée Van Engeland, *Civilian or Combatant? A Challenge for the Twenty-First Century* (Oxford: Oxford University Press, 2009), 121.

[3] Donald Rumsfeld has described the prisoners as the "worst of the worst" (Mark P. Denbeaux and Jonathan Hafetz, eds. *The Guantánamo Lawyers: Inside a Prison Outside the Law* (New York: New York University Press, 2009), 167, 311); George W. Bush used the phrase "bad men" about the Guantánamo prisoners in a 2003 press conference.

[4] See Barbara Harlow, who provides a detailed review of the "ever-expanding Guantánamo bibliography [...] of Guantánamo personnel, the camp's prisoners, their comings and (for some, at least) goings, their stories (life stories) that prevailing US policy has persistently,

University who has represented seventeen Guantánamo prisoners in habeas suits, points to the importance of such personal writing. Reflecting on his decision to edit and publish a collection of poetry written by Guantánamo prisoners and translated into English, Falkoff insists upon the "importance—and utility" of the poems in relaying the experience of dehumanization and challenging the normative articulations of the war on terror.[5] In other words, he sees these new texts making a significant intervention because in this "war," language itself remains a contested site. Political theorist Fred Halliday has explored how the neologisms of the war on terror played a significant role in shaping and controlling political events, as the Bush administration instrumentalized words to euphemize and justify the treatment of prisoners.[6] Guantánamo detainees, for example, were not being tortured, but rather subjected to "enhanced interrogation techniques."[7] Such evasive language helped screen not only Guantánamo's human rights violations, but also the desperation of the prisoners. Successful suicides at the prison were redefined as "asymmetric warfare" and so transformed into acts of war.[8] The military personnel at Guantánamo described suicide attempts as "acts of manipulative self-injurious behavior" or "hanging gestures," while a hunger strike was construed as a "voluntary fast" in order to depoliticize and undermine the protest efforts of prisoners.[9]

Against the military's ability to detain and stifle prisoners, we can see the efforts of lawyers to provide the Guantánamo prisoners both with a voice and with legal representation. This chapter examines the first-person accounts of attorneys, the so-called "Guantánamo Bar," that detail their experience as advocates working on behalf of designated enemy

---

consistently, sought to suppress" ("'Extraordinary Renditions': Tales of Guantánamo, a Review Article," *Race & Class* 52, no. 4 [2011]: 2).

[5] Marc D. Falkoff, "Conspiracy to Commit Poetry: Empathetic Lawyering at Guantánamo Bay," *Seattle Journal for Social Justice* 6, no. 1 (2007), 5.

[6] Fred Halliday, *Shocked and Awed: How the War on Terror and Jihad Have Changed the English Language* (London: Tauris, 2010), xii.

[7] Scott Allen et al., *Leave No Marks: Enhanced Interrogation Techniques and the Risk of Criminality* (Washington, DC: Physicians for Human Rights & Human Rights First, 2007), 2.

[8] Marc D. Falkoff, "This Is to Whom It May Concern: A Guantánamo Narrative," *DePaul Journal of Social Justice* 1, no. 2 (Spring 2008), 170.

[9] Ibid., 171.

combatants.[10] In their professional capacities, these lawyers have been instrumental in creating public awareness of Guantánamo and its contraventions of the rule of law. The chapter investigates the political function of their personal narratives, an opportunity for the lawyers to advocate in a very different way, in the proverbial court of public opinion through human rights networks. While not direct witnesses to the alleged abuses at Guantánamo, many of these attorneys nevertheless feel confident enough to present themselves on the world stage as both legal and moral authorities, not only presenting the "facts" but also extensive commentary upon human rights violations and the larger issue of how justice operates.

I seek to understand these lawyers' autobiographical narratives within the larger context of the "memoir boom" in the Anglophone world. As Julie Rak has observed, since the early 1990s, tens of thousands of memoirs by celebrities and unknown people have been published, sold, and read by millions of readers in the United States alone.[11] Part of the public's increasing interest in memoirs is linked to a fascination with the "real," especially major historical events of which personal witness accounts of suffering are emblematic. As Kay Schaffer and Sidonie Smith have argued, personal narratives are often taken up within international human rights campaigns and circulate as commodities: "a potent and highly problematic form of cultural production, critical to the international order of human rights and movements on behalf of social change."[12] Taken together, such texts contribute to what Schaffer and Smith elsewhere identify as an "evolving human rights regime."[13] This regime, Schaffer and Smith argue,

---

[10] Denbeaux and Hafetz, *Guantánamo*, 19. Many of these lawyers filed habeas appeals on behalf of their as-yet-unknown Guantánamo prisoners, whom they had not yet met. This posed specific challenges, not least getting the information about their names (from a variety of sources, including charities, non-governmental organizations, the media, families, etc.) and then having to obtain consent from their clients in a "closed" site that was not accessible without a high level of security clearance.

[11] Julie Rak, *Boom! Manufacturing Memoir for the Popular Market* (Waterloo: Wilfrid Laurier Press, 2013), 8–14. For more details of the "memoir boom," see also Leigh Gilmore, "Limit-Cases: Trauma, Self-Representation, and the Jurisdictions of Identity," *Biography* 24, no. 1 (2001) 128; Kay Schaffer and Sidonie Smith, *Human Rights and Narrated Lives: The Ethics of Recognition* (New York: Palgrave Macmillan, 2004), 13–20.

[12] Schaffer and Smith, *Human Rights*, 31.

[13] Schaffer and Smith, "Venues of Storytelling: The Circulation of Testimony in Human Rights Campaigns," *Life Writing* 1, no. 2 (2004), 4.

is produced dialogically between, on the one hand, "storytelling" and, on the other, "human rights platforms, discourses, and campaigns."[14]

As some of the Guantánamo lawyers themselves work within those same human rights networks, they certainly were well aware of the tactical uses of the autobiographical form. My argument builds upon the way these legal advocates leverage the genre of the personal story in order to campaign against perceived systemic injustice. In representing Guantánamo's atrocities to a larger public, their autobiographies appear as what Gillian Whitlock calls "soft weapons." Whitlock, implicitly building on Joseph S. Nye's concept of soft power, uses this phrase to suggest the political possibilities of life narratives, which can make "powerful interventions in debates about social justice, sovereignty, and human rights."[15] In Nye's account, "soft" power famously stands in contrast to "hard" military force: but, as Nye affirms, it "is not merely the same as influence [… and it] is more than just persuasion."[16] The distinction between the two definitions is pertinent to my argument: where Whitlock identifies the rhetorical power of life narratives, Nye emphasizes that soft power is "*attractive* power."[17] It enables desired outcomes not so much through castigation, critique, protest, or shaming, but rather through hope and idealism. As Nye puts it, "attraction often leads to acquiescence."[18] In the following, I examine how lawyers advocate through their personal stories not so much for their particular clients, but more for the *principles* of the law. Toward the end of this chapter, I explore how their advocacy appeals directly to an explicit American patriotism that interpellates readers as responsible citizens. American patriotism is central to the *appeal* and *attraction* of the attorneys' advocacy: in promoting a return to the rule of law, the attorneys simultaneously project a return to a moral authority that would reposition the United States as a "leader" in human rights practices.

---

[14] Schaffer and Smith, *Human Rights*, 5.

[15] Gillian Whitlock, *Soft Weapons: Autobiography in Transit* (Chicago: University of Chicago Press, 2006), 3. Whitlock also cautions that these narratives can be used to uphold propaganda and so are complicit in the "careful manipulation of opinion and emotion in the public sphere and a management of information in the engineering of consent" (3).

[16] Joseph S. Nye, "Soft Power," *Foreign Policy* 80 (Autumn 1990): 153–71.

[17] Ibid.

[18] Ibid. In contrast, Whitlock notes how life narratives produce a rhetoric of intimacy and "peaceful coexistence" (172), or empathy, particularly through "an exotic engagement with the Arab world" (95).

Since at least 2002, Guantánamo lawyers have been publishing and publicizing (through promotional lectures and events) autobiographical accounts about their legal involvement with the military prison complex. The "Guantánamo Bar," which is made up of about five hundred lawyers from various backgrounds,[19] from large corporate firms, the public sector, and academia, and at various stages of their careers, has taken on the *pro bono publico* work of habeas appeals for the Guantánamo prisoners. While not all attorneys involved with Guantánamo have written about their experiences, those who have published their first-person narratives have done so in many forms, including memoirs, personal essays, at least one diary, scholarly commentaries, newspaper op-eds, an electronic archive of lawyers' reflections, and a published anthology of personal stories. My chapter concentrates on the 2009 anthology *The Guantánamo Lawyers: Inside a Prison Outside the Law* (hereafter *The Guantánamo Lawyers*), edited by Mark P. Denbeaux and Jonathan Hafetz. This collection of short personal stories about Guantánamo has contributions from 113 American lawyers and covers the earliest legal interventions in 2001 (the filing of a Freedom of Information Act request to determine the identity of the prisoners) to the continued habeas appeals in 2009. Initially, the marketing "hook" for these narratives was their ability to penetrate the highly securitized space of Guantánamo—until then an inscrutable spectacle—to map the physical and social geographies and to reveal the myriad people and animals populating its grounds. For example, Denbeaux and Hafetz emphasize in their introduction this special privilege of access:

> lawyers remain the only people other than government officials and representatives from the International Committee for the Red Cross (who are bound to confidentiality) to see or speak to the Guantánamo detainees.[20]

Consequently, in contrast to prisoner testimonies, the eyewitness accounts of former guards,[21] and the carefully orchestrated visits of press representatives and public officials,[22] these lawyers' accounts function as a

---

[19] In his memoir, Stafford Smith estimates that the Guantánamo Bar consists of "almost five hundred lawyers" (*Bad Men*, ix). It is probable that this number has since increased.
[20] Denbeaux and Hafetz, *Guantánamo*, 2.
[21] For example, see Cucullu, *Inside Guantánamo*: a prison memoir about Cucullu's experience as a guard, which reads like an inversion of the prisoners' testimonies.
[22] Clive Stafford Smith, *Bad Men: Guantánamo and the Secret Prisons* (London: Weidenfeld & Nicolson, 2007), 172–74. Stafford Smith calls these "propaganda tours" (172).

counter-narrative by "outside" experts with "inside" access to the prison. Their status as lawyers adds a layer of authority that serves to corroborate the accounts of the Guantánamo prisoners. This is significant when considering the stigma and suspicion that linger around the prisoners themselves, even those who have been released without charge (most, for example, remain on the US government's "No Fly List"; many cannot be repatriated to their country of origin; all face skepticism, both about why they ended up in Guantánamo in the first place and as possible Muslim extremists, radicalized by their incarceration).[23] In contrast, the attorneys draw authority and legitimacy by emphasizing their *professional* loyalties to the law, above all. While bound by client confidentiality as well as by US censorship rules, the attorneys affirm over and over their commitment to the "rule of law" rather than to any partisan cause.[24] The valorization of the law frames their narratives as "the objective arbiters of a rights claim," whose own professional standing "determine[s] the truth-value of the testimony" of their clients.[25]

The attorneys' adherence to legal principles in general, and to habeas corpus rights in particular, suggests that they seek to move away from the broader (and fuzzier) concept of "human rights," and to reference instead a much more conservative tradition. Habeas corpus (Latin for "you shall produce the body") originates in the Magna Carta and represents "the single most important check against arbitrary and unlawful detention, torture, and other abuses" in the Anglo-American legal system.[26] With the weight of a 700-year history behind them, habeas cases assert the

---

[23] Jennifer Caseldine-Bracht, "Security, Civil Liberties and Human Rights: Finding a Balance," in *Guantánamo Bay and the Judicial-Moral Treatment of the Other*, ed. Clark Butler(est Lafayette, IN: Purdue University Press, 2007), 61.

[24] Perhaps for the reason of deflecting accusations of partisanship, the lawyers in Denbeaux and Hafetz's anthology almost uniformly refrain from describing the Guantánamo inmates as "prisoners," and instead elect for the less politicized (Bush euphemism) "detainee." I should also add that the Guantánamo lawyers too are subject to security clearance, monitoring, and censorship by the Pentagon. Denbeaux and Hafetz include a section in their anthology on this process: "Barriers to Representation" details the classification of the lawyers' meeting notes and client communications at Guantánamo. The material is not allowed to leave the prison; it is reviewed and, if approved, is sent on to a "secure facility" in Florida or in Washington, DC, where the lawyer has to go to access his or her notes, which are often redacted (*Guantánamo*, 109–30).

[25] Schaffer and Smith, *Human Rights*, 36.

[26] Jonathan Hafetz, *Habeas Corpus After 9/11: Confronting America's New Global Detention System* (New York: New York University Press, 2011), 6.

fundamental right to judicial review; habeas writs do not discriminate—"its protections have been invoked by common thieves and alleged enemies of state alike"—to ensure the lawful basis of a detention, by providing access to the judicial courts.[27] In the case of Guantánamo, habeas writs insist on the state's accountability and so challenge the "shadowy, global gulag of secret interrogation prisons" of the war on terror, where otherwise the "extravagance of violence" can continue unimpeded.[28]

Given the initial failure of the state to produce, in the form of criminal or even military trials, the bodies of Guantánamo detainees, many lawyers fought to produce their testimonies.[29] In the context of Guantánamo's secrecy, its military censorship, and the classification of most documents—including the notes the attorneys make within the prison—the lawyers frequently argue that access to information about *what* is occurring inside the prison complex is critical. For attorneys seeking to publicize evidence that their clients were not only being illegally imprisoned but were also being abused by the US military, prisoner testimony was key. Thus, lawyers like Falkoff operated as intermediaries, translating (in the fullest meaning of that concept, "a bearing across") the words of their clients to a global audience.[30] In Falkoff's case, these testimonies took the form of poems written by detainees—placing them in the long tradition of prison poetry that includes the writing of Bobby Sands of Northern Ireland's Provisional IRA. These poems, with their emphasis on the "I" of the narrating subject, described the experience of torture and trauma in deeply expressive terms and so supplied, in Falkoff's terms, "an opportunity for empathy."[31] Framed as a witnessing project, they are driven by the imperative to *show* a public the effects of imprisonment at Guantánamo on the human subject. In detailing the prisoner's suffering and fear of indefinite detention, they are "soft weapons," in Whitlock's version of the term.

[27] Ibid., 83.
[28] Anne McClintock, "Paranoid Empire: Specters from Guantánamo and Abu Ghraib," *Small Axe* 13, no. 1 (2009), 51.
[29] Military commissions were established at Guantánamo in November 2001; however, even military lawyers have called these commissions "rigged" (Denbeaux and Hafetz, *Guantánamo*, 173). Prisoners could only be defended by military-appointed defense council, the commissions used torture testimony as evidence, and the charges were often based on classified information (which was denied to both the prisoner and his lawyer).
[30] Yet this layer of mediation is further complication by the fact that most Guantánamo prisoners do not speak English. Denbeaux and Hafetz's anthology speaks to the importance of interpreters by including a subsection about their role (*Guantánamo*, 103–108).
[31] Falkoff, "Conspiracy," 6.

That is to say, the poems "describe experiences of unbearable oppression and violence across a cultural divide."³² In this mode, the Guantánamo poems viscerally capture the experience of the prisoners, humanizing these mostly Muslim men who are otherwise unheard and yet vilified in a western, public context.³³ The political threat of this endeavor is confirmed by the military officials' ongoing confiscation of the poetry written by the detainees. As Falkoff explains in his anthology, poetry was viewed as a "'special risk' to national security because of its 'content and format.'"³⁴

In the face of Guantánamo's increasing censorship, when even the poems of the prisoners were being prohibited, the personal narratives of lawyers themselves began to take on a special significance. Their stories about their time in Guantánamo, whether describing their attorney–client relationship or detailing the complex processes of security clearance to travel to Guantánamo to access their clients, reveal a larger perspective upon how a prison like Guantánamo continues to operate. With an eye to their implied audience, the lawyers critique the conditions *they*—as well as their clients—face. They list the material impediments and systemic resistance—both bureaucratic and ideological—to their work, and so make available a new set of information to the public (details that would be excluded or discounted within the juridical process). The discursive representation, in other words, supplements the legal work of representation. The British civil rights attorney Clive Stafford Smith declares this outright in the preface to his 2007 memoir, *Bad Men: Guantánamo and the Secret Prisons*: "Greater justice has been achieved for the Guantánamo prisoners in the courts of public opinion than in the courts of law."³⁵ Similarly, Falkoff recognizes the limits of the law and the need "to think creatively [...] outside of the boundaries we have defined for ourselves as lawyers."³⁶ Earlier, Falkoff praises the law as a narrative, specifically as a "drama" that "plays out [as] the defendant's story gets told [...] in legal briefs, supplemented by oral argument before a judge and the public."³⁷ However, this

---

[32] Whitlock, *Soft Weapons*, 56.

[33] Whitlock also uses the phrase "soft weapons" to call attention to its ambivalence: the "double-edged nature" of testimonial life narratives that, while poignant and powerful in their representation of oppression, "can be harnessed by forces of commercialization and consumerism in terms of the exotic appeal of cultural difference" (56).

[34] Falkoff, *Poems*, 7.

[35] Stafford Smith, *Bad Men*, x.

[36] Falkoff, "Conspiracy," 11.

[37] Ibid., 11.

narrative potential is foreclosed since legal appeals were met by at least two challenges: first, the closed military tribunals at Guantánamo, which ratified the status of prisoners as "enemy combatants" in order to prevent habeas rights; and second, the delaying tactics produced by the Pentagon's "bureaucratic maze" and its "calculated inefficiencies."[38] As Falkoff explains:

> not a single one of our clients has had his day in court [...] after six years of litigation, our clients continue to be denied access to the courts and the natural and appropriate venues in which to air their stories. We have been forced by necessity to find alternative ways to speak out, to assert our clients' innocence, and to affirm their essential humanity.[39]

These personal narratives about Guantánamo then provide one such "alternative" method. Their autobiographical act constitutes a challenge to what one attorney terms the "passage of time [...] GTMO's strongest ally."[40] Forming an elaborate paratext to Guantánamo's prisoner testimonies, the attorneys' personal narratives represent a call for public scrutiny of a dysfunctional judicial system. For example, a number of these personal stories appeared *after* the landmark 2004 Supreme Court ruling in *Rasul v. Bush*. This ruling upheld constitutional protections and asserted that Guantánamo prisoners had habeas rights. As Denbeaux and Hafetz's anthology demonstrates, the government initially ignored the ruling, and it "would take several years and three Supreme Court decisions for the United States... [for it] to begin to comply."[41]

I see the attorneys' personal narratives advocating strategically in at least three ways in response to the inadequacy of actual legal representation and the broader politicization of this *pro bono* legal work, which was publicly attacked as jeopardizing national security.[42] First, in their nonlegal narratives, the lawyers mediate the voices and experiences of their

---

[38] Denbeaux and Hafetz, *Guantánamo*, 42, 137.
[39] Falkoff, "Conspiracy," 11–12.
[40] Denbeaux and Hafetz, *Guantánamo*, 136.
[41] Ibid., 33.
[42] As one lawyer notes, the "fight for habeas has been as much a *political* struggle as a legal one, as the Republican-controlled Congress tried not once but twice to overturn the Supreme Court's decisions and strip federal judges of jurisdiction over the detainees' cases" (ibid., 200). Many lawyers received hate mail and death threats (ibid., 31). This vilification was prompted by Elizabeth Cheney's 2010 advert campaign, "Keep America Safe," against the "Al-Qaeda Seven," members of the Guantánamo Bar (Laurel E. Fletcher, Alexis Kelly,

clients. As habeas lawyers—who physically and legally represent their clients—there is a symbolic, if discursive, re-enactment that places the prisoner's body before the reader and, by extension, a public. Lacking the materiality of habeas corpus, the text fails to produce the actual body, but presents a *representation*, a signifier for the absent body that lacks its most fundamental rights. Second, the lawyer's discursive representation of events reveals the acts of concealment at Guantánamo, including not only the level of censorship, bureaucracy, and petty punishments by authorities, but also the physical condition of the prisoners. Denied access to prisoners' medical records, the lawyers instead write about the black eyes, bruises, and scars on the wrists of their clients, markers of guard brutality and prisoner desperation.[43] We can observe a proxy witnessing in these accounts, as representations of the prisoners' emaciated and battered bodies make visible the system of abuse at Guantánamo. Indeed, the notion of a public is critical to the efficacy of the law. As one contributor to the *Guantánamo Lawyers* anthology, a former judge, makes clear: the "program of torture [...] had to be carried out in places where the law and the public were both excluded."[44] Third, lawyerly self-representation challenges the vilification and smear campaigns to discredit their work as so-called "terrorist" or "al-Qaeda" lawyers.[45] The safeguarding of the rule of law in offshore sites like Guantánamo, in other words, is about holding the state to account and calling attention to the transgression of civil liberties. In these life narratives, the habeas work of US lawyers is regarded as an act of patriotism, what a number of them have called "*honorable advocacy.*"[46]

The legal frameworks of these life narratives invoke a particular social capital—the expertise, status, and presumed objectivity of the lawyers—

and Zulaikha Aziz, "Defending the Rule of Law: Reconceptualizing Guantánamo Habeas Attorneys," *Connecticut Law Review* 44, no. 3 [February 2012]: 624–26).

[43] Falkoff, "This Is to Whom," 173. One lawyer, Joshua Colangelo-Bryan, saves his client's life when, literally minutes after meeting with his client, he walks into the cell and finds him hanging by a makeshift noose, with his "body and face [...] covered in blood" (Denbeaux and Hafetz, *Guantánamo*, 285). After "months [... and] a fair amount of wrangling," Colangelo-Bryan receives the declassified suicide note, which is personally addressed to him (ibid., 287).

[44] Denbeaux and Hafetz, *Guantánamo*, 35.

[45] David J. R. Frakt, "Lawfare and Counterlawfare: The Demonization of the Gitmo Bar and Other Legal Strategies in the War on Terror," *Case Western Reserve Journal of International Law* 43, no. 1/2 (2011), 338.

[46] Benjamin Wittes, "Presumed Innocent?" *The New Republic*, March 24, 2010.

that shores up the aim of such narratives as a testament, "a historical record of Guantánamo's legal, human and moral failings."[47] The narratives, however, are animated by the personal motives, values, and loyalties that reorient the endeavor to challenge Guantánamo via the patriotic self. The genre of the personal or life story is important in this regard, since it puts emphasis on the authentic and is invested in the notion of representation as Truth. This presumed veracity helps explain the special role of life narratives as a "primary tool" of human rights campaigns.[48] Clive Stafford Smith, who has given public talks on the human rights circuit and is the founder of Reprieve, a charity that helps prisoners in the United Kingdom secure the right to a fair trial, draws on this real-life experience to authorize his account of Guantánamo. His memoir repeatedly reiterates his "practical experience in the *realities* of interrogation" and his "*real-life* experience."[49] It is not only what the attorneys see and experience, but also what they write about the prisoners in their legal notes that signifies their professional and authorial credibility. As one attorney explains, "notes [...] are our first tools for making our clients into real people. If we want their voices to be heard [...] we have to write down what they say."[50]

Certainly, a fuller picture of the prisoners emerges in Denbeaux and Hafetz's anthology, which includes the attorneys' meetings with their clients: Afghans, Pakistanis, Uighurs, Syrians, Bahrainis, Saudis, Britons, Algerians, Bosnians, Yemenis, Sudanese, Uzbeks, Tunisians, and Tajiks, imprisoned in Guantánamo.[51] Yet, unlike the lawyers, these prisoners are not like the anthology's implied reader. Instead, there is a distance set up between the representation of the prisoners and the American audience. Many of the accounts relate how initially the prisoners are presented as "superhuman" villains; the guards warn the lawyers that the prisoners will "gnaw the hydraulic wires of a C-17 transport plane," "lunge" for the throat, and shower them with "feces cocktails."[52] This rhetoric magnifies

---

[47] Denbeaux and Hafetz, *Guantánamo*, 5.

[48] Joseph R. Slaughter, *Human Rights, Inc.: The World Novel, Narrative Form, and International Law* (New York: Fordham University Press, 2007), xiv.

[49] Stafford Smith, *Bad Men*, 35, 41.

[50] Denbeaux and Hafetz, *Guantánamo*, 120.

[51] There was also an Australian, a Canadian, and a Somali held at Guantánamo. US citizens accused of terrorism—John Walker Lindh and Jose Padilla—were not held in the Cuban prison.

[52] Denbeaux and Hafetz, *Guantánamo*, 57, 70.

the prisoners; in the reality described by the attorneys, the prisoners are diminished, broken men: "weeping," "cowering," "as a caged bird," and "emaciated" from their hunger strikes.[53] The attorneys describe the prisoners in terms very close to those in which Julia Kristeva has theorized abjection, to indicate their "fragile states" and their "radical exclusion."[54] Based upon their meetings, the attorneys represent the prisoners as deeply traumatized. To give examples from three separate accounts, we are introduced to one client who "kept his hands in his face and didn't say a word"; another client "simply has worn down"; while a third finds he cannot talk about his experiences as "his voice broke and his eyes filled with tears."[55] These kinds of descriptions are manifold, amplifying the collective suffering of the prisoners. They highlight the prisoners as objects of pity, with despair inscribed in their weakening bodies, reflecting what one attorney describes as Guantánamo's "climate of despondency and hopelessness."[56] A vicarious traumatization emerges from these meetings, but it is rooted in shame or an affront to one's ideals.[57] One lawyer finds that her Guantánamo work causes her "grief"; yet it also represents a form of "solace," a symbol for the "fight for the soul of [her] country."[58] For another lawyer, the prison represents a limit experience that exceeds her ability to rationalize events: "when I contemplate the unthinkable human cruelty of Guantánamo […] I have no frame of reference for this point."[59] Another lawyer is "overwhelmed by a sense of loss" when she learns about her deceased client, a Guantánamo prisoner whom she has not yet met.[60] Her feelings about the incident—including the possibility of its prevention had she seen her client, as well as her anger over the mystery surrounding the "circumstances" of the death—motivate her "continued involvement" at Guantánamo.[61] Such personal stories affirm the anthology's purpose: that

---

[53] Ibid., 99, 81, 159, 275.

[54] Julia Kristeva, *Powers of Horror: An Essay on Abjection*, trans. Leon S. Roudiez (New York: Columbia University Press, 1982), 12, 2.

[55] Denbeaux and Hafetz, *Guantánamo*, 236, 240, 253.

[56] Ibid., 264.

[57] A number of the attorneys are haunted by what they see and experience in Guantánamo (ibid., 145, 198).

[58] Ibid., 26, 27.

[59] Ibid., 279.

[60] Ibid., 25.

[61] Ibid., 25.

it puts a "human face on what had previously been a legal issue."[62] Certainly, the reader learns a great deal about the thoughts and feelings of individual lawyers, so gaining insight into their need to mediate the voice of their clients; and yet, such a focus, at times, overshadows the abject prisoners, whose very helplessness implies lives that have already been forfeited.

As the full title of Denbeaux and Hafetz's anthology suggests, *The Guantánamo Lawyers: Inside a Prison Outside the Law* centers on a group of American lawyers who have mobilized to protect the rule of law.[63] The self in the personal narratives is an emphatically American self, who is personally repulsed by a vision of the United States' "moral failings [...] disdainful of its own best traditions and world opinion."[64] Guantánamo, as one attorney puts it, is a "cancer on the body politic."[65] This patriotic self is magnified in the anthology by the inclusion of stories from 113 lawyers to form a collective voice. Like the attorneys themselves, the reader follows the stories, which are "organized to take [her] on a roughly chronological journey of the Guantánamo detainee litigation."[66] The anthology includes the observations of seasoned attorneys who are appalled to see the state of their clients: "I have never seen anything like these conditions before."[67] One attorney compiles a list of the "Top-Ten Most Depressing and Frustrating Sights in GTMO," invoking the "American flag flying above it all" as the "most depressing" spectacle.[68] Others find it hard to believe that "American authorities would claim a right to incarcerate an individual, any individual [...] without a charge, without a lawyer, and without a trial."[69] These sorts of wide-eyed sentiments are relayed over and over; yet, in doing so, the anthology is careful not to affiliate with any particular American political party, in order to emphasize that this outrage reverberates across the political spectrum. One attorney stresses the importance of an "apolitical" involvement, working "with Guantánamo detainees to preserve their human rights, regardless of their guilt or

---

[62] Ibid., 19.
[63] Elsewhere, this mobilization is described as "rule of law lawyering" (Fletcher et al., "Defending," 647).
[64] Denbeaux and Hafetz, *Guantánamo*, 5.
[65] Ibid., 239.
[66] Ibid., 5.
[67] Ibid., 49.
[68] Ibid., 148.
[69] Ibid., 80.

innocence."[70] Another lawyer frames the advocacy as "fundamentally an 'American' issue," neither a left nor a right issue.[71]

The American ethos of patriotic *inclusivity* deployed in these narratives is fairly crude. *Patria* is saturated with melodramatic affect.[72] The accounts conceptualize the legal struggle over Guantánamo as a *moral* issue, with the lawyers' narratives modeling the right, rather than the wrong side:

> I was proud to be a part of the "Guantánamo Bar" and of this effort by so many lawyers to stand up for the principles that have made the American legal system the envy of the world.[73]

Such a statement conjures up a sentimental—and yet banal—discourse of national and social belonging that readers will easily identify (if not identify *with*).[74] In particular, the melodramatic virtues of patriotism are equated with ethical superiority, as is evident in one lawyer's statement, which emphasizes her "duty as a citizen, as a lawyer, and as a patriot to fight to uphold those values that define us as a nation."[75] These "principles" are reaffirmed variously across the anthology, asserting clichéd maxims like "I needed to fight for the soul of my country," we "violate the

---

[70] Ibid., 24. Indeed, there was concern that Guantánamo advocacy might represent a politically partisan cause. For instance, one lawyer is initially suspicious, thinking that the Guantánamo Bar would be a group "of hippie civil rights lawyers out of the 1960s," but is proud to see that the attorneys also come from "large, national, conservative law firms" (ibid., 19).

[71] Ibid., 39.

[72] I am using melodrama broadly here, though I draw on Peter Brooks' pertinent explication of the term as "the indulgence of strong emotionalism; moral polarization [...] reward of virtue [...] the pleasures of self-pity," as well as "the experience of wholeness" (11–12). Compelling melodrama, according to Brooks, is a concept that points to "stark ethical conflict" (12).

[73] Denbeaux and Hafetz, *Guantánamo*, 19.

[74] A similar patriotic sentiment is voiced in Rukhsana Mahvish Khan's collection of Guantánamo prisoner testimonies (*My Guantánamo Diary: The Detainees and the Stories They Told Me* [New York: Public Affairs, 2008]). A US-born citizen and student lawyer, Khan espouses the rule of law, but imbues it as inseparable from "the beliefs upon which the United States of America was founded" (xi). In particular, Khan views these beliefs as integral to the American Dream. She emphasizes how her parents, immigrants from Afghanistan, have come to the United States precisely "so that their children could grow up with all those rights and with the freedoms that exist here for everyone, no matter a person's background" (2).

[75] Ibid., 23.

core principles we stand for as a nation," and "we cannot forfeit our claim to moral leadership on the world stage."[76] These claims are pitted against the "false patriotism" that galvanized the war on terror.[77] They underscore the belief that the "values of the United States" represent "a fair system."[78] While this view of the United States calls to mind what Nietzsche called a "monumental history," the attorneys' stories are also careful to distance themselves from the Bush administration and its "abandonment of American principles."[79]

The narratives assert that defending the rule of law is the motivation for the Guantánamo Bar; but, in detailing their personal experiences, the attorneys also convey sympathy toward their clients, who face indefinite imprisonment under a regime of "sensory deprivation and engineered terror."[80] What their accounts express, however, is not a "profound fellow-feeling" for a human life, the subject of human rights that emerges out of narratives like the *Bildungsroman*.[81] Instead, these narratives operate as a relay for a "profound fellow-feeling" that is at once patriotic and benevolent, and that resonates with other (implicitly American) lives. The values espoused by the Guantánamo lawyers evoke, above all, positive connotations, proclaiming notions of legitimacy, transparency, openness, integrity, and fairness. They manifest, in other words, what Nye called "soft power"—an attractive idea of American justice. In his seminal essay on "Soft Power," Nye identifies "ideals" and "transnational ideas" as an "important source of power [... that blur] the distinction between *realpolitik* and liberalism."[82] Soft power is developed through its appeal: its attractiveness is fundamental to its ability to coopt others. The attorneys' set of values cherishes the ideals of impartial justice; though they appeal to their (American) readers, they also function as global exports with a political purpose. Nye outlines the way soft power can consolidate leadership and successful policy:

---

[76] Ibid., 19, 27, 267, 37.
[77] Ibid., 310.
[78] Ibid., 192.
[79] Friedrich Nietzsche, "On the Advantage and Disadvantage of History for Life," 1874, trans. Peter Preuss (Indianapolis, IN: Hackett Publishing Company, 1980), 9; Denbeaux and Hafetz, *Guantánamo*, 197; the lawyers also suggest the Bush administration is outright disobeying the law (310).
[80] Allen Feldman, "On the Actuarial Gaze: From 9/11 to Abu Ghraib," *Cultural Studies* 19, no. 2 (2005), 219.
[81] Slaughter, *Human Rights, Inc.*, 253.
[82] Nye, "Soft Power," 170.

If a state can make its power seem legitimate in the eyes of others, it will encounter less resistance to its wishes. If its culture and ideology are attractive, others will more willingly follow.[83]

Nye's original argument (since updated to account for the global age of digital technology[84]) was made in an uncertain post–Cold War future, where political commentators anticipated the decline of American hegemony. Soft power resolves this dilemma.[85]

To conclude, we can view the attorneys' personal narratives about Guantánamo as a currency, a form of soft power that seeks to regain legitimacy for the United States—a legitimacy that has been compromised since the creation of Guantánamo. At the same time, I do not want to downplay the importance of these personal narratives, which disclose to the public, and in great detail, the conditions at Guantánamo, as well as the complex governmental processes and legal contradictions that enable the prison to continue.[86] Nevertheless, the rhetoric of the collection, which remains invested in the moral legitimacy of the United States, is problematic, because it valorizes the American hegemony that in its various forms has retained its exceptionalism as well as its historical amnesia. At the beginning of the war on terror, this exceptionalist ideology was evident in President Bush's assertion: "you're either with us or you're with the terrorists."[87] At one level, the personal stories of the Guantánamo lawyers explode this rhetoric, by detailing the necessary interventions that disprove the "us" versus "them" dyad. Providing access to legal counsel and habeas rights protections are obviously significant here, though the challenge to arbitrary imprisonment demands a fuller historical picture of the structural racism and imperialism that often underpin such global injus-

---

[83] Ibid., 167.

[84] Nye, "The Information Revolution and Power," *Current History* 113, no. 759 (2014): 19–22.

[85] Nye opens his essay with his assertion that if "the most powerful country fails to lead" there would be severe "consequences for international stability" ("Soft Power," 153). In his 2014 essay, Nye suggests that, given the economic rise of China, soft power can enhance global stability and cooperation between the United States and China.

[86] A small part of the anthology also calls attention to Guantánamo as part of a global yet secretive prison network. I refer here to the infamous Central Intelligence Agency (CIA) "black sites," the secret detention centers where abducted prisoners are tortured and interrogated (Denbeaux and Hafetz, *Guantánamo*, 379–98).

[87] Bob Kemper, "Bush's Support Fades as Nation Moves On," *Chicago Tribune*, September 10, 2002.

tices. The personal stories, along with the organized public advocacy engineered by the Guantánamo Bar, in fact reveals the frailty of human rights, subject to the whims of a political power. In their call to principles and ideals of the rule of law, the Guantánamo attorneys resurrect the "us" and "them" specter, by reminding their readers of who "us" *should* be. In other words, the patriotism that frames their demands for habeas rights simply reinforces and legitimizes an "us" as a responsible power and a bestower of rights. In continuing to hold up the United States as this privileged site of human rights in spite of the evidence their own narratives have produced, the attorneys unwittingly obfuscate the "hard" power that enables the international sovereignty of one nation's so-called "moral leadership"—the very "leadership" that has produced the regime of torture and terror to which their clients are subject.[88]

[88] Denbeaux and Hafetz, *Guantánamo*, 37.

CHAPTER 14

Did We Survive Torture?

Mansoor Adayfi

In 2001, Mansoor Adayfi, originally from Yemen, was captured in Afghanistan and transferred to the custody of US forces in the country. He was rendered to Guantánamo (GTMO) soon after it opened in 2002, and he spent nearly fifteen years there without charge. In 2016, he was released to Serbia. In this final essay of the volume, Adayfi considers the difference between living through and surviving the experience of enforced disappearance, rendition, and torture. Speaking for himself as well as for other detainees who remain in Guantánamo or who have been repatriated, he explains that although he is alive, he is not sure he survived: parts of him are irreparably damaged, and, he writes, "I am still trying to escape."

Adayfi focuses on the role of writing and artistic production as a means of self-expression, self-preservation, and witnessing. And, although he focuses on the institutional and material constraints on artistic and literary self-expression in Guantánamo, it is clear that the act of writing this essay (which also includes transcribed excerpts from a recent video interview) is itself part of the process of reclaiming that right to witness. In terms of life

Mansoor Adayfi
(Guantánamo February 2002–July 2016)

M. Adayfi (✉)
Anonymous, Serbia

writing—and, we might add, self-portraiture—Adayfi's essay is both personal and collective. Written in the shifting pronouns of both a non-native speaker and thoughtful authorship, his style aptly represents his own experiences, those that he witnessed directly, and the experiences of men whose continued imprisonment or mental collapse prohibits their own testimony. In detailing the extraordinary restraints on personal expression within Guantánamo—for instance, using tea bags for ink and painting while being shackled to the floor, he simultaneously attests to the challenges and the importance of self-expression in aesthetic modes to survival.

* * *

Life is most beautiful, powerful and precious, wherever you are. I wanted to write about our torture at Guantánamo and even before we got there, but I found that would take a book. Instead I will give you a hint here without going into details. I saw and felt all kinds of pain. I lived it and still live with it. I spent years in those steel boxes, and what happened in those years can't be explained in these lines. Guantánamo affected us in every aspect of life. We carry scars in our souls, in our bodies, and in our lives. I lost teeth; I suffered a broken wrist, fingers, ankle, and damaged knees, but what is worse are the psychological, mental injuries. Mentally I am still there, and I am trying to escape.

We were in a place totally isolated from the rest of the world and from our families. Most of us were young, between sixteen and twenty-four years old. I had just turned nineteen when I arrived. We didn't know why we were held, why we were treated the way we were, why we were tortured, how long we were going to stay, or where we were to be sent. We spent years in isolation cells. Imagine being held in a stone box where all around you are strangers. You don't speak their language, and they don't speak yours. You can't communicate with anyone around you, and you don't know why you are there or what is going to happen.

To see people suffer around me, to watch them being abused and to have to stand by helpless and hopeless, sometimes was worse than my torture. Terrible moments happened almost every day. I remember the father of a child who kept crying, shouting out the name of his daughter, begging interrogators, guards, and camp staff to tell him about his child. Months and years passed, and there was no answer for him. Interrogators told him, "Cooperate with us if you want to see your child." Many of those who had families in Afghanistan or Pakistan suffered most. Interrogators withheld letters from or to those detainees, and they were told nothing or told that their wives had been raped and killed along with their kids.

The many years we spent in isolation, with different systematic abuses, were meant to destroy us and actually badly damaged us. We could not understand what was going on, and we just reacted to whatever was thrown at us. The interrogations and interrogators used every possible method to break us, to separate our minds from our bodies. They didn't just torture us and leave us, no, it happened again and again. New guards and administration, new interrogators, would come every year or so and would start with us from square one. Years later, I watched *The Hunger Games, Part 2*, where the tributes have to fight to the death in an arena designed as a clock and at each hour the tribute would be attacked. That was our GTMO arena program. The rules of the camps changed all the time. Despite its Standard Operating Procedures, Guantánamo detention had no standards. "You have no rights," we would be told.

One detainee asked a camp commander for his rights, for human rights. The answer was, "Here you have no rights."

The detainee then asked, "How about animal rights?"

"You are devils, and devils have no rights," came the reply.

At the beginning, we thought we would be in Guantánamo just for months. Then, when the first year passed, we said, next year. But many years passed. Some detainees lost their minds. The first one was an Afghan guy. He couldn't handle what was happening to him. He turned crazy, day and night, shouting, getting naked, eating his waste. He was treated with violence by the guards. "All of you will be the same, it's just a matter of time," the interrogators told us. They told us he had been given an injection that made him lose his mind. That was scary, and now we questioned and doubted everything—our food, water, anything given to us by guards.

I don't think we survived. I don't think that I survived. But we could stay alive. How did we manage to do that?

We all live on hope, no matter how or what or where. Hope is the most important survival skill. At Guantánamo, we had a special kind of hope—our faith, and we believed that everything is the hand of Allah. We became stronger in faith when the camp administration tried to steal the little hope we had. Everything suggested that we should be hopeless: knowing nothing, facing constant threats, seeing others go mad. But it was either die or try to survive, and each comes with a price.

From 2002 until 2010 we lived in isolation cells which I call stone boxes. Do you remember what I said at the beginning about life? "Life is most powerful, beautiful and precious." Life is all we get. Some detainees tried to fight back, but fight what and against whom? We felt powerless. Some detainees just ignored whatever happened, or they lived in a different world and struggled back and forth. All of us were fighting back, but it was not us, it was the life within us, that powerful, beautiful and precious life. Our life did all it possibly could to survive.

How detainees managed to shift their minds out of that hell was different from person to person. In 2010, we were given access to classes, computers, art, sports, TV, and books. We were moved to a communal camp. Some started taking classes in art, in English, in computers because they were interested, and some just to keep busy. But still we were nowhere, still in prison, still in fear of what would happen, still in fear of the unknown, but that fear was silent.

Some detainees started to paint about their lives, feelings, and emotions, about their hopes and fears. Things they couldn't possibly put in words, they put in shapes and colors. Their behavior changed, and they were more relaxed with painting.

But art and writing in Guantánamo had a difficult history. We imagine that artists sit in a room, drinking coffee, or listening to music, that they are sitting somewhere that has a very nice view. In Guantánamo, it was different. I remember in the early days, some detainees used to steal pens from the International Committee of the Red Cross (ICRC), some detainees got pens from the guards, and they wrote on toilet paper. Remember we were limited in everything. We had ten sheets of toilet paper a day. Detainees used to draw, to write, or to try to learn English on that toilet paper. We had inspection every single day, and people would take the tissue and try to hand it over to other detainees during inspection. If a guard caught you with a pen or that toilet paper, it would be confiscated and we would be punished.

Some detainees were smarter. At that time, we had "ready meals" that included a small bag of tea. Detainees used the tea as an ink. They would mix it with a little water and then fold the tea bag to use as a pen to write or draw on their toilet paper. People would also write or draw on the walls with a plastic spoon or a small stone from the rec yard. Each individual detainee had his own language and his own way to express his feelings.

Even after 2010, we had limited time for class. We were not allowed to have the supplies outside the classroom. In the class, detainees were shackled to the ground, guards watching, cameras everywhere. The instructor would provide detainees with the materials they needed. You had to concentrate because there were detainees around you, speaking different languages, some practicing English, some who just came for conversation. It was very difficult to hold onto the emotions for a painting, especially to do a longer work. You were only allowed to have at most two hours or ninety minutes a week, and it could take weeks or months to finish one painting. Detainees would work on a small part of a drawing, then pause and look at it for a few days before going back to it. It wasn't as though they were sitting and looking out upon a beautiful view.

Some detainees managed to smuggle to their cells some of the materials for drawing. And they got caught. It was an unspoken war between the administration and detainees. What was the problem with letting detainees have those materials? The administration would say it's a security issue. But there is no security issue.

I remember one detainee from Pakistan who was a very good painter. He used to ask for materials, but no one would give them to him. He would tell the guards, "You know what, I don't want food. Please take the food away. Please, I don't want clothing or medicine. Just bring me my colors and art supplies. I need to paint. This is my escape gate from this hell." When they refused to give him materials, he turned to some spices that came from his family through the Red Cross. He mixed them together and made his own colors. I saw in his cell the paintings he made with these spices—ginger, coriander, chili.

I asked him, "How do you manage?"

He said, "Spices. Don't worry, we improvise."

Art or writing wasn't easy to do there, but we did it. We got forty-five minutes in art class, there weren't many materials, and most of the time detainees' belongings were confiscated. But still, we made a lot of art and works out of cardboard and other materials we could find. Detainees made decorations, cabinets, tables, shelves, ships, planes, and other things. Some detainees covered their cells with beautiful paintings. I would go there and look at the paintings, and looking at the paintings would take me on a lovely journey out of GTMO.

In 2013, four of us wrote a book in Guantánamo, an illustrated feasibility report in English and Arabic called "Yemen Milk and Honey Farm." We studied how to create a business that would grow and sell milk and honey, what equipment we needed, how much money we needed to get started. We even designed a website. We drew detailed illustrations. We figured out how to bind the pages together into a book. It took many months. When it was finished, we had a party in our cell block to celebrate. While I was there, I also worked on another book, not just about me or about other detainees, but about everyone there as human beings. I wrote about everyone and everything: detainees, guards, camp staff, ICRC, lawyers, animals, the sea, the buildings. I wrote about how the detainees live their lives there. There were forty-eight nationalities among the detainees when I was there: different countries, languages, traditions, cultures, customs. I wrote about how we detainees lived together, how we communicated, how we reacted. I wrote about life between the detainees and guards: how the two groups communicated and how they understood each other. It was sad. Imagine: most detainees don't speak the language of the guards. The guards only speak English, but some detainees speak only Arabic, Pashto, Urdu, French, Persian. When there is no communication, there are a lot of misunderstandings and problems. I tried not to put the reader in one track and one perspective, but instead to tell many small stories. When I was writing the book, I would let the guards, other detainees, camp staff, doctors, psychologists, officers, ICRC, lawyers, younger people, older people read what I was writing. I would ask them, "What do you think?" And I would study their reactions. I tried not to tell just my story, but to tell a more complete story about life inside. I want readers to live the moments in Guantánamo and to piece together the story for themselves.

Guantánamo wasn't just about torture and abuse. There was something bigger and beautiful there. It was life. There was life, love, good moments, bad moments, sad moments, happy moments. Everything was there, including hope. Some guards and camp staff even tried to help some detainees who were suffering. One guard would bring candy or chocolate for a young detainee, saying "Hi, you are going to be OK. I have brothers just like you." Some detainees made gifts for guards. Guantánamo wasn't just about detainees or guards. It was about us as humans regardless of our backgrounds. All simply was because of life and the beauty of life.

I don't know if I'm a writer, but I like to write. Sometimes I can't sleep and I feel a powerful urge to write. I think we are all painters, painting our lives. I hope that I can make a very good painting. It will have a small spot that is Guantánamo, but I think that will make it more interesting.

Epilogue: From Solitude to Solidarity

Dianna Ortiz, O.S.U.

On a scorching, steamy day in June of 1998, a small group of women and men from Africa, Asia, North America, and Europe met for the very first time in Washington, DC. Little did we know that this encounter would give birth to an organization, the Torture Abolition and Survivors Support Coalition International (TASSC), and would forever link us as a global community of torture survivors.

During our initial gathering, we realized that we shared much in common. The brutality that we had experienced, and mystifyingly survived, had changed our lives forever. Belief in ourselves, in the human family, and in the God we worshipped appeared to be gone. In a sense, we were like seeds of a dandelion, each carried by the wind and scattered to a foreign land.

We recognized that many, if not all of us, had been walking a silent journey. The realization that we were not alone gave us reason to believe that we were not powerless and that it was possible to restore a semblance of order in our shattered lives. Being able to share our vulnerabilities and the hardships of living a life of solitude was like an invitation to "to wash in the Pool of Siloam" (John 9:7) and to see the world around us with new eyes.

We recognized that, like ourselves, other torture survivors were fleeing brutal wars and trudging through foreign lands in search of a safe haven. They were living among us—in our neighborhoods, in our places of worship, and in our streets—searching for a welcoming and supportive community.

How, we asked, was it possible to have others understand our lives after torture, if we, ourselves, were constantly struggling to grasp the psychology of torture: its purpose; its immediate and long-term effects; and the political and social institutions that create, practice, and endorse this crime against humanity?

In the fall of 1998, TASSC opened its doors to anyone who had fallen victim to torture. Its mission was to create a global community of survivors and to offer unconditional support to those whose lives had been shattered by torture as they healed their physical wounds, reclaimed their self-dignity, rebuilt trust in humanity, renewed their lives' purposes, and re-established a sense of community.

In a blink of an eye, trust emerged among strangers. We caught glimpses into each other's souls and shared how torture had impacted our lives, the lives of our loved ones, and the lives of our communities. We dared to share the sudden visits of our torturers who came to us in our dreams; the haunting screams of those tortured beside us; and the indescribable fear that engulfed us when we saw a person in uniform, when a cloud of cigarette smoke drifted (wafted) in our direction, or when harmless questions asked by others took us back to our interrogations.

As wanderers in a strange land, we began to share how people of goodwill expected us to let go of the past and to move on with our lives. Many survivors expressed how they struggled to convey to spouses and partners, to family members, to friends, and to colleagues that we were, indeed, *living* life, considering the appalling violence that we each had sustained. Avoidance of dank basements, phobias of another person's touch, fear of coming face to face with one's torturers, consumption of cup after cup of coffee to stay awake as a way to escape the nightmares, frequent showering to wash away the traces of the perpetrator's odor, and social withdrawal and loss of interest in life were, all too often, perceived as abnormal, destructive, and unhealthy behavior. For survivors, these reactions were as normal as breathing air: a natural human response to an extremely abnormal experience of torture. They were not symptoms of weakness or psychological instability; in reality, these responses were survival skills that kept many of us alive.

Oddly enough, many of us were tormented by two burning questions: Why were we "chosen" as designated survivors while others—who endured similar, and perhaps even worse, cruelty—died in the hands of their torturers? Why was there a deafening silence surrounding the crime of torture in today's world? In response to the lack of outrage over the widespread use of torture, TASSC provided a platform for survivors to speak their truth, to speak on behalf of those who had been silenced, and to advocate for the abolition of torture by raising awareness of its impact on the tortured, their families, their communities, and society as a whole. From the outset, TASSC promulgated that the strongest and most effective voices in the campaign to abolish torture were survivors. Who better than the tortured to speak of this atrocity and its complicated aftermath?

In the early days, a definitive goal of TASSC was to close the door on torture; in so doing, the global community of survivors would have accomplished its main objective: the worldwide abolition of torture. How naïve we were to assume such a quixotic responsibility.

Nearly twenty years have passed, and still the doors of TASSC remain open. Every day, women, men, and children of all ages, ethnicities, nationalities, faith traditions, and political ideologies make their way to the place they call "home." Social service, government, and medical and mental health-care agencies continue to offer legal, medical, housing, food, and employment assistance to survivors. Many of TASSC's allies have joined survivors to work to end torture through education, advocacy, and public speaking. This volume represents one more space where survivors and advocates have come together for the same goal: to work to end torture by witnessing it, analyzing it, and demanding its worldwide abolition.

One may ask, "Did TASSC succeed in its mission to rid our world of torture?" My answer is a definitive no! Despite a series of international conventions and prevention instruments, the use of torture persists. It is widespread and systematic; it is practiced not only by oppressive regimes during armed conflicts, but also by countries with purportedly democratic and stable political systems. In the fight to end terrorism, many governments have opted to legitimize torture as a method of investigating potential terrorists and protecting national security. Torture does not discriminate and knows no boundaries. No national emergency or threat, however dire, ever justifies its use. From the moment of its inception to the present, TASSC has committed to shining a light on the silence and indifference surrounding torture and its long-lasting effects on asylum seekers, refugees, and the broader community. The work of TASSC members and allies in this book represents one more expression of that commitment.

As one member of TASSC's global community of survivors, I recognize that the memories of my torture will forever remain with me. I am of the opinion that one never heals from torture—torture's ghost will constantly dwell within each of us. We will never forget the brutality that was done to us and to others, nor will we forget those who were silenced by their torturers. Many of us will learn to live with the memories, the flashbacks, and the aftermath. We look past the tragedy of our torture and refuse to allow those dark moments to define who we are or what path we will walk. Survivors of the early days and of the present will continue to struggle, to question, and to fall into pools of despair, but together we will *rise*. Broken bones will mend, pulled teeth will be replaced, scars will fade, and many of us will return to a comparatively normal life. Like tall dandelions, we will grow in the sun and dance to the harsh beat of the wind of injustice, all the while scattering seeds of new life and a promising hope of a day when the world will be free of torture.

Index[1]

A

Abu Ghraib, 100, 143–145, 154, 156, 200–203
Activist, ix, x, xii–xiv, xvi, xvii, xix, xxiv, 3, 21, 25, 28, 37, 40, 41, 44, 71, 93, 109, 128, 130, 139, 184, 186, 187, 191, 192, 199–203, 205, 208
Affect/affective, xvi, xvii, xx, xxvii, 95, 137, 158, 166, 185, 190, 199, 208, 226
Alleg, Henri, xv, xvn3, xvi, xxi, xxin13, xxiii–xxv, xxivn19, xxvn22, 199
  See also Question, *The*
American Psychologists Association (APA), 59, 60, 111–113, 117–133
Améry, Jean, xix, xixn8, xixn10, xxi
Amnesty International, ix, x, 28n13, 62, 62n1, 72, 79, 198, 198n17, 205
Argentina, xixn10, 8, 34, 140, 147, 157, 159–161, 166, 167, 169–173, 175, 177, 201n21
  See also "Dirty War"

Aristizábal, Hector, xvii, xviii, xviiin5
Argentinean Forensic Anthropology Team, 169
Argentine Forensic Anthropology Team, 175, 177
Aristotle, 189
Art/artistic production, xxn11, 137, 140, 142, 169, 199, 201, 205, 209, 231, 234, 235
Artist, 1, 140, 170, 178
Artistic, 137
Asylum, 62, 63, 66, 66n3, 68, 72–76, 81–83, 87, 89, 90, 104, 105, 132, 146, 239
Athey, Stephanie, xviii, xviiin7, xix, xixn9, 1–3, 2n2, 73, 73n2

B

Baráhéni, Réza, 204n23
  Les Saisons en enfer du jeune Ayyâz [*The Infernal Days of Aghaye Ayyaz*], 204

---

[1] Note: Page numbers followed by 'n' refer to notes.

Betrayal, 3, 4, 10, 37, 38, 40–46, 69, 111–136, 203n22
Blindfold's Eye, The, 82n10, 91n2, 113, 199
Boltanski, Luc, 189, 189n11, 209n30
Bush, George W., xxv, 109, 120, 123, 144, 155, 156, 201, 213, 213n3, 214, 218n24, 221, 227, 227n79, 228, 228n87

C

Center for Multicultural Human Services (CMHS), 91
Center for Victims of Torture (CVT), 91, 131
Central Intelligence Agency (CIA), 24, 112, 119, 120n15, 122–124, 122n21, 123n22, 123n23, 124n25, 127n33, 133, 143–156, 198, 228n86
Citizen, xvii, 21, 27, 66, 81n9, 82, 84, 116, 127, 144–146, 154, 185, 188, 194, 196, 212, 216, 223n51, 226, 226n74
Coalition for an Ethical Psychology, 112, 120, 120n14, 133
Coetzee, J. M., 1
Cohen, Stanley, 188–190, 188n5
Collective memory, 140
Collective witnessing, xx, 137–140
Communist Party of the Philippines (CPP), 37, 38, 41–45
Community of healing/communities of healing, 59, 71, 75, 86
Compañera/compañero, 147
Convention Against Torture and Other Cruel, Inhuman or Degrading Treatment, United Nations (1984), 208n29

D

Dark chamber, xviii, 1, 1n1, 3
Denbeaux, Mark P., 213n3, 215n10, 217, 217n20, 218n24, 219n29, 219n30, 221, 221n40, 222n44, 223, 223n47, 223n50, 223n52, 224n55, 225, 225n64, 226n73, 227n79, 228n86, 229n88
  See also Guantánamo Lawyers: Inside a Prison Outside the Law, The
Desaparecidos, 159–161, 164
Detainee, ix, 25, 27n9, 28, 32, 33, 42, 111, 120, 139, 142, 155, 160, 211, 212, 213n1, 214, 217, 218n24, 219, 220, 221n42, 225, 231, 233–236
"Dirty War", xixn10, xxvii, 140, 157, 169
Disappearance, ix, xixn10, xx, 44, 137–144, 147, 156, 157, 170, 171, 175, 231
  See also Enforced disappearance
Dorfman, Ariel, 191
Dostoyevsky, Fyodor, 191, 203
  The Brothers Karamazov, 191, 203

E

Electric shock, xxv, 154
El Mozote/El Mozote massacre, 169, 177–180
El Salvador, xii, 46, 86, 140, 154, 155, 161, 169, 174, 177, 181n5
Enforced disappearance, xx, 137, 139, 140, 157–168, 170, 231
Enhanced interrogation, xxv, 100, 111, 119, 120n15, 123, 214
Étienne, Gérard
  Le Nègre Crucifié [*The Crucified Negro*], 204
Evidence/evidentiary, xv, xxii, 22, 44, 72, 73, 75–82, 86, 88, 107, 108,

114, 120, 121, 124, 125, 133, 138–140, 150, 152, 156, 169, 175, 177, 193, 196, 198, 200, 201, 206, 219, 219n29, 229
Expertise, x, xiv, xvi, xxvi, 2, 57, 58, 61, 105, 127, 222

F

Falkoff, Marc, 213, 213n1, 214, 214n5, 214n8, 219, 219n31, 220, 220n36, 221n39, 222n43
Fanon, Frantz, 205
Farabundo Martí National Liberation Front (FMLN), 180, 180n4
Fear, 8–16, 38, 50, 63, 65, 76, 81, 81n9, 82, 90, 97, 109, 113, 130, 133, 135, 171, 173, 201, 203n22, 219, 234, 238
Feinstein, Diane (U.S. Sen.), 123, 123n22, 123n23, 126
Forché, Carolyn, xx, xxn11

G

Geneva Conventions, xxvi, xxvin24, 120, 156, 213
Genocide, ix, 46, 145, 165, 172, 177–179, 181, 187, 188, 192
Ghost house, 21, 25–32, 34
Guantánamo, 58, 117, 119, 141, 142, 198, 203, 211–229, 231–236
"Guantánamo Bar", 214, 217, 221n42, 226
Guantánamo Lawyers: Inside a Prison Outside the Law, The, 141, 211, 213n3, 217, 225
Guatemala, 46, 49, 132, 138, 143–146, 148–151, 153, 154
Organización Revolucionaria del Pueblo Armado, 146
Guilt, xi, xxvi, 12, 13, 33, 65, 83, 84, 113, 175, 225

H

Habeas corpus, xixn10, xxvi, xxvin24, 161, 211, 212, 218, 222
Hafetz, Jonathan, 213n3, 215n10, 217, 217n20, 218n24, 219n29, 219n30, 221, 221n40, 222n44, 223, 223n47, 223n50, 223n52, 224n55, 225, 225n64, 226n73, 227n79, 228n86, 229n88
See aslo Guantánamo Lawyers: Inside a Prison Outside the Law, The
Halliday, Fred, 214
Health professionals, 53, 57–70, 79, 93, 109, 112, 120, 123, 124
Herman, Judith, 93, 93n9, 99, 99n33
Trauma and Recovery, 93
Hoffman Report, 124, 129, 133
Human dignity, 10, 62, 66, 69, 172, 207
Human Rights and Narrated Lives: The Ethics of Recognition, 215n11
Human rights workers, xn1, xi–xiv, xvii, xix, xxiv, 43

I

Ignatieff, Michael, 188, 188n2, 190, 190n14
Imagination, xx, 25, 48, 49, 140, 183, 186–188, 190–192, 202, 203, 205, 206
Impunity, xxvin24, 10–12, 163–166
Independent Review Relating to APA Ethics Guidelines, National Security Interrogations, and Torture, 119, 119n10
See also American Psychologists Association (APA)
Institutional/institutions, ix, xvi–xx, xxii, xxiv, xxv, 1–3, 5, 7, 40, 57–60, 71, 72, 77, 78, 78n6, 82, 88, 111–130, 132–136, 151, 178, 184, 192–195, 206, 207, 231, 238

International Committee for the Red Cross, 217, 234
International Convention for the Protection of All Persons from Enforced Disappearance, United Nations (2006), 139, 157
Interrogation, xxi, xxv, xxvi, 3, 17, 27, 31, 37, 42, 61, 62, 64, 66, 100, 113, 117–119, 122–129, 127n33, 132, 145, 152, 184, 197, 198, 200, 206, 207, 208n28, 214, 219, 223, 238
Intersubjective, 137, 138, 140
Iraq, 46, 90, 143, 154, 173, 174, 174n1, 200

K

Kaplan, E. Ann, 5, 5n5
Karski, Jan, 187
Kravtchenko, Victor, 187
Kristeva, Julia, 224

L

Latin American Federation of Families of the Disappeared (FEDEFAM), 157, 160–164, 167
Lawyer, xiii, xvi, xix, 48, 74–77, 80–82, 87, 142, 155, 158, 162, 211–229, 236
Life narrative, xvii, xviii, 139, 212, 213, 216, 216n18, 220n33, 222, 223
Life writing, xiv–xxviii, 2, 58, 138, 141, 231–232
Luban, David, 133
 Torture, Power, and Law, 133

M

Madres and Abuelas de Plaza de Mayo, 158, 159
 Hijos (Children) de Plaza de Mayo, 167

McAfee, Ambassador Marilyn, 148, 150–152
McCain, John (U.S. Sen.), xxvi, 126, 155
Madres and Abuelas of Plaza de Mayo, 165
Martial law, 37, 40, 73
Mayer, Jane, 59, 59n2, 117n5, 123, 133, 134n43
Memory, 39, 44, 49, 50, 65, 91, 103, 140, 169–181, 239, 240
Menchú, Rigoberta, xx
Mental health, 53, 73, 75, 78, 81, 88, 91, 93, 109, 114, 117, 124, 127, 239
Military Commissions Act (2006), U.S. Congress, xxvi, xxvin23, xxvi–xxviin24
Military dictatorship, 167, 168, 171–173, 175
Moeller, Susan, 188
Mollica, Richard, 87, 87n12
Mukasey, Michael, xxv
Muslim Brotherhood (MB), 24–26, 30, 33, 34
Mutua, Makau, 57, 57n1

N

National Child Traumatic Stress Network (NCTSN), 130, 134
National Consortium of Torture Treatment Programs (NCTTP), 78, 79, 79n7, 99, 100, 131n41
National Institute of Mental Health (NIMH), 114–117, 131, 132
Non-governmental organization (NGO), ix, xi, 49, 79, 161, 162
Non-survivors, xn1, xii–xiv, xix, xxiii, xxiv, xxvii, 54, 55, 114, 131, 132, 135, 136
Nye, Joseph S., 216, 216n16, 227, 227n82, 228, 228n85

O

Oliver, Kelly, xxii–xxiv, xxiin16, xxiiin17, xxivn18, 137, 137n1, 138
Organization of American States (OAS), 148–151, 153, 161
Ortiz, Dianna, Sr., 82n10, 91n2, 113, 115, 154
  See also Blindfold's Eye, The

P

Pain, ix, xi, xiii–xv, xvii, xviii, xxiii, xxvii, xxviii, 3, 8, 12–16, 21, 28, 30–32, 37, 38, 40–46, 51, 61–63, 65, 67, 80, 84, 90–94, 97, 99, 99n30, 102, 103, 106, 109, 113, 131, 135, 140, 154–156, 171, 172, 175, 179, 185, 188, 190, 198–200, 207, 208, 232
Paraguay, 7, 8, 9n1, 10n3, 12, 15
Pay Any Price: Greed, Power, and Endless War, 122, 122n20
Peace Advocates for Truth and Healing (PATH), 38, 43–45
Pearlman, Laurie Anne, 94, 94n14, 95n15, 97, 97n27, 98n29, 103n36, 109, 109n45
  See also Trauma and the Therapist
Pedagogy, 140, 183, 193, 206
PENS, *see Report of the Presidential Task Force on Psychological Ethics and National Security*
Perpetrator, xv, xvii–xx, xxiv, 1–3, 8, 22, 33, 44, 45, 57, 68–70, 127, 159, 162, 163, 172, 186, 199, 201, 203, 238
Perquin, 169, 178, 179
  See also School of Art and Open Studio
Phenomenon/phenomenology, xiv, xvi–xviii, xxii, xxiii, 11, 13, 18, 24, 46, 65, 159, 162, 166

Philippines, the, xix, 3, 37, 38, 40, 43, 44, 46, 73
Physicians, xi, xiii, 63, 66n3, 74, 75, 80, 93, 109, 112, 121n18, 125n29, 145, 147
Physicians for Human Rights, 66n3, 112, 120–122, 121n18, 122n21, 124n25, 125, 125n29, 132, 214n7
Political, xi, xii, xiv, xvi–xx, xixn8, xxii–xxv, xxvii, 1–5, 7–9, 10n3, 11, 14, 15, 17, 18, 21–25, 30, 37, 40, 43, 44, 46, 57–59, 67, 73, 74, 76, 81, 87, 90, 104, 109, 115, 127, 130, 139, 158, 160, 163, 172, 178, 183–185, 187, 196, 197, 199, 201, 202, 206, 212, 214–216, 220, 225, 227–229, 238, 239
Prisoner, xxvi, 3, 4, 8, 13–18, 22, 24, 28, 32, 63, 79, 96, 99, 107, 117, 118, 144, 147, 148, 150, 152, 153, 156, 168, 176, 200, 203, 212–214, 213n3, 213n4, 215n10, 217–225, 217n21, 218n24, 219n29, 219n30, 226n74, 228n86
Professional, ix, xiii, xiv, xvi, xix, xx, xxiv, xxvi, 2, 15, 30, 31, 49, 57–73, 79, 89, 93, 95, 109, 111–130, 132–136, 212, 215, 218, 223
Program for Survivors of Torture and Severe Trauma (PSTT), 89, 91, 91n3, 99, 106
Proxy witness/proxy witnessing, 141, 211, 222
Psychiatrists, xiii, 2, 7, 61, 75, 205
Psychological, xvi, xvii, xxiv, 2, 7, 8, 11–14, 16–19, 29, 32, 58, 59, 61, 62, 72, 79, 89, 95, 104, 105, 111, 113, 118, 119, 121, 132, 133, 147, 156, 189, 232, 238

Psychologists, xi, xiii, xix, 58–60, 75, 82, 86, 87, 89, 91, 103, 104, 109, 111–113, 117–129, 121n19, 124n26, 124n27, 125n29, 131, 132, 236
Psychologists for Social Responsibility (PsySR), 112, 120, 121, 121n17, 124n26
Psychosocial, 1, 2, 8, 79, 87, 142

Q
Question, The, xvn3, xxi, xxin13, xxiv, xxv, 77, 82, 207

R
Redress, xviii, xx, xxi, 2, 4, 37, 38, 40–46, 43n1, 137–142, 159
Rejali, Darius, xvi, xviin4, 5
Religion/religious, xix, xxii, 3, 12, 17, 21–23, 25–30, 32–34, 76, 81, 90, 91, 102, 128, 158, 178
Rendition, 168, 231
Rendition, Detention, and Interrogation program (RDI), 140
Report of the Presidential Task Force on Psychological Ethics and National Security (APA 2005) (PENS), 111
Response-ability, xxii–xxiv, 138
Rhetoric/rhetorical, ix–xiv, xvi, xix, xxiv, xxvii, 4, 57, 138, 199, 200, 212, 216, 216n18, 223, 228
Right to genetic identity, 167
Right to know, 164–165
Risen, James, 120n13, 121n16, 121n19, 122–124, 122n20, 124n27, 126n32
    See also *Pay Any Price: Greed, Power, and Endless War*

Rome Statute, International Criminal Court, 163
Roustang, François, 9, 9n1, 9n2, 13, 17

S
Saakvitne, Karen W., 94n14, 97, 97n27, 98n29, 103n36, 109, 109n45
    See also *Trauma and the Therapist*
Salvador (dir. Oliver Stone), xi
Sartre, Jean-Paul, xxiv, xxivn19, xxv
Scarry, Elaine, xx, xxn12, 3–5, 3n3, 21, 199
Schaffer, Kay, 215
School of Art and Open Studio, 178, 179
School of the Americas, 24, 153, 201
Secondary trauma, xxiii, 92, 94, 95, 99, 100, 102, 103, 105, 106
    See also Vicarious trauma
Senate Intelligence Committee Study of the Central Intelligence Agency's Detention and Interrogation Program, 112
Sexual, xxvii, 41, 80, 90, 130, 156, 200, 201
Shaffer, Kay, 215
    See aslo *Human Rights and Narrated Lives: The Ethics of Recognition*
Smith, Clive Stafford, 217n19, 217n22, 218n25, 220, 220n35, 223, 223n49
Smith, Dorothy, 72n1, 77n4, 78, 78n5, 78n6, 215n11, 215n12, 216n14, 218n25
Smith, Sidonie, 215, 215n11
    See also *Human Rights and Narrated Lives: The Ethics of Recognition*

INDEX   247

Soft power, 216, 216n16, 227, 227n82, 228, 228n85
Solidarity, xvii, xxxiii, 2, 4, 9, 13, 15, 38, 46, 47, 64, 84, 86, 159, 160
South Africa, 114, 134
Spiritual, 33, 61, 62, 64, 67–68, 93, 98, 101, 102, 103n36, 106, 172, 181
State Department, U.S., 138, 148, 150–152
Stroessner regime, 2, 9
Sudan, xix, 3, 21–23, 25–27, 29–34, 99, 101
Suffering, x, xiv–xvi, xxii–xxv, 1–4, 8, 12, 15, 17, 22, 29, 31, 32, 47–49, 54, 55, 58, 59, 61, 62, 64, 67, 68, 80, 89–91, 109, 152, 158, 160, 179, 188–190, 208, 215, 219, 224, 236
Survivor, ix, 2, 7, 21, 38, 47, 58, 61, 71, 89, 112, 137, 143, 157, 237

T
Taylor, Diana, xxi, xxin14, xxiin15, xxvii, xxviin26
Terror, ix, xxv, 8, 9, 41, 42, 50, 59, 62, 66, 111, 122, 123, 139, 141, 143, 152n2, 154–156, 168, 172, 173, 187, 196, 198, 208, 213, 214, 219, 227–229
Terrorism/terrorist, 173
Testimonial/*testimonio*, xii, xiii, xvi, xix, xixn10, xxiv, xxvii, 4, 38, 47, 65, 67, 68, 92, 143, 144, 187, 188, 192, 199, 209, 220n33
Testimony, xv, xvii, xxii, xxiv, xxvin24, 5, 47, 48, 51, 55, 58, 66, 68–70, 81, 90, 138, 144, 173, 174, 177, 183, 187–191, 196, 212, 213, 217–219, 217n21, 219n29, 221, 226n74, 232

Therapeutic/therapy, xxiv, 15, 47, 72, 73, 87, 90, 95, 97, 103, 106n40, 109, 132, 135
Ticking bomb, 208
Torture Abolition and Survivors Support Coalition (TASSC), xn1, xi, xiv, xxvin24, 4, 38, 46–49, 51–55, 59, 71–77, 79, 81–86, 88, 113, 132, 237–239
Torturer, xviii, 1, 8, 11–14, 16–19, 21, 28–34, 45, 50, 63–69, 73, 82, 84–86, 94, 96, 99, 100, 102, 103, 105, 116, 135, 152–155, 195, 196, 198, 199, 203n22, 204, 205, 207, 238, 240
Torture Victims Relief Act (TVRA) (1998), U.S. Congress, 72, 79, 132
Translate/translation/translator, xxiv, 1–5, 47–55, 82, 90, 130, 191, 194, 199, 204, 213n1
Trauma, ix, xiv, xv, xxiii, 4, 13, 16, 42, 46–55, 63–65, 67, 69, 75, 76, 79, 86–90, 92–95, 93n4, 94n12, 97–106, 108, 109, 113–115, 129, 130, 132, 134, 160, 196, 199, 219
Trauma and the Therapist, 93n8, 94n14, 97n27, 98n29, 224
Trust, xix, 9, 17, 18, 43n1, 48, 49, 54, 55, 58, 64, 67, 95, 101, 116, 124, 132, 151, 170, 179, 238
Truth, xvi, xxi, xxii, xxviii, 2, 38, 44, 45, 50, 68, 82, 85, 94, 97, 112, 116, 118, 124, 133, 135, 141, 145, 147, 152, 153, 159, 161, 164–165, 172, 177–178, 183, 189, 191, 196, 197, 202, 206, 218, 223, 239
24, 196, 199, 202, 209n31

U

U.S. Senate Intelligence Committee Study of the Central Intelligence Agency Detention and Interrogation Program, 122

V

Vicarious trauma, 92, 93, 95, 97n25, 108

W

War on terror, ix, xxv, 59, 62, 66, 111, 119n8, 122, 123, 139, 141, 143, 155, 168, 187, 198, 198n18, 208, 214, 219, 227, 228

Waterboarding, xxv, xxvn22, 27, 46, 58, 100, 154, 155, 195, 198n18

Wellstone, Paul (U.S. Sen.), 115, 117, 130, 131

Whitlock, Gillian, 216, 216n15, 216n18, 219, 220n32, 220n33

Witness/witnessing, xiv–xxviii, 2, 4, 5, 42, 44, 45, 47–55, 57–60, 66, 69, 74, 76, 81, 89–109, 112, 113, 127, 131, 133, 137–141, 143, 144, 147, 152, 153, 157, 170, 183, 185, 187, 208, 211–213, 215, 219, 222, 231, 239

Worrying, 131

Druck:
Customized Business Services GmbH
im Auftrag der
KNV Zeitfracht GmbH
Ein Unternehmen der Zeitfracht - Gruppe
Ferdinand-Jühlke-Str. 7
99095 Erfurt